TRIBUTES

TRIBUTES

Personal Reflections on a
Century of Social Research

Irving Louis Horowitz

Routledge
Taylor & Francis Group

LONDON AND NEW YORK

First published 2004 by Transaction Publishers

2 Park Square, Milton Park, Abingdon, Oxfordshire OX14 4RN
711 Third Avenue, New York, NY 10017

Routledge is an imprint of the Taylor & Francis Group, an informa business

First issued in paperback 2017

Library of Congress Catalog Number: 2003048418

Library of Congress Cataloging-in-Publication Data

Horowitz, Irving Louis.
   Tributes : personal reflections on a century of social research / Irving
   Louis Horowitz
      p. cm.
   ISBN 0-7658-0218-X (cloth : alk. paper)
      1. Sociology. 2. Sociology—Philosophy. I. Title.

HM585.H67   2003
301—dc21   2003048418

ISBN 13: 978-0-7658-0218-7 (hbk)
ISBN 13: 978-1-138-51749-3 (pbk)

Render to all their dues:
tribute to whom tribute is due;
custom to whom custom;
fear to whom fear;
honor to whom honor.

Paul, 13:7

Even unto them will I give in my house and within my walls
a monument and a memorial…that shall not be cut off.

Isaiah, 56:5

Contents

Preface: A Tribute to Vocation

Over the course of my approximately thirty-year career in academic life and more than a decade of scholarly editing, I have had the good fortune to meet or correspond with at least a dozen of the fifty-three figures paid tribute to in this extraordinary book. Three died before I was born, and two others died when I was ten and eleven years old. The garnered sheaves collected here, ranging in time over the second half of the twentieth century, establish a benchmark for earning the privilege of paying tribute. In this collection of reminiscences, reminders, and reconsiderations, the alliterative and operative come together in such payment.

It is worth reminding that the kind of tribute exemplified in this book is possible only in relations of authority; in relations of power, bribe and "protection" are more apt. The affective side of tribute is acknowledgment, esteem, and honor, all of which combine in what is humanly and freely given. It is rare these days to see freedom in this way, but there it is: a tribute is evidence of a world of accomplishment in which we are free to praise those whose accomplishments are not only worthy but also superior in ways that no menacing chill of equality can alter. Here is an entire work devoted to the informing and nonconforming realities of social science, so often, and too often, thought of as itself a tribute to equality. But this cannot be, or at least, with human will and effort at its base, cannot be for long. Instead, taken together, all of these great and greater—known and lesser known—figures form a single diversity called social science, with many tributaries flowing into it from philosophy and science, from politics and civil service, from business and journalism, from all of these and more.

Social science cannot be greater than the sum of its contributors. It is not a quest for theological certainty anymore than it is a servant to politics. Certainly such quests and such service characterize some who have been part of it, but what ought to interest a reader of these tributes in particular is how seamlessly their orchestration, by Irving Louis Horowitz, intends us to enter into debate and conversation, one by one and one on one, with each person addressed. We must read them to know them. Nothing could be plainer about Irving Horowitz or about his vision and vocation of social science than this single fact, that in treating each person with civility and decency, even disagreement can be the highest tribute, and then, only because this is social science, not faith-based anything. The faithful may say that this is not possible, and they have a point. But only up to a point can the charge be made that social science lacks coherence because it inevitably portrays competing, indeed, opposite visions of the good and the possible. Without competing visions, disagreement is heresy. And for our times, the achievements of all social science are bound soul and sinew to democratic life, and to the competing principles that make our living together more or less possible, even satisfying.

This book does not contain a sentimental or sour note in its movements among so many virtuosi, whose qualities of mind and character are what they are. Why should we be so interested in them, if we are not also interested in ourselves being (as well as not being) like them? Max Weber, in "Politics as a Vocation," put the matter clearly enough when he observed, "Vanity is a very widespread quality and perhaps nobody is entirely free from it. In academic and scholarly circles, vanity is a sort of occupational disease, but precisely with the scholar, vanity—however disagreeably it may express itself—is relatively harmless; in the sense that as a rule it does not disturb the scientific enterprise. With the politician the case is quite different." Weber contended that the two deadly sins of politics are for the politician to mistake himself for his cause and to become irresponsible, enjoying power "merely for power's sake." It is possible to imagine that had Weber encountered Daniel Patrick Moynihan, he might have considered another way of understanding the potential for greatness between scholarship and politics, however rare such greatness may actually be. It is also possible to imagine that had Weber lived to see, first the hard totalitarianisms of Stalinism and Nazism and later the soft totalitarianisms of McCarthyism and multiculturalism, he would have considered how vanity produces bullies whose little powers may not produce big problems but who are nevertheless the bane of existence to those who believe in the scientific enterprise. At least in democratic politics, the electorate decides. In academic life, the problems seem more insoluble because if the claim is maintained that the personal is political, then Weber's neat separation between vanity and the scientific enterprise cannot hold. Such is the triumph of ideology under conditions of decomposition, a failure of the social-scientific imagination as it cedes itself to politics and the politics of vanity.

In this sense, all the figures presented in this book have been "activists"—just not in the received sense of purveyors of ideological demands. Instead, they have been activists for the truth, always separate from such demands, but never unaware of them or their influence. C. Wright Mills is sentimentalized by far too many as a great sociological critic, in a spirit of criticism that is now so hackneyed and so dumbed-down that it would require something of a miracle to save that spirit from those who praise it the most. Nevertheless, it is precisely Horowitz's reading of Mills that allows for that possibility, acknowledging Mills' enthusiasms while reminding us how timeless his sociological imagination remains and how instructive it could be, if only we place Mills in his time rather than to take the specific criticisms he made in his time as the substance for critiques of our own present difficulties.

The same holds true for that spirited rebel, Hans Eysenck, whose dedication to experimentalism brought him both praise and disdain along the same ideological fault-lines that are familiar to anyone caught within them. Eysenck's writings on tobacco are a case in point. The enormous cultural shift in custom that followed tobacco's condemnation as unhealthy forty years ago put a once prominent American industry on the chopping block. As the most affordable and convenient drug delivery device to have ever been invented, the cigarette may no longer be sublime, but it is likely to be around for a long time to come. What Eysenck was caught up in was nothing less than a whirlwind of uncertainty about how to assess the causal links between cigarettes and health over and against what sellers hoped would not be found and what health experts believed had been found decisively. Perhaps a disinterested social science is impossible under such circumstances, but skepticism about the sellers and their opponents is a healthy thing for social science in the long term when it comes across such controversies.

If space permitted, I should say something more, too, about the contributions of such great thinkers as Robert Nisbet, Russell Kirk, Lewis Feuer, Hannah Arendt, W.E.B. Du Bois, David Riesman, and others now living. Nisbet, in his *Degradation of the Academic Dogma*, recognized what was coming in the next thirty years before anyone else did. Kirk's *The Conservative Mind* has only grown in stature and influence fifty years on. Feuer's *Ideology and the Ideologists* tells more about the psychology of power than any book written since *The Prince*. For all the controversy surrounding Hannah Arendt, her ideas and arguments are engaged with no less enthusiasm today than a half-century ago. Du Bois' disappointments in the world diminish in the face of his confidence in human possibility in the same world. And David Riesman, whose career took him to the elite pinnacle of higher education, never lost touch with the sensibility of democratic individualism and its strong identification with achievement, but not ascription. How can anyone reading these tributes deny to any of them their own fair share of achievement?

What readers of this splendid collection of personal and intellectual accounts will enjoy the most, I believe, are the insights provided by Irving Horowitz's encounters with both the limits and mortality of all concerned. Ideas may be immortal, but no one I know can say whether this or that idea is immortal. I suspect that publishers of ideas know this best of all. There is nothing more sobering about the mortality of ideas than to discover one's book is out of print. It is impossible not to acknowledge that so many of the tributes given here are to the many people over the past forty years whose ideas have achieved that limited immortality of remaining available in print because of the good offices of Irving Louis Horowitz and Transaction Publishers. The costs borne by the publisher are recouped in the remarkable pantheon of thinkers and writers on display here. This is a book of the ideational lives neither of saints nor of sinners, but of those whose life's works have mattered first to Irving because they matter most of all to his vision of social science. It is a family album, and it is fitting that the man touched by all of them should show them off now with pride and affection.

Jonathan B. Imber

Introduction

There is a nebulous kind of writing that escapes easy characterization. Books, essays, articles, reviews, and even op-ed pieces are easily identifiable. But statements made for special occasions, usually memorial services and remembrances of people recently or remotely departed, do not fit into these "boxes." Locating the thread between "chapters" becomes more a matter of reader impressions than authorial intentions. I suspect too that the failure to acknowledge this type of work as a legitimate activity, even a socially necessary one, is a function of the pain and sorrow of transition and finally loss itself. In such somber circumstances we are far happier doing the honoring than acknowledging the worth of those being honored.

There are other reasons why such writings at the literary margins usually remain obscure. So often the comments of the living about the elderly or the dead are laced with self-reflection and, unhappily, self-promotion. In addition, such addresses often emphasize the personal and the private, making some effort to connect the living and the departing. Too often the result is not only incidental writing, but also trivial writing. For what matters, what counts in memorial statements—whether delivered orally or in writing—is the reason for the gathering to begin with. What makes an individual merit special attention in a world in which dying is tragically routine?

For those people in the social and behavioral sciences for whom the empirical is king, or who want only to learn hard lessons about the history and conduct of the research process, this sort of informal collection of materials may well seem dismaying for its inherently unsystematic characteristics. For when all is said and done, eulogies and reflections of this sort have more to do with the literary than the scientific tradition. In these we reflect on the character of the person, the esthetic dimension of his or her writings, and the moral purposes—if there are any—of the person being honored. In short, memorializing the venerable departed is not quite the same as criticizing and confronting adversaries in the marketplace of ideas.

Self-reflections exhibited in quasi-public statements about friends are inevitable. To eulogize others is to come face to face with the transience of individual life as such. Yet the purpose of such memorial statements is to somehow accomplish the reverse: to snatch permanence from the jaws of transience. What is it that remains intellectually alive after the bodily remains have been interred? It is less than pleasant to reflect on one's own destiny. We want for ourselves what we extend to others: permanence, even immortality. So our tributes to others are not exactly untouched by the vanity of those who live with the power of ideas. Tributes may prove to be a poor substitute for the exercise of actual power based on physical force, but it is worthier to honor the bearer of truths than the master of arms.

It may be simpler to define this effort by what it excludes rather than what it contains. To start with, other than the year of birth (and, alas, death when necessary), there are few dates given. This is not an encyclopedia of social science or a who's who of its founders. Nor is it a dictionary of terms and their inventors. The world has an ample supply of such reference volumes. I also wanted to avoid any sense of this being an exercise in necrology. Death notices usually contain information on starts and finishes. At the risk of driving readers to precisely such reference works, I decided to keep this volume as informal as the subjects involved permitted. I would prefer criticism of the text as somehow lacking in precision than the opposite charge of it being excessively pedantic or emotionally remote.

These deliveries, commentaries, and eulogies were often delivered in an informal context of taken-for-granted sensibility, with an audience that knew the timeframe in which the figure being honored worked, or in some happy cases, continues to work. As a consequence, these remarks are rarely rounded, full-bodied appraisals that present a complete listing of the contributions of the people being honored. They offer, or at least they attempt to offer, insight into how ideas and experiences are transmitted from person to person. In Western culture we may not always venerate the generations that came before us, but in a myriad of ways, from establishing canons of important figures to erecting pantheons for the honoring of such individuals, we still must come to grips with the cultural tradition that binds generations. Memorial services, festschriften, birthday celebrations of the venerable, awards in the name of the famous, all function in such a manner. So this volume is constructed, and hopefully will be received, as a contribution to what makes the culture of the social sciences viable, and in some figures, sufficiently worthy to invite imitation and improvement.

However much we fancy ourselves the inventors of our own thought, the best of them are often a digest and a reflection of the work of many others. We are not so much discoverers of new ideas as transmitters of old ideas retooled and refashioned to address the challenges of a contemporary age. That this simple fact is easily overlooked is surprising, given the fact that as teachers, we take for granted our role in the continuation of culture—which, after all, is what we social scientists mean when we speak of the canons of social science. Such a canon is the composite of experience. Even as we each work hard to define our own uniqueness, the culture itself draws us in an opposite direction, toward common concerns of all those who accept the limits as well as the benefits of social research.

Certain technical problems arise in trying to create a composite picture of the sort exemplified by this volume. How should one demonstrate respect and appreciation for the work of others without falling prey to eclecticism—to a fawning celebration of different viewpoints that hardly fit with one another? The best one can hope for is a composite picture of influences yielding something of a mosaic. This volume seeks to display reverence for ideas collectively, although I may have serious doubts, even deep reservations, as to the veracity or worth of some. In assembling such a collective portrait in a single volume I have come to better understand the role of civility and generosity of spirit in appraising the work of others.

The esthetics of the scientific process have a dimension of their own: One can admire the elegance with which an idea is constructed, and respect the logical development of a work whatever its premises may be. This itself becomes a factor in the evaluative process. Scholars make mistakes. They sometimes live lives of quiet desperation, even moral dissolution. We are constantly confronted by the duality of the product and the person. We perceive the value and design of the work performed in a lifetime, as distinct from the values and designs of the person who performed such work. We all wish our heroes to be whole, consistently virtuous in practice as well as preachment. Once in a while, this actually occurs. But such wholeness, such saintly characteristics, is rare in the lives of actual figures. Even the best are touched by vanity; even the worst have aspects of divinity. This duality is the fundamental challenge for one offering appraisal of friends and colleagues of a lifetime.

One brings to such underground musings a sense of personal experience. Private motivations, small or large, also play a role in estimating the contribution of those people we actually knew. In my case, such knowledge has much to do with attitudes toward the publishing environment. Some wanted more free copies than they were entitled to receive; others were anxious to broaden their circle and willing to pay for the privilege of doing so. Some perceived copyeditors as inherent enemies of the literary race, others saw such often-anonymous figures as saints in the publication process. Some saw the publication of their work as the end of their involvement with the publisher; other were quite willing, even anxious, to contribute to the post-publication marketing process. The publication process is highly revealing, even of intimate details of family life, children, pets, travel, and team preferences.

I daresay that my own publishing role contributes enormously to an appreciation of the academic performance and scholarly worth of others. How could it be otherwise since so many of these tributes are also tributes to authors with whom I have worked in my publishing activities—for ten years as external social science editor at Oxford University Press and for forty years as editorial director of Transaction Publishers at Rutgers University? For an academic such as me, working on publishing requires more than a touch of schizophrenia, and multiple roles are not easy to manage. But on balance, my dual life as professor and publisher has proven to be a great help to seeing the social science world and its many contributors fair, square, and whole.

In this sense, scholarly publishing was also a wonderful preparation for recognizing the differences between form and content, and more pointedly, to an appreciation of the fact that the quality of the work done by others only partially rests on a theory of verification. The other part rests on the practice of esthetics. I would like to believe that the finest minds in the social research process have also been its best writers, those best able to present their work for public consideration. This, of course, is not universally the case, yet I am pleased to note that it is far more often the case than one might expect. What we respond to in others is that happy blend of intellectual exactitude and esthetic design that somehow finds a role in public service—or at least public display. It is that balance between the analytic and synthetic, however individually arrived at, that serves as a unifying feature for my selection of tributes for this volume.

It might well be the case that such a distinction between the esthetic and the intellectual, or more to the point, the personal and the professional, is disconcerting to some and a violation of ideological rigor to others. Those for whom political principles, such as they may be, override all other considerations will surely be dismayed by the apparent eclecticism of friends and associates herein represented. But I fail to see how civility and decency in human discourse is possible if we select ideological purity as a litmus test for evaluating the work of others. This is not in any way to deny my own deep-seated beliefs in evaluating the work of others. It is to reject the absurd notion that the position I hold or that are held by others can ever form the basis of human friendship. To make such personal demands as the grounds for intellectual association is as foolish, and as fanatical, as making intellectual similitude the bases for personal association.

At the same time, into the mix of evidence and esthetics, one must always include the moral bases of belief. We might like to think of the social sciences as sharing with the physical sciences a sense of evidence based on a common core of methodology. However, the ability of so many important people in the varied fields to focus on moral ends, or at least ethical consequences, is the true unifying element above and beyond esthetic sensibility. For while these figures may or may not have a strong predilection to policy suggestions and prescriptions, all seem to share a unique appreciation of the moral bases of human judgment.

The late Stephen Jay Gould best expressed my own feelings in the matter. In *Wonderful Life*, he spoke of *Homo sapiens* as a "wildly improbably evolutionary event well within the realm of contingency." This is a depressing prospect to some, but for him it was "exhilarating, and a source of both freedom and consequent moral responsibility." If this sentiment is the case for paleontology, how much more is it so for students of the human condition? So what I will leave the reader is a personal hurrah, not a professional summation. This is a series of quite personal, but not especially intimate, recollections stimulated by the work of others. It is to be taken in small doses and with caution. It may well be that in the beginning is the word. But at the end there is the tribute.

Now that this long odyssey has come to a climax, or at least a conclusion, I have to be clear and admit a truth—one nervously lurking in the shadows of my mind for some time. This is as close to an autobiography as I am likely to get. For despite every possible ruse and effort to avoid the pitfalls of egoism, of self-centered reflections imposed on others, there is the irreducible fact that these are all, or nearly all, people who I knew and cared for. In many case, they are people who deeply influenced my life—whether through mentoring, gentle coaxing, or simply in a willingness to exchange ideas and opinions.

Autobiography is a reflection of two great epicenters of the person: the inner life of the mind and the external life of social and intellectual exchanges. To be sure, there is precious little of the former in *Tributes*. These statements were not designed for delivery as self-revelation. But in going through these profiles in miniature, I see much of myself: who I am, what I was, and why I worked hard to become better at the craft of social research. So many of these scholars and friends are now deceased that the sense of finality, of rupture, hangs as a dark cloud over these pages. One memorializes the dead, but one talks only to the living.

Given the nature of this effort, it is only fitting that a broad disclaimer be entered as to what *Tributes* is not seeking to perform. First, this is not a history of the social sciences in the twentieth century. Too many entries are of a personal nature that may not be part of any enduring history of the various disciplines. Even more telling at this level, is the fact that many figures of great prominence are not included. Among these are people with whom I have no contact, and those whose work is in areas entirely remote from my base of knowledge. Second, this is not a comparative study of intellectual elites. I make no effort whatever of comparing or contrasting any of these people. They are treated sui generis, for contributions that they made on their own and in their own time. Third, there is no assessment of ascriptive features of the people examined. How many men or women, how many Americans or Europeans, how many Jews or African-Americans, simply have no bearing on measuring their individual contributions. Of course, such elements are dealt with as contextually relevant to understanding contents. But beyond that, the reader is free to make his or her own judgments of such elements.

With very rare exception I knew these people personally – some intimately more often than not in passing. Living a life that constantly crosses over from scholarly publishing to academic professing was and remains a tremendous source of pleasure in my life. It allows for knowing people in special circumstances of work in progress no less than thoughts in passing. The big exception is the entry of Karl Popper and Ludwig Wittgenstein. Both were such huge influences on my early thoughts about social research and the logic of social science that I decided to make an exception. The occasion of their singular meeting in debate gave me the chance to reassess their importance on my work, and more, put in perspective how the actual course of intellectual history has treated each of these extraordinarily able, if troubled, individuals. In the case of the Lynds, I did not know Robert. But I did have the opportunity to interview on several occasions, his widow and partner, Helen Merrell Lynd for their joint entry in the *Encyclopedia of the Social Sciences*. I do not think that this violates the self-imposed rule that the entrants in *Tributes* be known to me as a person as well as a scholar.

Ever since the publication of my childhood memoir on growing up in Harlem, *Daydreams and Nightmares*, Kind readers have asked me if this was but the first step in autobiography. I said no then and reiterate that again. Most academic autobiographies are so terribly self-centered, so focused on the world as seen from a singular perspective that they fail as literature and even more emphatically as narrative. But in doing *Tributes* it soon became apparent that my own life is very much entwined with the achievements of others. Indeed, my infatuation with the history of ideas is doubtless an expression of my admiration for these special people. But it is also a way to put myself in a world beyond myself. I want *Tributes* to serve as an expression of who I am, but only in a context of respect for what other people have made me. We all live in a private world of angels and devils, those we admire and those for whom we have sharp criticism that spills over into anger or criticism. This is a work about academic angels and personal admiration. I will leave for to others the hard task of summing up what is wrong with our world – at least on this occasion.

It needs only further emphasizing that this is not intended to be a formal history of social science as a whole or discipline by discipline. It is a fragment in the lives of others as they impinged on myself, or at least as I imagined them. As such these statements may be skewed, even at times, deeply flawed. But nothing in the volume is done with malice or an attempt at "sitting on the shoulders of giants." I do not want to be in the position reputed to be that of

Sandor Ferenczi, who in a fit of false modesty spoke of himself as sitting on the shoulders of a giant—in his case Sigmund Freud—the speaker who he was about to introduce at an early gathering of international psychiatrists. The great man responded to such fatuous praise by saying, yes, that sitting on the shoulders of a giant is an understandable position, but for a person to lodge his lice in the hair of another is a far less acceptable situation.

I would like to be viewed as a man among men, and yes, in certain cases, among women. I was in dialogue with these people during their lives; painfully, I remain so in their absence. I hope that this is sufficient, if not a necessary, justification for this volume of tributes—to people of great talent who for the most part were neither giants nor pygmies, but creative talents who helped forge a century of intellectual and cultural work that we call the social sciences. I hope that in the act of reading this set of profiles, others can join in this endlessly wonderful game of coming to terms with our selves. No higher purpose can be obtained than this fusion of who we are and how others made our existence possible and meaningful.

Acknowledgements

Before leaving the reader to his or her own devices, I want to make clear a few of the changes from the original text as either written or delivered. While the substance of each narrative remains unaltered, for the purpose of making the volume stylistically consistent as well as user friendly I have eliminated references that were carried, often at the insistence of scholarly publications in which a good deal of this material originally appeared. This paraphernalia has been replaced with a listing of several major books by each of the people under examination. In doing so, I have avoided referencing specific editions or even languages of first appearance in order to provide a sense of informality.

Other changes have been of a more cosmetic variety. I have given each person a caption, or title if you prefer. These were often not in the original eulogies or commentaries, and again, it is an effort to highlight a particular aspect of the person under discussion, and avoid the appearance of a necrology. It simply seems to me that, especially in an informal, and highly personal series of statements, some sense of context is called for. There is a fine line between the private statements made at intimate gatherings and public statements made for a reading audience. It goes without saying that they spill over into each other—at times with unintended consequences. I ask the reader to accept a volume of tributes where hard lines and clear-cut distinctions are not easily maintained. This sort of effort obviously makes demands upon the reader that are unfair if not downright presumptuous. I can only hope that the results make for a worthwhile reading experience that parallels my own sense of a worthwhile writing experience.

Irving Louis Horowitz
July 12, 2003
Rutgers, The State University of New Jersey

1

Hannah Arendt:
Juridical Critic of Totalitarianism

Hannah Arendt was born in Hanover, Germany, of German-Jewish parentage in 1906. She was educated in Koenigsberg and later Heidelberg. After fleeing to France from Germany in the late 1930s, she immigrated to the United States in 1941. She was naturalized as an American citizen in 1950. Most of her life was spent in the academy. She was a Guggenheim fellow in 1952-1953; visiting professor at the University of California at Berkeley in 1955; the first woman appointed to a full professorship at Princeton in 1959; and visiting professor of government at Columbia University in 1960. From 1963 to 1967 she was university professor at the University of Chicago. And in 1967, until her death in 1975, she served as university professor at the New School of Social Research. It is fair to say that Arendt was an intensely urban person, and that being proximate to San Francisco, Chicago, and New York meant at least as much to her as the university affiliations as such.

The publication of *The Origins of Totalitarianism* in 1951 established her as a major figure in postwar political theory. In that work she attempted to provide a unitary approach to totalitarianism as such, seeing differences between National Socialism and Communism as of lesser significance than the organizational and cultural linkages that such systems have with each other. Such systems have a common base in the leadership principle, in single-party politics based on mass mobilization rather than individual voluntary participation, and not the least, in a nearly insatiable desire to expand from nation to empire—whether directly through military adventure or indirectly through political infiltration.

Anti-Semitism functioned differently in Germany under Hitler and in Russia under Stalin, but they had the same common roots: the existence of disparities between social classes and the need for objectifying an enemy responsible for all shortcomings and defeats suffered by nations and systems. Arendt's powerful critique of anti-

Semitism was directly linked to her participation in Jewish affairs once she came to the United States. She served as research director of the Conference on Jewish Relations between 1944 and 1946; and then as executive director of Jewish Cultural Reconstruction in New York between 1949 and 1952, or just prior to her fame and assumption of the round of university posts mentioned earlier.

Arendt's views on genocide extended far beyond her *Eichmann in Jerusalem* volume. Indeed, unconstrained by journalistic narrative, she developed a general theory of totalitarianism, in which the subject of genocide was thoroughly explored. In defining Nazism, she argued against the idea that it is simply a distorted extension of Western culture as such. "Nazism owes nothing to any part of the Western tradition, be it German or not, Catholic or Protestant, Christian, Greek or Roman.... On the contrary, Nazism is actually the breakdown of all German and European traditions, the good as well as the bad."

Arendt, rather than view genocide as a special property of Germans or Austrians (or any other people), considered it as nihilism in action, "basing itself on the intoxification of destruction as an actual experience, creaming the stupid dream of producing the void." Not a few of Arendt's critics consider this formulation as apologetics, a way in which she was able to reconcile personal relationships with politically conservative mentors and lovers like Martin Heidegger with a larger series of politically liberal, and sometimes radical, claims. But whatever the truth of such strongly biographical claims, her views on national types are well within the mainstream of twentieth-century social theory.

The single most important element in *The Origins of Totalitarianism* as it pertains to genocide is the idea that the prospects for mass murder and selective mayhem are embodied in the structure of totalitarianism as a system rather than the special national characteristics of any particular people. The forms of totalitarianism may vary—Nazi, Fascist, communist—but the content allows for genocidal acts whatever the ideological proclivities of the extremist regimes may proclaim.

The ground for such genocidal actions is prepared by the denial of citizenship, of political and legal rights of the victim class. In a brilliant examination and support of Edmund Burke's critique of abstract arguments of human rights that are divested of concrete sentiments of those natural rights that spring from being part of a nation, Arendt notes that "The survivors of the extermination camps, the inmates of concentration and internment camps, and even the comparatively contented people, could see without Burke's arguments that the abstract nakedness of being nothing but human was their greatest danger. Because of it they were regarded as savages and, afraid that they might end by being considered beasts, they insisted on their nationality, the last sign of their former citizenship, as their only remaining and recognized tie with humanity." And in a stunning conclusion to the segment on imperialism, Arendt points out "That a man who is nothing but a man has lost the very qualities which make it possible for other people to treat him as a fellow man." And this stripping the Jews of legal rights through deprivation of the rights of citizens *per se is* the essential necessary (if not sufficient) condition for genocide to take place.

There is an ambiguity in her formulation, in that at times, it is the size and power of government as such that provides the seeds for totalitarian rule, while at other times, it is the cultural and psychological conditions that define prospects for totalitarian domination. So it turns out that totalitarianism depends on the assumption of power by the extremists at a point in time when state machinery is "frozen" and unable to remain a process. But it also turns out totalitarianism is made possible by the widespread installation of fear and what she calls "total terror." And the totalitarian system is one in which victims and executioners alike are selected without regard to personal conviction or sympathies, but only in terms of rigid "objective standards," that is, who is a Jew and who is an Aryan.

The Origins of Totalitarianism ends on a creative ambiguity, one hardly restricted to Arendt. A great deal of argument within political theory after World War Two focused on just such an examination of the causes of extremism and the breakdown of law and democratic order. We need to know whether it is politics or culture that defines the limits of power. Otherwise, not only are we limited in understanding or responding to such ultimate horrors as the Holocaust, but also the nature of democratic options as such remains in precarious limbo. For we need to determine whether totalitarianism is but an extension of political processes of mobilization and massification as such, or something quite different and antithetical to those processes.

Arendt attends to this ambiguity in a work that appeared a decade later. After *The Human Condition*, which might well be seen as an interlude rather than continuation of the earlier arguments about totalitarianism, is a tribute to her fine German mentor, Karl Jaspers. She returns squarely to the problem of totalitarian systems and political change in what may well be her most underrated effort: *On Revolution*. Indeed, this work too is dedicated to Jaspers. In it she noted that he, uniquely, in *The Future of Mankind* "dared to face both the horrors of nuclear weapons and the threat of totalitarianism." *On Revolution* addressed the world one step further. With the nuclear powers at a stalemate, revolutions had become the principal political factor of the time. To understand revolution for her became the key to unlock the future.

While *On Revolution* does not directly address issues of genocide, in coming to a psychological profile of political absolutism, a sense of how the "passions" and the "taste" for power lead to the genocidal state emerges, and Arendt does illumine new directions. She takes Robespierre's theory of revolutionary dictatorship as the quintessential model of the European encounter with politics, an encounter that ends in anti-politique. "The thirst and will to power as such, regardless of any passion for distinction, although characteristic of the tyrannical man, is no longer a typically political vice, but rather that quality which tends to destroy all political life, its vices no less than virtues." With the appeal to the political as a framework for rational discourse—the sort of unique qualities that endeared American and British civilization to Arendt—there can be no democratic society. So that even in Revolutionary France, from 1789 to 1794, the shouts of the day were "Long Live the Republic," and not "up with democracy."

Arendt remained in all her works the jurist, the legal analyst. Her concerns were to plumb the depths of legitimacy, not as an abstract discourse on nationalism, but as an effort to review the grounds that permit a people to survive even harsh and tyrannical conditions. In this she was neither a conservative nor liberal, at least not in any conventional sense of those concepts. To be sure, this difficulty in easy characterization may be that property in Arendt that has proven most irritating as well as elusive to critics.

For example, Arendt saw in modern conservatism (in contrast to the writings of ancient Greek philosophers) a profound two-hundred-year response to the French Revolution, seeing it as a polemic in the hands of Edmund Burke, Alexis de Tocqueville, Eric Voegelin, and their modern followers. Liberals, for their part, were doomed to provide an uneasy rationalization for a totalitarian revolution they could not quite understand, accept in full, or reject. But the ambiguity of such formulations notwithstanding, in this way she compelled a fresh reading of historical events of enormous magnitude.

It is questionable, and not at all certain, that Arendt had her causal ducks in a row on this theme. It would seem that Jacob Talmon, who also wrote on *The Origins of Totalitarianism* at the same time and with remarkably similar conclusions, was closer to the mark in suggesting that the radical segment of the French Revolution, and of the French Enlightenment before that, were the real source of polemics—both as a style suited to ideological thinking and as a substantive way to treat political power. But that said, it may well be that conservatism for so many years did reveal reactive rather than proactive tendencies. It did so until that point in time when it was once more linked to mass politics and political party life in America. But of course, Arendt died just at that point in time when the transformation of conservatism from a class-based theory to a mass-based practice was commencing. But these are considerations within democratic cultures that were far removed from the monolithic works of totalitarianism that allows for genocides.

As someone steeped in classical German legal philosophy, the juridical order of things was critical to Arendt throughout her career. The legal system is that logical artifact that both makes possible and calls forth the loftiest aims of human beings, and, at the other extreme, prevents or at least curbs the implementation of their most venal desires. These strongly ancient Jewish and classical Greek appeals to the legal as the logical were invoked by Arendt to illustrate the survival of the human race and its function to limit anal ultimately thwart the totalitarian temptation behind the genocidal invocation.

The various strands in her thinking on law and the social order come together in her "report" on the Nazi destruction of the Jewish people, *Eichmann in Jerusalem*, to which we now turn. The most explosive statement on the trial of Adolf Eichmann that was held in Jerusalem in 1961 after his capture by Israeli security forces in Argentina was unquestionably the book written by Arendt entitled *Eichmann in Jerusalem*. The work originated in a commission by *The New Yorker* magazine to cover the trial and was finally written up in the summer and fall of 1962 while Arendt served as a fellow of the Center for Advanced Studies at Wesleyan University. The book itself was published in 1963 with a 1964 version that carried a post-script and a reply to critics.

The work has been subject to such repeated and withering assaults and no less fatuous praise from sources remote to Arendt's way of viewing and thinking that it is not amiss to look back to the text itself. The biggest surprise in store for the viewer is that the overwhelming burden of the book is a straight legal narrative of the trial of one man in one courtroom for specific crimes against one people—the Jewish people. The Arendt volume shares the position of the Israeli judicial system: that Eichmann was guilty of heinous war crimes and that Israel as the representative of the Jewish state and its people had every right to execute the culprit.

The largest portion of *Eichmann in Jerusalem* is taken up with exposition and narrative: moving from the character of the German judicial system and its corruption under Nazism, to a biographical profile of Eichmann, onto the stages in the development of the Nazi plan for the genocide of the Jewish people leading up to the Wansee Conference. The next large portion of the work is taken up with a series of brilliant historical sketches of deportations. The first wave came from Germany Austria and the Protectorates. The second wave came from France, Belgium, Holland, Denmark, and Italy. This was followed by a third wave of deportations, from Central Europe, especially Hungary and Slovakia. At the level of historical sweep, the Arendt volume stands side by side with the works of Lucy Dawidowicz and Raul Hilberg.

The controversial elements are actually restricted to the Epilogue and the Postscript. Indeed, even Arendt's description of the Nazi killing centers at Auschwitz, Bergen-Belsen, Theresienstadt, and her recitation of the evidence and eyewitness accounts of the Holocaust follow a familiar path. There is not effort to dismiss, denigrate, or become disingenuous about the existence of the Holocaust, or even that it was a warfare aimed at the specific liquidation of they Jewish people. To be sure, it was the very specificity of the Nazi crimes against a particular subset of humanity that permits Arendt to reason that Israelis courts had full jurisdiction in the matter of the disposition of Eichmann, no less than the precedent set by the Allied courts after World War Two, in the Nuremberg Trials. Hence we must look at the ethical and the psychological aspects of the Arendt volume for an answer as to why her work aroused such passions among scholars, politicians, and Jewish communities the world over.

The problem inheres in the subtitle rather than the title: *A Report on the Banality of Evil*. The choice of words was not accidental. Arendt was in search of the why of the Holocaust even more than operational details. She aimed to understand how this colonel in the Nazi SS could perform such a hideous role in modern history, show little remorse, yet also display keen analytical insight into the trial processes no less than the killing fields he helped organize and supervise. Arendt located the problem and her answer in terms of the nature of the bureaucratic mind—a world of operations without consequences, information without knowledge. In this strict sense she felt that banality was the most appropriate single-word description of Adolf Eichmann.

And while not even Arendt's most bitter opponents would accuse her of being a Holocaust denier there is a problem with the word banality. It strongly implies the mundane, the ordinary, the everyday vulgarities experienced by all creatures—great and small. To use such a term to describe Eichmann thus appeared as a form of clever apologetics making him into an everyday functionary—interchangeable with other unimportant people and their passive followers. At the same time one might point out that for Arendt there is also a banality of goodness. In this category one might easily place Oskar Schindler—womanizer, profiteer, Nazi Party member, and savior of one thousand Jews from the ovens of Auschwitz. It was Arendt's special ability to appreciate the mixed motives from which human beings operate that accounts for good and evil alike. In this sense her Kantian philosophical roots served her well as a student of the Holocaust.

The question thus arises, and Arendt admits to it, whether the trial was actually intended to punish a single person for his specific crimes or a symbolic assault on the totalitarian regime that existed in Germany between 1933-1945. In response Arendt argued that the use of the word banal meant nothing more or less than a factual description of an evil man but not a deranged one, an ambitious bureaucrat rather than a dedicated ideologue. Arendt observed of the judges in the trial "a conspicuous helplessness they experienced when they were confronted with the task they could least escape, the task of understanding the criminal whom they had come to judge." As might be imagined, this only rubbed salt into a wound—one that has neither healed nor even abated.

Arendt placed her finger on the soft underbelly of the trial, not only of Eichmann, but of his likeness: to single out the most monstrous of perverted sadists and yet claim that he was intrinsically little else than a cog in the Nazi war machine, a figure representing the entire Nazi movement and anti-Semitism at large. While this might have passed with a disturbing nod, Arendt's further claim was that the physical extermination of the Jewish people was a crime against humanity, perpetrated upon the body of the Jewish people. In other words, it was the nature of the crime, not that it was perpetrated against the Jewish people, that was subject to punishment. Once again the issue was joined between Arendt and her critics since there was a subtle denial of the uniqueness of the Holocaust in the long history of human savagery.

Arendt's careful outline of how the Wansee Conference decisions to exterminate the Jews to make Europe *Judenrein* or Jew-Free is chilling and numbing. It is among the best writing she was able to muster. And if there were strange elements such as linking Eichmann to the Kantian precept of obedience to the law and a moral obligation, the actual savagery and fury of the Nazis and their more than willing helpers among the occupied nations can hardly fail to elicit a powerful response in readers even now.

The one element that did arouse additional anger was a subtle equation of the victims with the victimizer. The participation of Jews and Zionist emissaries in bad bargaining, and at times even in bad faith efforts to save Jewish souls by trafficking in monetary and commodity bribes to the Nazis, while not condemned by Arendt, are dealt with in less than sympathetic terms. That transport lists to concentration camps were often put together by Jews that sent many to their deaths and preserved the lives of some has been well documented. But in Arendt's hands, such acts of complicity only deepened the notion of "banality" as a common feature of the tormentors and the tormented.

One can say that Arendt's report *cum* book is a landmark in the psychology of the Holocaust. *Eichmann in Jerusalem* provides a foundation that makes possible a political psychology of Nazism far beyond earlier works—even of her own efforts to study the nature of totalitarian power and mass movements. If *Eichmann in Jerusalem* was found even by its admirers, such as Stephen Spender, as "brilliant and disturbing," and by Hans Morgenthau as "troubling our consciences," it is because the psychological profile makes the Holocaust not a special event but a common human failing of civility and decency; induced by either an absence of or a breakdown in governance as a response to the human need for tranquility. Arendt wrote a work on Jews worthy of a German scholar and a classical Greek humanist. Whether the work captured the ultimate tragedy of the Jewish people in the twentieth century or even the imagination of the Israeli citizens at the time remain open issues. But whatever turns out to be the ultimate judgment, this is clearly one of those rare works in which the object of the discourse is of great significance along with the subject of investigation.

Works by Hannah Arendt

Between Past and Future: Eight Exercises in Political Thought
Eichmann in Jerusalem: A Report of the Banality Evil
The Human Condition
On Revolution
The Origins of Totalitarianism

2

Raymond Aron:
Tribune of the European Intelligentsia

It is both daunting and dangerous to write a review of Raymond Aron's work. Here is a figure who wrote hundreds of journalistic articles for *Figaro, L'Express, Commentaire,* an equal number of articles and essays for professional journals, and several dozen books, at least some of which, starting with *The Opium of the Intellectuals,* helped to shape post-World War Two thinking. I do not believe that any serious person could take issue with the judgment of E. A. Shils that "no academic of this century—certainly no academic social scientist, with the possible exception of John Maynard Keynes—was so widely known and appreciated as Raymond Aron." Certainly, no other social scientist has been so universally honored in his lifetime. At the time of his death in October 1983 he had received as many emoluments and awards as he had book titles to his credit—no easy feat even in this age of easy academic celebration. Yet, even for those who admired him, questions remain as to the lasting nature of his intellectual achievement, and whether it is equal to his political acumen or moral probity.

History, Truth, Liberty is the second collection of Raymond Aron's essays to appear recently. The first, *Politics & History,* was published several years earlier. A third collection of essays, promised for 1988, is to be called *Sociologists, Power And Modernity.* Doubtless, still others will follow, given the indefatigable spirit of his heirs and assigns. Indeed, a solid broad cross-section of his journalistic or editorial writings would help give us a clearer picture of his day-to-day activities.

The reason for this posthumous outpouring, I would argue, apart from his towering importance as a scholar, is Aron's qualities as an essayist. For in truth, Aron is as much a child of Montaigne in stylistic terms as of Tocqueville in substantive terms. Despite his exhortations to the strictly rational, Aron wrote the sort of essay that epitomizes writing in relatively brief form that contains a moral lesson

11

more than an empirical datum. In this respect he is markedly distant from the contemporary sociological article. Each of the twelve essays in this volume, for example, contain more or less well defined examples of pitfalls to be avoided if not always paths to be followed.

So much was Aron the essayist, even the journalist in the best sense of that word, that a large-scale effort, such as *Peace and War: A Theory of International Relations*, was less than successful. Details drawn from the current events of the late 1950s and early 1960s kept getting in the way of Aron's Clausewitz-like effort at synthesis. In part at least this is due to an innate liberalism in Aron that was far deeper than any imputed conservatism. In any context other than France, this would have readily been recognized. But in an ideological environment often defined by the polarities of an abstracted Marxism and a crude if concrete Gaullism, Aron's essentially prudent and mediating efforts seemed an alien and intrusive force in French politics. But liberalism entered into the sinews of Aron's analysis, as when he notes in his essay "On the Morality of Prudence" that "we have tried to make the analysis of international relations independent of moral judgments and metaphysical concepts"—in other words, apart from the very linkage that is the shank of all conservative ideology.

It is important to have these selections from the work of Aron if for no other reason than to rescue him from the iconographic tradition to which he is increasingly subject. Essays and introductions on Aron's thought tell us a great deal about his dedication to French national interests, the Judaic tradition, his indomitable will in the face of personal misfortune, public obloquy, his *pessimiste jovial* and/or his *optimiste triste*. But in this display of necrophilia it is all too easy to lose sight of the actual themes to which Aron repeatedly returned; the strengths that made him such a powerful moral voice and alas, the weaknesses that made him more widely renowned as commentator than as synthesizer.

The core of *History, Truth, Liberty* is less concept-oriented than people-saturated. Individual greats uniquely embody important concepts. Thus, in the paper on "Tocqueville and Marx" we are given the brilliant insight that a "purely political revolution, one that does not modify the social infrastructure, does not allow man to realize himself because it confuses the genuine man with the worker locked into his particularity and because man is in conformity with his essence...." Aron comes down on the side of democratic liberalism:

the trinitarianism of bourgeois citizenship, technological efficiency, and the right of every individual to personal choice. The struggle between liberal democracy and socialist construction is seen as a historical dialogue between Tocqueville and Marx. But, of course, this is a contemporary French reading of the past. In England, the same struggle was locked in the bosom of John Stuart Mill, who embodied both liberal and socialist principles. In Russia, different varieties and strains of socialist politics embodied this struggle over the goals of democracy, with well-known disastrous consequences. In the United States liberal and conservative struggles were conducted as if socialism were an exotic European import. This is not to say that Aron was wrong in his judgments. It is to say that his formulations were all too often limited as well as informed by a continental elitism.

In the analysis of the West and the East, the chapters of this book which take up the penultimate and largest segment demonstrate well the strengths and weaknesses of Aron's continentalism. For in his understanding of the ideological roots of the problem of conflict, the Soviet empire's insistence on historical triumphalism and hence liquidation of the democratic West, the sources of tactics and strategies must be worked through. For as long as this commitment to the inevitable destruction of the West remains the basic agenda as well as telos of Marxism-Leninism, then all notions of accommodation must be tempered by a dual realism: the dangers of nuclear conflict (which require appropriate technical responses) and the threats to Western survival (which require appropriate ideological responses). But it remains problematic that "the day the Soviets have the same right to read, write, criticize and travel as Western nationals, the competition will have become truly peaceful." Even given such rights, and the movement is currently in such a direction, the likelihood of peace breaking out is slender. For different interests often preempt similar ideologies. And on this does Aron's attempt at synthesis come to a screeching halt.

But this is to draw attention to the weakest aspect of Aron's legacy. His enormous strength is as a political moralist par excellence. It is simply exhilarating to read Aron on the distinction between a philosophy of history and a theology of history in "Three Forms of Historical Intelligibility"; the role of the conduct of warfare in and of itself apart from the origins of a conflict or the diplomacy of a peace treaty in producing the most far-reaching social consequences as in

"The Intelligibility of History"; and the plurality of meanings and motives in real history in contrast to the monism of meaning in fanaticism disguised as the inevitable future, as in the great essay on "On False Historical Consciousness." If one may be forgiven an illiberal mandate on a liberal spirit: no student should be permitted to enter the field of historical studies without reading and knowing Aron's probing essays on history and its enemies, the sociological messianists.

Even the essays on presumably sociological themes gathered in the fourth and sixth segments are more an extension of Aron's historical concerns than with the actual conduct of empirical research. Thus, in "Science and Consciousness of Society" Aron makes clear the distinction between fairness and objectivity, criticism and dogmatism, individual heroism and collective suicide. And throughout, the examples of Soviet history and Marxist historiography are the foils upon which truth is lanced. Likewise, in the chapter on "Social Class, Political Class, Ruling Class" Aron instructs us with scalpel-like precision, and quite properly on the ambiguity of categories and the pluralities of meanings in real world contexts. And in the final segment on "Max Weber and Modern Social Science" we are instructed in the relativity of benefits and injuries, the richness of total history in contrast to the poverty of national chauvinism, the need for rationality in a universe dominated by irrational impulses. It is to Aron's credit that he sees the weaknesses in Weber's relativism without claiming to have answered such questions as are raised in the Weberian corpus, without sitting on the "shoulders of a giant" as would a gnat in the hair of another man. Aron's modesty was as genuine as his achievement: to see the problem, to state the problem, and to do so even if no answers are presently forthcoming. For it is the essence of rationality, of his rationality at least, to see the struggles of our time as a problem that needs the best efforts of rational people—even if that rationality should come up short in its struggle with the beasts who would be angels.

In reviewing this selection of Aron's essays (indeed other essays as well) one is repeatedly confronted with the European conscience wrestling with problems of democratic liberalism. But it seems to me that Aron did so with an arsenal of ideas that was only half-full. Tocqueville and Weber are set upon to do battle with Marx and Lenin. But in some strange way it was the Anglo-American tradition, of which Aron was acutely aware (but more on practical than on theoretical terms), that gave the answer to totalitarian regimes and systems. Whether or not Jefferson or Mill, Lincoln or Churchill, or more recent examples of the Anglo-American or constitutional tradition confronted the evils of Soviet totalitarianism as ideology, they did expose those evils in economical and political practice. In short, Aron's "West" had two components: the continental and the constitutional if you will: the former he knew best, the latter applied his teachings best. On this anomaly does Aron's work come to rest. Aron was a paragon of virtue and a beacon of light—for those "Cartesian" anti-theorists so highly prized and praised by Tocqueville in *Democracy in America* and an irritant and mystery for those European theorists who could not accept the realities of democracy that lacked a metaphysical shroud. Aron's great strength, and unique contribution, was to live comfortably in a world striving for democracy, while lacking adequate theories, rather than to opt for pure theories that yield so little in the way of practical liberties. In this, Aron was the true child of the French Enlightenment and the perfect critic of a German Romanticism that promised so much and yielded the free spirit so little.

Works by Raymond Aron

In Defense of Decadent Europe
Main Currents in Sociological Thought (2 volumes)
The Opium of the Intellectuals
Politics and History
Thinking Politically

3

Digby Baltzell:
Private Paradoxes and Public Losses

There is something patently absurd about trying to encapsulate the life of a scholar who lived eighty years, and worked up until the end, in a few brief minutes. Yet, these occasions somehow call forth just such absurdity. I think this custom continues more to give comfort to the living than to promote understanding of the dead. That is as may be, I feel no desire to break tradition—certainly not at the expense of a major figure in the ranks of social science and social history.

I was neither a student nor colleague of Digby's—at least not in the strict empirical sense. We were personal friends, and through the aegis of Transaction we have served as his major publisher for the past decade. Digby and I spoke of social concerns and of private fears, of political items and intimate matters. Surprisingly, we agreed on so many points of darkness and light that we very rarely argued. He had a sharp wit and yes, a sharp tongue. Happily, I shared in the former and was spared the latter.

To me Digby was, and remains, less an enigma than a paradox, a series of paradoxes. He offered no great synthesis, no single flash of light to illumine the world. Rather, his life and work provide uncomfortable illustrations that what we hold as commonplace often turns out to be extraordinary, and what we view as unusual is just as frequently routine. Digby did not pound out a theory of culture. He rather wrote within a cultural tradition that made sense out of the paradoxes that haunt our age.

Digby wrote of Philadelphia gentlemen, but with the cutting edge of a New York educated plebeian. He compared elites of Boston and Philadelphia, but with the sharp eye to the failings of all elites when it comes to servicing the needs of everyman. He put to the fire the so-called Protestant Establishment, knowing full well that its moment of dominance was fast fading. He excoriated the commercialism of modern sport, knowing full well that the days of the gentle-

17

man athlete had passed. And finally, even furtively at times, his mind was locked into examining patricians, but he practiced the ethnography of the rich with the heart of a plebeian.

In the hands of a lesser scholar, such paradoxes would have dissolved into a jumble of words, yielding a barrel of books without meaning. But therein lay Digby's secret: he could look at intimate phenomena and historical events, and tease out large-scale implications and social meanings. Indeed, I have come to believe that he was a better Weberian than most who tout themselves that way, simply because he examined the relationship of economy and religion not by thinking about Protestantism as a whole, but by looking at Quakers and Puritans in specific cities, in specific political configurations, in specific economies. By starting with real people in their historical contexts, Digby saw the long past, and as a result he understood the empirical present.

There was of course a literary gambit in all of this. He was not especially concerned with causal priorities and cultural linkages. And if Digby left certain big issues in sociological theory unresolved in his writings, one always walks away having a workmanlike explanation for the way things are. Why Philadelphia, despite its political advantages, was unable to capitalize upon them. Why sports became transformed within a century from a Jamesian moral equivalent to war, to its opposite, a warlike equivalent to morality. Why economic power and even educational background did not automatically translate into political domination or cultural control. In short, Digby's paradoxes became our illuminations.

What I loved most about Digby was his ability to transcend that which he knew to be true or false in favor of what he wanted to be right or wrong. Like Nietzsche in *The Uses and Abuses of History*, Digby well understood that the loss of innocence is not an argument in favor of coarseness or vulgarity, and the loss of power is not an argument in favor of its unbridled exercise by others. Perhaps he was too close to the traditions of the past to appreciate the excitements of the present. But his was a special vision in which the past mediated the present and informed our sense of the future—without tea, sympathy, or ideology.

I do not favor any more than Digby did, the oft-cited remarks by Santayana that those who forget the past are condemned to repeat its mistakes. Digby had too much skepticism about unilinear and unilateral theories of history to accept such a formulation. Rather, I think he would say, like Freud, we are so much a product of our past, so much a part of our culture, that whether we like it or not, present and future, like history, religion, and economy, simply roll over into one another. Digby said it best when he wrote in the new introduction to our edition of *Philadelphia Gentlemen*: "Anyone, finally, with a sense of history knows that all ages have their troubles and these give rise to feelings of loss compared with some supposedly more settled era.... As Abraham Lincoln once put it, if we are lost in the woods, we begin to find our way by retracing where we have been."

With Digby's death, we have the ultimate paradox: we have him (at least in his writings and in our memories) and we miss him—wondering in what nook and cranny he would have next illumined society and history. Given the futility of such idle speculation, we can at least retrace where Digby went in his spectacular life in order to better understand where we all going. As a personal footnote, when I run the spell check on the word processor, "Baltzell" comes up as "ablaze." I rather suspect Digby, being a wordsmith, would like to know that he went out on such a "correction."

Works by Digby Baltzell

Judgment and Sensibility
Philadelphia Gentlemen
The Protestant Establishment Revisited
Puritan Boston and Quaker Philadelphia
Sporting Gentlemen

4

Ernest Becker:
An Appreciation of a Life

During the final years of his life Ernest Becker knew death as a handmaiden. Cancer is a condition of permanent biological confrontation in which dying becomes a way of life. Ernest's extraordinary talent was the ability to translate experience into reason, the everyday expression of disaster into a social science expression of tragedy. In this regard, his final work, written and released just prior to the end, *The Denial of Death* (1973), parallels that remarkable personal document by Stewart Alsop, *Stay of Execution* (1974). Becker's final study concerns the meaning of death and not the management of dying. It centers on a universal property that unites the human sciences—the effort to overcome the inevitable. Becker was never content with observation cut asunder from interpretation. This work closes the circle he began in *The Birth and Death of Meaning* (1962). It is right and just that he should have been posthumously awarded a Pulitzer Prize on May 6, 1974.

In a lesser talent, professional marginality dooms a scholar, placing him between the many schools of social science. Becker knew this full well, and willingly ran risks for his integrated science of man, in which Pragmatism, Personalism, Marxism, and Freudianism were a four-fold metaphysical table. Although he was trained in cultural anthropology (receiving his doctoral degree from Syracuse University in that subject) he preferred the kind of theorizing favored by an inherited cultural sociology. The *Geisteswissenschaft* of a Dilthey more than the cultural anthropology of a Boas stirred his imagination. *The Structure of Evil* (1968) rather than the structure of the family or tribe stirred his soul.

Becker claimed as his domain the science of man, while those fragmented, or better, fractured social scientists, simply saw this preference as an occasion to exclude him from their specific domain. Psychiatry at Syracuse University, sociology at the University of California, and social psychology at San Francisco State College cast him loose. His soul finally came to rest at Simon Fraser University, with its special integrated department of political science, anthropology, and sociology. During the final burst of radical energy of the late 1960s, Becker came to a department which, if it did not exactly meet his criteria for an integrated scientific vision of humanity, at least gave him the material sustenance and the critical intellectual mass required for his effort.

I first met Ernest at Syracuse University during the summer of 1961, where I was serving a visiting stint in Paul Meadows' sociology department. It was an interesting and lively group, including S. M. Miller, Blanche Geer, Irwin Deutscher, with many special programs that were later to be of decisive importance in the study of income gaps and national poverty. But the quintessential group of innovators at Syracuse was a peculiar group of social psychiatrists lodged in the medical school, headed by Tom Szasz, Ronald Leifer, and Ernest Becker, whose appointment was in the Department of Psychiatry, the State University of New York, Upstate Medical Center, located in Syracuse. This special School of Medicine, rather than any of the social science or business policy schools, contained the greatest amount of novelty. From this point in time, Ernest evolved his ideas concerning an integrated vision of the science of man. I confess that then, as now, I remain unconvinced by his pragmatized version of overcoming alienation by a return to the *kulturkampf als Geistewissenschaft*. But his intellectual demeanor was so gentle and his passions so deep, that it was hard not to take his effort with the utmost seriousness. For whatever its exact content, Ernest did anticipate by a full decade the current round of intellectual discontent with the fragmentation and frustrations brought about by the previous automatic acceptance of functionalism as a way of social science life.

During this period I had the privilege of knowing Ernest personally, and I learned that he had wit as well as wisdom. His ability to regale a group, in accent and anecdote, was such as to make one wonder why he insisted on such an austere public image. Perhaps he felt that too much lightheadedness and levity were already a hallmark of academic affairs, or, as is more likely the case, he simply felt that keen sense of the public and the private—a distinction that many outstanding intellectuals have been forced to live with. In any event, he was an intensely private person; even his cancer illness was known only to a handful. His work, while reflecting a growing interest with the interplay of life and death, showed no traces of self-indulgence or self-pity. His illness became a source of information as well as imagination.

My favorite of his essays was, first, his extraordinary statement on "Mills' Social Psychology and the Great Historical Convergence on the Problem of Alienation," in *The New Sociology* (1964). It was an outstanding reinterpretation of the idea that mental illness is linked to educational breakdown; specifically, that the Freudian conception of neurosis might best be interpreted as a case of maleducation, or miseducation in the things that are vital to personal survival. As he put the matter in a later work, *Angel in Armor* (1969), "Character armor refers literally to the arming of the personality so that it can maneuver in a threatening world." This approach tied into a Marxian view of consciousness as a precondition for political liberation. This essay formed the basis of his later work on *The Revolution Psychiatry* (1964). I still feel that this represented a far more intriguing effort at synthesis than the eros/thanatos dialectic taken by other left-oriented figures in the early sixties—for it carried the possibility of rebirth and reform within real persons and not just the metaphysical interplay of giant thought systems.

The review-essay Ernest wrote for *Transaction/Society* entitled "Biological Imperialism" (1972) on *The Imperial Animal*, by Lionel Tiger and Robin Fox, was typical of his independent frame of mind. Far from taking the easy road of criticizing the book for its ill-timed male chauvinism (by virtue of its automatic and unfounded assumption that the hunting culture was specifically male dominated, and therefore spilled over into the management and control of the household or the community itself), Becker chose to develop a careful but devastating critique of the biogram model employed by Fox and Tiger. Nonetheless, he was careful to note the values of linking disciplines (from biology to zoology on one side to ethnology and sociology at the other side) in an effort to better understand the historical foundations of sex differentiation as well as all forms of social stratification. This piece was revealing because it showed that the idea of culture, the root and branch of cultural anthropology, remained at the heart of things for Ernest. Even in the integrationist attempt to frame a science of man, his intellectual origins were clearly expressed. Perhaps this is the inevitable consequence of all efforts at synthesis that start from the idea of a special social science, be it anthropology or sociology or economy.

Ernest was not a political radical, certainly not in any commonsense meaning of that term. Never did I hear him offer a tsk-tsk here and a pshaw-pshaw there about the awful truths of life and death as reported in newspapers. Indeed, his earlier background in the U.S. Foreign Service ill-suited him for any sort of political role. But in searching for a scientific synthesis that would amplify experience without violating the complexities of daily living, he attracted the radical sectors of the student body and professorial estate to his classes and causes. From Syracuse, to Berkeley, to Simon Fraser, people sensed a radicalism of content buried beneath a peculiar conservatism of style. This combination was to become Becker's intellectual badge. Here too, the mosaic of the man was best expressed in his constant search for the roots of twentieth century tragedy: technological growth brought at the price of genocidal destruction. Through this dialectic, Ernest was able to identify with the main movements of his time, against war in Asia, for racial equality in the United States, without the conventional parochialisms that made these movements themselves obsolete in victory. His anguish was the breakdown of synthesis in the present century, and his understanding was that the realization of equity would be the precondition for any renewed effort at universal synthesis—in fact as well as in theory.

Ernest Becker's abilities as a teacher are legendary. Probably not since F. O. Mathiesson has the higher reaches of academia known such a powerful, charismatic teacher. When the department of sociology at the University of California chose not to retain him on a permanent basis (it was said that he was not a professional sociologist), he received the unique honor of a teaching offer from the student body. Ernest became the first teacher chosen by his students directly without administrative support, and paid by them through Student Union funds. Fortunately for Ernest, and perhaps for the Student Union itself (which might have come into a serious jurisdictional dispute with the California Regents over such a disbursement of its funds), he received an interim appointment at San Francisco State, itself in the twilight of its own radicalization.

After arriving at Simon Fraser University one year later, Becker had to choose new sides between radicals fighting their dismissals and other radicals who, because they had been retained, chose not to fight. The issues at Simon Fraser were complex, and the scars deep. Ernest remained outside of this battle, although he tacitly supported the claims of those dismissed. We all want our heroes to be larger than life, to come out at the bell fighting and to do the righteous work of the Lord on every occasion. This was not the case with Ernest. By the time he reached Simon Fraser, the bloom was off the rose of the radical sixties. The issues had become cloudy and interest in student rebellion had waned. In any event, Ernest had never claimed a radical posture and hence had little compunction about absenting himself from radical campus politics. Shuttling about in academic life for two decades might also have played a part in dulling his appetites for internecine struggles, especially during a period of sharply failing health. No apologies are called for; yet no false deities should be constructed either. Ernest was man, not superman; humanist scholar, not socialist activist.

To all of us privileged to know Ernest Becker, the loss will be real and great. He well understood the idea of culture as a transmission belt, or as he called matters: "stones in the edifice." He knew this both through anthropology and through religion. Immortality for the humanist is rendered in the ongoing tradition of the new, in the people who use and even abuse works of the past. In eight books and countless more articles he set forth the premises of his integrationist view of the social sciences. His efforts to move beyond the positivist critique of meaning into new sources for the discovery of meaning made Ernest a contributor to liberation in that special, some may say vain, sense, in which the idea of social science is itself isomorphic with the idea of reason. Whatever the life of reason demanded—action or contemplation—it was the appeal to evidence as an architectonic of knowledge that ultimately renders meaning possible. Ernest was prepared to run his risks as part of such a framework of intellectual redefinition and redemption.

Let me end with one of Ernest's favorite aphorisms (from Pascal). It well expresses the special dialectic of the man. "Deliver me Lord, from the sadness at my own suffering which self-love might give. But put into me a sadness like your own."

Works by Ernest Becker

Beyond Alienation
The Birth and Death of Meaning
The Denial of Death
The Revolution in Psychiatry
The Structure of Evil

5

Herbert Blumer:
The Pragmatic Imagination

In academic life, there are people who are known for their writings, others for their teaching skills, and still others by the impact of their personalities. Despite the substantial achievements of Herbert Blumer in all three areas, he best fits into the last category. He was, for me at least, *Homo Americanus*, the personification of the American encounter with social science. Unlike so many others who owed their training and even sentiments to the European experience, Herb seemed to emanate from the American soil. It hardly does justice to speak of him as a member of the Chicago School of Interactionism, as if he was some abstract participant in the long march of partisan schools of ideological thought called "isms." He was the personification of the city of Chicago as such. It isn't every day that the field of sociology could boast an All-Pro football player (for the Chicago Cardinals), a negotiator of major labor management disputes (as in the wartime settlement between the government and U.S. Steel), and someone who was at home in the world of capitalist magnates like Benjamin Fairless and communist anarchists like Emma Goldman. If that made Herbert Blumer a larger than ordinary life that is because he was just that—a large sized personality encased in a large framed body.

Although he spent his final years at the University of California at Berkeley, he shall forever be identified with the University of Chicago, and the pragmatic tradition that it fostered between 1925 and 1952. The primary influence was the person of George Herbert Mead, and to a lesser, but significant degree, the work of Jane Addams in education and John Dewey in philosophy. Indeed, Herb was jealous of his own place in the pragmatic pantheon. While he shared with others a benign liberalism, a faith in the curative powers of learning and a naturalistic vision of the world in general, it was Mead who captured his imagination. The twin notions of social interaction at one level, and creative emergence at another, both derived from

Mead—which he took to be the mission of social research to expand upon.

In his writings, relatively sparse though they were for so senior and well known a figure, Herb spent more time puncturing holes in the theories of others than in formulating a world view of his own. He was the enemy of pretentiousness at the emotional level and tendentiousness at the ideological level. I confess to having thought of him as my adopted father in sociology. For while the most powerful influence on me was through philosophy and the work of Abraham Edel, the work of Blumer was less well structured but one I found to be more exciting. Emergence did not mean the transition from capitalism to socialism—whatever that idiotic phrase turned out to be— but change in status, in situation, and in structure. Blumer's sense of emergence derived from the process of multiple interactions. As such, the chain of events is as much a wide-open universe in the future as in the past. There is little room for pessimism or optimism in social research, for the obvious reason that such emotions rest on a belief that we can know the direction of events yet to happen. The social process was for Herb the source of emotional pleasure and no less than the actual meaning of events.

This is the case since both meaning and emotion are properties of behavior more than of any presumed intrinsic property of things. Indeed, so central was this to Herb's thinking that it defined the difference between the human sciences and the physical sciences. It was perfectly satisfactory for him to adopt a materialist view of matter, but it was equally unsatisfactory to make human assessments in the same terms. Since the human being, and by extension human society, is neither a function of mechanics nor operates behind the backs of men—like some hidden hand in Adam Smith or some unseen historical forces as in Karl Marx—such thinking is not only reductionism, but downright subversive of the sociological enterprise. Such mysticism smuggled into human events as moral imperatives or historical forces are modes that make explanation in social research the object of derision among ordinary mortals who know better.

Social interaction is the source of social order. It is the sense of communion that makes possible doing things together that otherwise cannot be done alone—that includes everything from science, to religion, to politics. The variety of responses to such collective needs creates the grounds for social institutions—and these in turn are wildly different formations that reflect the character of people. It is true enough that Herb sometimes downplayed and even disparaged searches for uniformity in behavior, even when such commonalties might be present. But more often than not, such a search produced sterile generalities that moved people in search of knowledge away from behavioral variations into an artificial set of constructs that placed living creatures into the straitjackets of dead theories. This type of rigorous pragmatism often placed him at odds with colleagues in the social sciences. Coming at a time when the discipline of sociology was intent on gaining a measure of legitimacy and even respectability, his thinking was at times belittled as crude and unsophisticated—a throwback to a pre-scientific era.

But such criticisms were unwarranted on several levels. First, Blumer's notion of interaction was just that. He shrewdly observed those action theorists (such as Erving Goffman) for all their acuity and brilliance lapsed into subjectivism, into a form of psychological hedonism that rested not on evidence but on intuition. It is not to deny that notions like "cooling out the mark" or "hustling" do not exist—of course, they exist. Rather, the task of the sociological is how such impulses and instincts play out on the canvas of social life. The entire framework of interaction, as it plays out in the empirical life and personal careers of individuals becomes the field upon which the sociological is examined. To do otherwise is to reduce social science to a series of a priori judgments that may satisfy the thirst for uniformity, but sacrifices the prizes of empirical examination.

Blumer carried these theoretical discussions into areas of major discourse. For example, he held that the notion of social development—so wildly popular after World War Two—was more myth than reality. To start with, people in the developmental field rarely were able to disaggregate the social from the political or the economical. The culprit was the idea of development itself—the weird notion that things move in an ever-upward direction and worse, that there is a moral good that attaches to development that somehow eludes the notion of change as such. For Blumer, change sufficed. Indeed, the dynamic exchange of change and order is a defining rod of the method of doing social research. Social institutions are a consequence of this exchange, this interaction engaged in by the human species. In this way, Blumer advanced the cause of social science as assuredly as did Weber and Schumpeter in their respective calls against imposing moral straitjackets and political ideologies on the conduct of the research performance.

The other areas in which Blumer weighed in heavily against scientism, or better said, physical reductionism, are the issues of social science in the conduct of public policy. Herb did not write very much, especially in his later, post-Chicago years. But he was enervated, or better said, aggravated by the Project Camelot scandal (the civic action program first aimed at Chile) by its presumptuous notions, by its belief that political movements can be fostered by foreign powers in search of political advantages. The Project Camelot affair became a metaphor for what went wrong in Vietnam, with its substitution of theoretical game models and civic action agrarian reforms for anything approximating the study of real people, with needs and traditions of their own. He saw such modes of reasoning, sponsored by huge federal agencies, as dangerous wishful thinking based on stereotypical concepts of the behavior of others. In this he was quite right. Indeed, in private conversations, Herb would often say to me that most policies are made in problem-solving settings. The need to get beyond a hurdle or a series of hurdles counts far more than predetermined ends in view by those who wield the levers of power. Of course, he was right on this—even if such an admission can hardly be envisioned, since it would result in a sharp reduction of funding access and sources.

Other than an early 1933 monograph with Philip Hauser on *Movies, Delinquency and Crime*, I am under the impression that his only other co-authored efforts were those he did with me. Both of them were aimed at Congressional testimony: one on the conduct of social research and the other on the establishment of a National Social Science Foundation—that would stand apart from the current National Science Foundation. It is fair to say that the search for a NSSF never had a chance, since the social scientists themselves were fearful that such a break from the establishment agency of scientific research and theory would result in isolation and a sharp reduction of influence. That said, the testimony we provided did lead to a sharply enlarged role for the social sciences within the National Science Foundation—perhaps all that could be expected. But the testimonials reflected the strong feelings that Herb had against sociological reductionism at one end and fatuous model construction at another. My own reasons for taking strong positions on these issues were less methodological than political. Like many others, I felt that the lines between scientific theory and social application had become so polluted that the end result was both bad sociology and even worse policymaking. Herb shared these sentiments, but he had a keener sense of the epistemological sources of how the corruption of science took place.

Perhaps the greatest honor Herb bestowed on me was not so much personal or even consenting to co-author a few papers, but his willingness to serve as the first chairman of the board of Transaction Publishers. After breaking with Washington University, and retaining ownership as a private enterprise dedicated to the public good, which took place in 1968—roughly five to six years after our origins—the need for legitimacy and capital became urgent. Herb responded at both levels. He was an original donor of substantial monies for our publishing venture, and I should add that Herb was not a wealthy man—a series of marriages that went sour saw to that—so his fiscal support was especially appreciated. But he did more: he also became chairman of a nascent board of directors of Transaction. He can never be fully repaid for such an act of generosity.

And what an ideal appointment this turned out to be! Herb Blumer could read a balance sheet in its most intimate details, plucking out the incongruities, the source of operational weakness from the numbers. I suspect that his activities as public panel chairman of the War Labor Board in World War Two and even more so his chairmanship of the Board of Arbitration for U.S. Steel may have honed his skills in these arcane areas. They were certainly a good deal more advanced than my own reluctant training in basic accountancy at Peerless Willoughby in New York during the heyday of McCarthyism! He served as editor of *The American Journal of Sociology* for more than a decade between 1942-1953, as president of the American Sociological Association in 1956, and editor of the sociology list at Prentice Hall Publishers for more than thirty years. Herb was in short the ideal candidate for the chairmanship of Transaction: He brought to the table worldliness, a powerful force in the profession of sociology, and a deep commitment to public welfare and public service.

Beyond all of this, I felt close to Herb as a person. He was a big man, with a chiseled set of facial features. In his hands and in his size one saw the contours of the proverbial football player. He told me that his grades at Chicago were not always up to par. He would play semi-pro ball on a Friday night, a pickup game for sizeable money on Saturday afternoon, and a Sunday professional game for the Cardinals. It was a world in which you played offense and defense. The squad size consisted of about fifteen men—four reservists carried in the event of injuries and body tears (which were frequent), and at the end of the day walked away with a week's pay for only (!) three days of work—or play—depending on one's attitude to the game. His was a background that I could understand, although in all candor, at the level of athletic prowess I was no match for his legendary achievements. Herb was stubborn but never mean, sure of himself but never dogmatic. He was a big man who in the act of committing himself to sociology made that field a little bigger and a lot more important. He smoked too much, lived too hard, and perhaps loved too easily. But he fulfilled his mission on Earth, and in so doing demonstrated the distinct nature of the human organism as a creative force.

Works by Herbert Blumer

Critiques of Research in the Social Sciences
Industrialization an and Agent of Social Change
Movies and Conduct
Symbolic Interactionism: Perspective and Method

6

Claude Brown:
Going to the Promised Land

Reading the obituaries on the death of Claude Brown (who died of a lung-related ailment on February 13, 2002) made me realize that such postmortems can be cruel and careless as well as comforting. One would think that what made *Manchild in the Promised Land* an important, nay, landmark, work, was that it is—as one obituary put it—"the tale of a boyhood spent among killers, drug addicts and prostitutes." The same syndicated obituary speaks of the book as "evoking Harlem's astonishing culture of violence." Even the death notice of the American Booksellers Association in recounting the passing of Brown speaks of *Manchild* being a "controversial book that exposed mainstream audiences to the stark realities of drugs and violence experienced by blacks in the 1940s and 1950s."

If these features are all of what distinguishes *Manchild in the Promised Land*, then it would not have sold more than four million copies in English and been translated into fourteen foreign languages. Nor would this explain the continuing interest in the book. It is indeed a memoir that takes some liberties with realities. Brown himself contributes to this by the use of pseudonyms for his characters, declaring that "all the names in this book...are entirely fictitious." *Manchild* ends on the same note of ambiguity. In describing to his father the cuttings and the killings he saw so frequently, his father in turn would raise doubts. "Dad would say 'Boy, why don't you stop that lyin'? You know you didn't see all that. You know you didn't see nobody do that.' But I knew I had." Indeed, he had. As the author of a memoir of growing up in Harlem, I can attest to the fact that children see a great deal more than adults imagine.

My own life in Harlem—from birth in 1929 to expulsion during the Harlem riots of 1943—preceded that of Claude Brown by nearly a decade, and in cultural terms by what seemed to be a century. There were differences as well as similarities. The biggest similarity was that life was lived in the streets, not the houses. The biggest difference was that the drug culture had displaced the alcoholic culture—and with devastating impact. I can attest to the essential accuracy of Brown's classical text. Indeed, although he wrote a second work, *The Children of Ham*, Brown shares with Ralph Ellison's *The Invisible Man* strong identification with a single work. To read Brown and Ellison as authors "bookending" Harlem's special history is to learn much about black life as a whole, but even more importantly, it is to see American urban life evolving as a stratified mosaic. Sometimes the phrase African-American is employed as a shorthand assertion of a special culture and a denial of a mainstream existence. But in fact, Ellison and Brown each tell an American story—not a pretty one, but an important one, and even a hopeful one.

The writing in *Manchild* is so stunning, so sociologically on target, that it merits at least a few excerpts. Brown's observations rival an earlier generation of ethnographers, but he has a sharper eye for detail and intimacy than say William Whyte had in *Street Corner Society*. His evocative description on the explosion of drug use in the 1950s hardly needs commentary. "It was like a plague, and the plague usually afflicted the eldest child of every family, like the one of the firstborn with Pharaoh's people in the Bible.... People were more afraid than they'd ever been before. Everybody was afraid of this drug thing, even the older people who would never use it. They were afraid to go out of their houses with just one lock on the door. They had two, three, and four locks. People had guns in their houses because of the junkies. The junkies were committing almost all the crimes in Harlem. They were snatching pocketbooks. A truck couldn't come into the community to unload anything any more. Even if it was toilet paper or soap powder, the junkies would clean it out if the driver left it for a second.... Then money became more of a temptation. The young people out in the streets were desperate for it. If a cat took out a twenty-dollar bill on Eighth Avenue in broad daylight, he could be killed. Cats were starving for drugs; their habit was down on them, and they were getting sick.... Harlem was a community that couldn't afford the pressure of this thing, because there weren't many strong family ties anyway. There might have been a few, but they were so few, they were almost insignificant" (pp.180-81).

Claude Brown was not exempt from this. He was "cut out to be in jail" like so many other Harlem young people. It was a mark of manhood, of pride, and security. Prisons were a good deal less dangerous than the streets. But Brown was also the product of the Wiltwyck School for Boys. It was there that the larger picture became clear. He was indebted to Eleanor Roosevelt, the founder of Wiltwyck, and absorbed in the life of Albert Schweitzer. In Aggrey House, he encountered supportive German Jewish immigrants like Mrs. Meitner, whose family was destroyed in the Holocaust. Sociologists often mock the absence of scientific rigor in the work of social welfare personnel, while radical revolutionists think of social work as a dangerous palliative, as if any meliorative approach to human suffering is worse than the suffering itself. It was Claude Brown's unique capacity to reject fanaticism of all types, political and theological, and his acceptance of life as a series of small steps forward, which ultimately defines *Manchild* and transcends an incomplete life. Wiltwyck was not heaven, but neither was it the prison hell of Woodburn, "the Rock," or "the Tombs." Those who have lived the "life" are less likely to fall prey to religious fantasies predicated on quotidian nightmares. They are also less likely to fall prey to chic sociological sophistries that hold the drug culture to be some kind of "recreational" reverie that can be readily "managed" by skillful users.

The secret of Claude Brown was precisely his analytic skills coupled with street smarts, or better said, a desire for self-preservation. There was "Billy Dobbs" and the search for a way out—first in the Muslim faith and then in the Coptic faith, in Ethiopia as the Garden of Eden. The street women showered their affections on Claude Brown, giving him "a little bit of tenderness." Claude's lasting "childhood" was that he could not "stand to see others suffer." His "manhood" is that he constantly had to "prove himself." The driving force in the book and in the life is the contradiction between childhood and manhood—hence the wonderful word "manchild." This was mirrored in the larger life of the city: between migration to Harlem from the Village, and back again. It was a shuttle that permitted him to experience all kinds of people and do all kinds of things. But a shuttle is a moving object, and that was indeed what Claude Brown always remained, a moving object. His relationships with "Dixie," who was turning tricks in Harlem, later with "Judy," the white, Jewish girlfriend, mirrored a man constantly "hiding out" from an uncertain environment. A man without dreams, but with fears. And here one feels the coming to life of Ellison's people.

If being a boy and a man at the same time was Claude Brown's contradiction, then the resolution was often attempted in his acute understanding of women. His writing on girls turned into drug addicts, whores, and prostitutes revealed a side of Claude Brown that set him as a man apart. Being soft, tender and sympathetic in fact resolved his contradictions on the ground if not in abstract terms. In an especially poignant moment, Brown writes, "even though I had been out there in the streets and had met all kinds of people, I hadn't learned to accept people, not really accept them." Having an epiphany is one of the charms of the book. And he had many of them! Indeed, every time he traveled "uptown" he learned things. "The best way to look at Harlem was to be on the outside and have some kind of in." And the "more I learned, the more beautiful it [Harlem] was." This is not a perfect book by any stretch of the literary imagination. People march in and out of the narrative in a wildly random fashion. They disappear only to reappear much later in the book. The stream of consciousness is not the best way to develop a rational model of writing. Then again, its form mirrors precisely the chaotic background of its author. His was an existence resolved far more often in the death and wasting of friends than in the triumph of life or in a career in public service. Harlem was not, is not, a moral playground of moving on up. Neither was it, or is it, a place of human degradation. Harlem is the capital of black America, where life is precious but tenuous, and ethics is chewed off in small pieces. It is not a place where "masses" constantly protest, and even less a place where "elites" gather to set national agendas. It is pure and simple, as Claude Brown constantly reminds us, a community—a spirit as well as a place.

In the final analysis, the success, nay the worth of *Manchild in the Promised Land* was a function of Claude Brown's arrival as just a plain *man* in a turf not so much promised as full of promises. This in turn rested on a shaky foundation of racial consciousness that itself could never quite eliminate the worth of a transcendent human consciousness. For in the last analysis, this is a book of hope built upon the sands of despair. I suspect that the book sold so well to so many because its author may have been reared on the mean streets, but was himself a nice man, a reflective man, a caring man. He can now rest in paradise—where promises are fulfilled and everyone, from Greenwich Village to Harlem, is treated fair and square.

Works by Claude Brown

The Children of Ham
Manchild in the Promised Land

7

Morris Raphael Cohen:
End of the Classical Liberal Tradition

Books of old essays and reviews, including for the most part the essays in *The Faith of a Liberal*, when measured in centennial terms, are old. They are not readily favored by the reading public. Most of these writings were prepared in the 1920s and 1930s. Indeed, they rank with the *festschriften* as all too often the least read and least purchased form of book. How much more must this be true the second time around. Thus, a volume of this sort must have a hugely compelling intellectual reason to be reissued in the closing decade of the century. I think this is the case with M. R. Cohen's essays on liberalism; and I shall dedicate the remainder of this essay to trying to prove the point.

Before doing so, a few brief remarks about the author are in order. I was too young to know M. R. Cohen personally, or to have him as a professor at the City College of New York. The closest I got was to his son Felix, whose fine course in the philosophy of law was taught at City in alternate years. But while I used the source book that Felix Cohen put together, the actual course was taught by Abraham Edel—the brilliant ethical theorist who spent the bulk of his academic life at City, and whose student I was privileged to be between the years of 1947-1951.

The philosophy department at the City College of New York was Morris Raphael Cohen's department. Although Harry Overstreet was chair through most of the Cohen years—1912 until his retirement in 1938—he was clearly the dominant intellectual figure for most of these years. That the department fractured on political grounds was inevitable given the climate of opinion in the 1930s. Still, the quality of mind from Abraham Edel in moral theory, to Daniel Bronstein in symbolic logic, to Philip Paul Sullener in the history of ideas, to Henry Magid in political thought, and finally, to Yervant A. Krikorian in philosophical psychology was extraordinary. The department honored the memory of Cohen precisely by the steady stimulus provided by a contentious group. In its soul, the department illustrated the lessons of liberalism: civility in dealing with one another and equity in dealing with students. We all learned the legends of Cohen, because whatever persuasion his progeny turned out to be, they reflected and refracted his sense of the bracing character of an honest exchange of ideas.

The Faith of a Liberal is, in part at least, a misnomer. In fact, the volume reflects the faith of a philosopher—one with intense curiosities and sentiments about subject matter ranging from American literary history to the history of the exact sciences. Still, the essays on liberalism that bracket the volume give substance to the title. Some deeper appreciation of how his personal odyssey is reflected in his public concerns is a necessary prelude to understanding the contents of Cohen's liberalism.

Cohen was born in Mink, Russia in 1880. He came to the United States at the age of twelve in 1892. Doubtless, Mink, a center of both the Jewish enlightenment and classical Hebrew learning, had an enormous and lifelong impact on Cohen. Long before it was fashionable, if indeed it has ever been fashionable, he championed Jewish interests. In 1933, responding to the emergence of Hitler and the German Nazi state, he founded the Conference on Jewish Relations, an organization that assumed responsibility for scientific research on Jewish problems. In 1939, he founded *Jewish Social Studies*, which remains a central organ on the subject to this day. Both his autobiography, *A Dreamer's Journey*, published in 1949, and a posthumous collection of briefer pieces, *Reflections of a Wondering Jew*, issued a year later, document his lifelong involvement in Jewish affairs.

In *The Faith of a Liberal* such interests are reflected in his choice of heroes: Spinoza is the "prophet of liberalism"; of the "three great judges" Cohen singles out, two are Jewish, Brandeis and Cardozo; the final "heroic figure" who is singled out for special attention is Albert Einstein. But the key to Cohen's vision of the place of the Jew in American civilization is contained in his essay first published in *The New Republic* in 1919, or immediately after the First World War. He does not deny the "tribal" aspects of Zionism. Indeed, he gives it a painfully accurate rendering. Cohen concludes, however, by noting that "Zionism has rendered the supreme service of increasing men's self-respect, and has helped men to realize that they must be ready to give of their own past experience as well as to accept. For this, the American ideal of civil and political liberty still provide a fair field."

This quintessential search for a level playing field links Cohen's faith in a liberal Judaism with his commitment to law and justice as such. To be sure, it is his work in legal philosophy that remains pivotal to this day. His book *Law and Social Order* is anticipated in the essay on "Constitutional and Natural Rights in 1789 and Since." Here he separates himself from the conservative notion that the courts limit themselves to decision-making in terms of the literal words of the Constitution. This "fiction" only relieves law of taking responsibility for critical decisions, and serves to justify the terrible disparity of power and responsibility. For Cohen, the empirical foundations of decision-making determine the interpretation of law. And beyond that, anticipating the social consequences of decision-making distinguishes totalitarianism from liberalism.

Cohen's powerful sense of the law as active may well have been fueled by his no less deep sense of injustice. Although he was a graduate in philosophy of the City College of New York, that revered institution with which he maintained a lifelong love affair— never mind association—and was later a graduate of the philosophy department at Harvard University in 1906, he went to work in the mathematics department at City College. It was only six years later, in 1912, that he was allowed to enter the philosophy department. But his involuntary exile was not an unmitigated disaster, since the years of association with mathematicians gave Cohen a feeling for logic and scientific method that often escaped others who had uncritically embraced pragmatic philosophy.

To be sure, Cohen came to scorn those who had a "popular science" image of actual processes involved in experimentation and research. He may have been declared by the *Columbia Encyclopedia* as "one of the most important American philosophers since William James," but he was in fact far more beholden to Charles Sanders Peirce's "realism" than to either Jamesian or Deweyan varieties of pragmatism.

Throughout his life, in almost Kantian fashion, he identified with science as an end in itself, or at least with a concern to establish all possible causal linkages, great and small. Neither Peirce nor Cohen believed for a moment "that action was the ultimate end of man." An implicit juxtaposition of Peirce against James and Dewey—against a philosophical tradition "centered about man's psychologic nature and moral duties"—was leveled by Cohen as ultimately narrow, impoverished, and illiberal. His own sense of science was of something that rises above a sense of immediate urgency. And he invokes authorities from Plato to Spinoza to identify the love of wisdom as nothing short of the conduct of science and mathematics. I think it fair to say that in his vision of the scientific, Cohen was far closer to the conservative tradition he eschewed than the modem liberalism he claims to have embodied. Just how his legal empiricism coincided with scientific rationalism remains a problem, not just for Cohen, but for modern intellectual history as a whole. For if law is but a thing-for-us while science is a thing-for-itself, just what hope is there for a unified or integrated vision of the moral order?

Increasingly, Cohen's revulsion for doctrines of activism were further fueled by the rising tide of authoritarianism, right and left, that enveloped the 1920s and the 1930s. At a time when it was hardly fashionable, Cohen wrote his famous essay "Why I Am Not a Communist." It remains to this day a blistering indictment of a Soviet regime no less than of Leninist ideology. Ultimately it was the intellectual disdain of fanaticism and irrationalism that made any possibility of lining up with communism possible. And in one of his typical literary asides, he notes of the choice between Communism and Fascism, "I feel that I am offered the choice between being shot and being hanged." Liberal society, American society, should not be compelled into a false choice, since neither variety of totalitarianism exhausts human possibilities. And liberalism is ultimately a matter of human possibilities.

Whether speaking of Alexis de Tocqueville's *Democracy in America* or Vernon Parrington's *Main Currents in American Thought*, Cohen loved that word "possibilities," for in it he saw the essence of Americanism as such. And here is where science and literature intersect: in problems of the nature of knowledge. The critical and skeptical spirit of American literature and science makes for distrust of tempting generalizations or self-evident truths—but it also makes possible the liberal imagination. In an interesting note on the Russian character, he speaks of the Russian interest in concrete science and general mysticism, but notes a void in the area of "abstract questions of scientific method." To be sure, the same void can be described by Cohen as a sense of liberalism as well. In this, he is part of a long line of American thinkers who linked the scientific method with the liberal spirit—even if that linkage could not always be nailed down in theory.

His final essay, "The Future of American Liberalism," is the only statement Cohen wrote specifically for *The Faith of a Liberal*. This should be taken as a measure of its importance. It is not a simple essay, for Cohen is at some pains to square liberalism with *political* individualism and *economic* collectivism. In this piece on a liberalism triumphant, he reflects more the New Deal philosophy that emerged triumphant at the end of the Second World War, than that of a theorist in search of new vistas. Cohen could say that "We need a certain amount of sociability," and follows this immediately with the Millsian concern that "nevertheless too much sociability is inimical to thought." There is, consequently, a certain strange platitudinousness that envelops Cohen's last writings on liberalism— as if a sense of closure of the old liberal verities was at hand, and a corresponding fear that the new liberalism would not exactly foster his vision of "free thought" and an "enlarged vision of the good life."

It is not unfair to say that Cohen was caught up in the Greek ideal of the good life and the American ideal of the practical life as well. How ancient thought and modern industrial society coalesced makes for an uneasy alliance. Cohen could not, indeed did not, resolve the issue. Perhaps the problem is labels as such—for if the world is not exhausted by communism and fascism, neither is it exhausted by liberalism or conservatism. In his highest moment of achievement, Cohen understood as much. For the much vaunted "Socratic method" stood in contradistinction to the Platonic definition of the Socratic dialogue.

Cohen's essay and *The Faith of a Liberal* as a volume ends with the triumph of the process over the decadence of the structure: "So in life there is growth and decay. In human history there are ups and downs. There are periods of flowering and periods of decay." "There is no use," Cohen concludes, "in thinking that any one movement of history, or of human life, will continue forever." Liberalism ultimately consists in this sense of openness, or at the least an absence of closure. In this, Cohen's collection of essays remains a marvelous, vital guide to the perplexed. It is a tragic reminder, if any be needed, how far down the path of totalitarian temptation even the blessed vision of liberalism has traveled. Indeed, even the best systems of thought fail to continue forever.

Cohen was part of that special generation that created the classical liberal tradition; or at least transplanted it to American soil. The first half of the twentieth century revealed a liberalism positioned *between* fascism and communism, or if one prefers, between the political right and left. Like others of his time, Cohen had a lasting and innate suspicion of ideological extremism and psychological exaggeration. He envisioned liberalism as the natural handmaiden of a scientific worldview, but one that was also tolerant of religious belief in the way that the scientist is appreciative of the limits of exact knowledge. For all of his sense of epistemological differences with people like John Dewey and the pragmatic tradition generally, he shared with his philosophical cohort common concerns in education, law, and literature. Indeed, he also shared with them the American dream; albeit, as an immigrant Russian Jew, without the aristocratic nativism of either the New England tradition of a Ralph Barton Perry or for that matter the frontier spirit of a Vernon Parrington. Liberalism has many mansions for Cohen and even a plurality of authentic voices and posture. What gave liberalism its resilience was less a code of conduct or a system of beliefs than those forms of conduct it eschewed and those systems of belief it condemned.

In an age in which liberalism has become part of the polarity—the anticonservative side of the discursive axis—Cohen's sort of liberalism as a positioning between extremes may seem somewhat archaic, even eccentric. But in Cohen's day and age, it was the quintessential approach to life and letters. It made sense of the world for whom notions of equity and liberty were the best, perhaps only, guarantors of minority rights and majority rules alike. To the extent that such an old fashioned notion remains valid, Cohen's work will continue to occupy a special place in American intellectual history.

Works by Morris Raphael Cohen

The Faith of a Liberal
An Introduction to Logic
Law and the Social Order
Readings in Jurisprudence and Legal Philosophy
Source Book in Greek Science (with I. E. Drabkin)

8

James S. Coleman:
Chance, Choice, and Civility

A book by so eminent and courageous a figure as James S. Coleman merits attention whatever its chosen subject matter. And when such an effort is prefixed by the word "foundations" it deserves special note. For whatever value this effort may possess, it may be expected from a person who has spent a lifetime doing serious thinking—his own thinking. Indeed, there is a rather quaint naivete in Coleman that I happen to share, a presupposition that honest research will triumph over every variety of distortion: from public ideology to personal neurosis. It is one of the charms of Coleman and his work that he holds firm to this Enlightenment canon of objectivity and its rewards.

One of my first recollections of Coleman is his giving a report in 1968, a follow-up report on the impact of busing, school desegregation, and "white" flight from the inner cities. As he was delivering his remarks at a gathering of the American Sociological Association, a banner bearing a swastika was unfurled behind the podium signaling disapproval of Coleman's "nefarious" admission of what everybody in the United States, except the ideological extremists within the profession, knew to be the case: that racial differences in elementary schooling remained a social fact, and inequality in educational opportunity was not dissolved by the mandated busing policy. And while I do not recollect an effort to remove this hideous slander in the form of a banner against Coleman's "politics," it did not prevent Coleman from completing his address in a calm and compassionate manner without as much as an acknowledgement of this disgraceful effort by a small faction of "guerrilla" and "insurgent" sociologists to inhibit free and honest speech at a professional gathering. While this weird episode of nearly a quarter century ago remains peripheral to the work at hand, it must be said that Coleman continues to write with a single-minded belief that the purpose of social science is to gather facts, to present them in the most adroit manner possible, and to let the chips, or the evidence, fall where they may. In this historical sense, the triumph ultimately belongs to Coleman, since he is now president-elect of that self-same association.

It would have been worthwhile had his *Foundations* opened with some sense of this commitment to a scientific naturalism and the limited intent of this enterprise. Instead, this important book is encumbered by exaggerated, epigonic praise that also adorns the promotional literature issued by Harvard University Press. Coleman's own claims to "address the question of the peaceful coexistence of man and society, as two intersecting systems of action" (p. 5) is ambitious enough, without needing the adornment of puffery bordering on empty-headed flattery. While encomiums are hardly original in promoting a book, in this instance they have the peculiar impact of drawing this reviewer's attention to those very aspects of Coleman's *Foundations of Social Theory* that are on shakiest ground. In so doing, the fatuous paeans of praise make the task of reviewing the book both easier and harder. Easier in that one can discard the debris and settle into a consideration of the book on its merits; more difficult, in that this reviewer's praise of the book for its actual worth, falls so far short of the lavish remarks made in pre-publication comments that his sentiments may seem tepid and rendered even half-heartedly.

Let me begin with an unequivocal statement. I urge all serious social scientists to read this book. The enormity of the enterprise, coupled with the essential decency of the author, earn the book serious treatment by everyone in the field. That said, what exactly is that "field"? To ask the question is to expose the central nerve endings of this volume to critical examination. To help garner an answer, it will be precisely my aim to review positive elements of the text against a backdrop of claims made on its behalf. That Professor Coleman for his part may, in fact, be an innocent victim of the exuberance of enthusiasts is a fact of authorial life. When one writes a magnum opus, one must live with claims to immortality no less than denigrations consigning a work to the historical dustbin. We should begin by clearing away some of the claims as a mechanism to permit us to get closer to this text and its author.

To start with, there is the entirely foolish and dangerous assertion in the descriptive cover copy, perhaps written by the publisher with or without the consent of the author, that *Foundations of Social*

Theory "promises to be the most important contribution to social theory since the publication of Talcott Parsons' *The Structure of Social Action*." Many extraordinary works have appeared since 1936, starting with Karl Mannheim's *Ideology and Utopia* in that same year, and proceeding through *The American Dilemma* by Gunnar Myrdal in the 1940s, *History of Economic Analysis* by Joseph A. Schumpeter in the 1950s, *Power and Privilege* by Gerhard Lenski in the 1960s, *Anarchy, State and Utopia* by Robert Nozick in the 1970s, and ending with *The American Political Economy* by Douglas A. Hibbs in the 1980s. René Koenig's extraordinary volume, *Die Geschichte der deutschen Soziologie*, which appeared only last year, can be thrown into the stew for good measure. While these and many other works have advanced the cause of social theory these past fifty-five years, such a goal is clearly beyond a single text to resolve. It is perhaps time for the social sciences to move away from the search for magical formulae, the single message that will resolve and wrap up all past issues.

It is true that an entire segment of Coleman's work covers "Structures of Action," but no claim is made for a general theory of social action. Rather, the first two segments owe far more to Peter Blau and exchange theory than to Talcott Parsons and general theory. It is scarcely an accident that, save for a single reference to Parsons, no analysis is made of *The Structure of Social Action*. On the other hand, there are far too few references to Peter Blau's *Exchange and Power in Social Life*. This, I suspect, is a function of Coleman's "linear system of action" which takes place in a wide-open social universe of interests, policies, mechanisms of control, relations of authority and trust, and above all, a world of choice.

Preoccupied as Parsons was with nineteenth-century European systems of thought, from Emile Durkheim to Max Weber to Vilfredo Pareto, he was enamored of determinist frames in which actions take place. The boxes of Parson's pattern variables remained hermetically sealed, not to be opened until *The General Theory of Action* in which the irrationalities and indeterminacies of Freudian psychiatry were admitted—albeit on an ad hoc intellectual basis, and for the most part through a side door marked Paretan residues. Because Coleman makes fewer metaphysical demands on social theory than did Parsons, he is also in the more enviable position of letting in fresh breezes, to air not only a variety of theories, but a variety of practices as well.

A second claim made for the Coleman text, and this time identified as the words of Jack Goldstone, is that *Foundations of Social Theory* "provides the finest solution I have seen to the vexing micro-macro problem in social science." I suspect that Coleman himself would like to believe these words of praise. But he is betrayed by his own text, for it is precisely his inability to link social history with social theory that puts at grave risk any effort at unified theory. Let us look closely at Coleman's chapter on "The Conflict between the Family and the Corporation." Since this is singled out as a highlight of the book, doing this cannot rightly be called a reviewer's selective perception. Coleman writes (and here it is necessary to quote him directly):

> In modern industrial society there have come to be two parallel organizational structures: a primordial structure based on, and derivative from, the family; and a newer structure composed of purposive corporate actors wholly independent of the family. The primordial structure consists of family, extended family, neighborhood, and religious groups. The purposive structure consists of economic organizations, single purpose voluntary associations, and governments. The primordial structure is unraveling as its functions are taken away by the new corporate actors.

One could argue the empirical point by noting that family, community, and religion are not dissolving. To be sure, such micro systems are sometimes aided and abetted by corporate structures that need stability in the private life of corporate actors, no less than the loyalty of such actors in daily affairs of management. It is troubling that the private and the public are so reified in Coleman's work, that the very nuances one imagines would be made by a sociologist are simply vacated. Of course, such reification is the high road of pluses and minuses, of ratio measurements in which an efficient equilibrium is imposed upon inefficient functions. Rather than argue the empirical point, since in fact, this is Jean-Jacques Rousseau's observation made so brilliantly and poignantly in *Discourses on Human Inequality*, I would draw attention precisely to Coleman's inability to resolve the contradictions between the "vexing" micro-macro problem in sociology. For if the micro is Coleman's stand-in for the individual, and the macro serves that role for the corporation, then what are those mechanisms for bringing the two together, once community and family are dissolved by theoretical fiat? This and a host of other dualisms are left quite intact as fixed theoretical polarities rather than grounds for empirical explorations. What we do not get is an attempt to understand that both family values and corporate structures are subsumed under a new variety of individualism—one in which the corporate life does not replace family life—but rather both are displaced in the rush to be defined as "a person." The demands of various movements for racial and sexual equality are not just for collective representation of general interests. They are demands for being counted as an individual—no more and certainly no less. Neither the corporation nor the family are in a position to deny this new surge of individualism—sometimes criticized, as by Christopher Lasch, as a heightened egotism, but just as readily viewed as an extension of constitutional demands that equity requires fair results no less than fair starting points.

Coleman does not make an effort at such synthesis and does not take us beyond a rather desultory set of observations. He leaves the woman shifting "her daytime locus of activity from the primordial structure, the family, to the purposive structure, the world of corporate actors." Here the dualism is simply left in peace. Little effort is made to situate women in varieties of individual self-definition; and no effort is made to understand that the post-industrial, modernist corporation is precisely bent on accommodating, or at least coming to terms with, a world in which corporate identities are even less well respected, and more interchangeable by far than familial identities. The formalization procedures introduced by Coleman have the effect of dampening interest in those sloppy elements in social life that fall outside the parameters of rationality. Components of social theory, such as public choice, are highly rationalized as "a set of roles that players take on...rules about the kind of actions that are allowable for players in each role...rules specifying the consequences that each player's action has for other plays in the game" (p. 11).

The gaming analogy appears repeatedly, as in the discussion of collective behavior, whose difficulties for "programmed strategies" are seen as interrupted by "asymmetry in an iterated prisoner's dilemma" which makes explanation higher than in a world that assumes a "tit for tat strategy." In other words, irrationalities are reduced to "panics and crazes" (pp. 211-219) to be overcome by "reward structures for members of a hostile crowd." The eleven "predictions" about collective behavior are actually propositions about the social control of crowd behavior—without respect to the content of the demands for change or assertions of injustice. In what sense are riots at Attica, demonstrations at Tiananmen Square, and bank panics on Wall Street, similar? We are not told because civil behavior does not descend to such baser levels of thought in Coleman's text. Rather, we are provided with models of similitudes at such high levels of abstraction, that the possibilities of counterfactualization are highly improbable. Instead, just when problems become real, we are swept along into general theorems about effective social norms.

Coleman has made wide use of the public choice models worked through in economics by James Buchanan, Gary Becker, and others. And I, for one, find this a refreshing coming-to-terms with how individual and social elements are fused in the public sector. But the rational choice model itself has a wide variety of problems that Coleman does not address, starting with the degree of volition in personal choice and ending with the systemic limitations of such a model in dealing with public decisions. This is a shame, since this micro-macro management system might have been a framework for showing how sociology can augment, amplify, and correct economic utility visions of rational choice. Instead, this system is employed by Coleman to negate sociological levels of explanation in favor of an equilibrium model derived from post-Keynesian economics.

As a result, an intellectual crisis is manufactured: Sociology is subsumed under economics for every important area of public life. Studies of self, individual, norms, authority, power, collective action, bureaucracy, and revolution "yield to formal models of the dynamics of social systems," as Michael T. Hannan obligingly states in his promotional blurb on the book. But at what tremendous costs and consequences! For the dynamics are drowned in formal systems common to economic equilibrium. And the price for this formal elegance is the transformation of hard social theory into what Coleman himself describes as "The Mathematics of Social Action." It is exactly this sort of economic linearity, this interchangeability of utility functions, this impersonal interchange system of corporate actors and collective decisions that has led economics into its current quagmire. To push sociology in this direction, to mathematicize social functions, is entirely possible, even plausible, but the price is a level of abstraction that yields "theory" only as a formal system, not as guidelines for prediction or experimentation. The hard equations thus disguise a soft approach to social theory.

As a consequence, what we have is a stunning outcome to this ambitious work of social theory: a series of platitudinous statements that does not so much end the book as exhaust what the author has to say about the subject matter of human society. The presumption is that the higher the level of abstraction, the greater the yield in predictions. This volume, however, becomes instead a sourcebook in the fruitless search for a social physics, with assertions at the level of the sun rising every day, rather than a sourcebook of social theory that helps explain specific national structures, specific economic systems, specific political regimes. If theory in social science cannot be applied directly and organically, then its worth is obviously subject to intense scrutiny.

A thread of tautological theorizing runs throughout *Foundations*. Even the conclusions remind us that "the value of resources in a system of action is the sum of actors' interest in the resource, each interest weighted by the actors' power...." Thus, if a specific issue is perceived "correctly," the problem becomes one of evaluating the public good problems as determined by resource availability and played out by individual and corporate actors. The problem with this construct is not the absence of such levels of behavior, but whether or not they actually exhaust, or more pertinently, really address the social life. And whether by accident or design, in the hands of Coleman, foundations become reductions and reductionism as a method becomes the stuff of social theory.

Thus, we have "macro" as little more than public choice economics and "micro" as little else than behaviorist psychology. If this book were entitled *Foundations of Economic Psychology* the work would have to be described as a true synthesis of the literature, a classical restatement of the fault lines for working in the interstices of both disciplines. But the work is enticed *Foundations of Social Theory*. Hence the reader ought to be informed what are the sociological, political, and cultural elements at work in such a theory. Except for a broad restatement of his own writings on social welfare and education, Coleman does not offer the reader broader guidelines.

We are expected to feast for an entire third of the manuscript on a restatement in "The Mathematics of Social Action" that can best be described as a brilliant reworking of the propositions stated, in narrative form, in the first two-thirds of the book. Without offering an empirical demonstration of the truth or worth of the propositions as such, all it proves is that formalized propositions take less time and space than sheer narrative. But I suspect that this is not what Coleman set out to accomplish.

At some levels, this emphasis on formal procedures works to Coleman's advantage. Such is the case when he criticizes, quite properly, weaknesses in Max Weber's theories of social organization. Coleman indicates his "deviations" from Weber and points to the latter's inability to address fully problems of motivation in corporate life, issues of incentive payments that modifies hierarchical arrangements, or the rise of managerialism, in which actual operations of the corporation are vested in non-owning individuals. This point, made by James Burnham many years ago, does not quite come to terms with the persistence of proprietary rights in determining the life and death of corporations (pp. 424-425). This material, largely derived from the work of Herbert Simon and James March and other organization specialists, does not eliminate annoying problems of ownership in corporate life, but it does remain the best part of Coleman's book, in that it addresses problems in classical business theory within a meaningful context. The same can be said for his summary of the literature on the how and why the state "replaces the family as the major social welfare institution of society" (pp. 579-609), although he totally omits any analysis of the voluntary or "third sector" of the economy.

The corporate structure and how it displaces the family network is the empirical hub of Coleman's work. Everything else is either in the nature of embellishment, or simply not considered. But what if this dichotomy of individual and corporation turns out to be wrong, incomplete, or as is already evident, too loosely stated? What then becomes of the "theory" on which this text is broadly based? Clearly, anything other than neat bivariate frameworks become encumbrances to theory and, hence, the drive toward a positivist reductionism becomes unavoidable, if not downright tempting.

Coleman is led to simplify major issues. The discussion of authority systems is framed in terms of weakening or strengthening authority, withdrawing or adding to mechanisms of control, compliance or non-compliance in the structure of society—whether those of the state or of the corporation. Sometimes, Coleman speaks of them in the same voice as parallel systems of power and authority. Legitimacy becomes critical since it is at this level that individuals (micro) and collectivities (macro) link up in the fine mesh of social action.

Coleman defines the parameters of his work early on by reference to "metatheory," but upon inspection, this effort to "construct models of the macro-to-micro and micro-to-macro processes" turns out to be little more than a Benthamite utilitarianism. The great breakthrough in studying the marriage squeeze problem turns out to be viewing marriage "as taking place in a kind of market, but one that is quite special, with each actor having only one commodity—himself or herself—to barter and with exchange rates governed by the constraint of monogamy, which prevents variations in quantity to achieve equal value in exchange." Leaving aside the rather quixotic, dare one say profane, aspect of this definition of a sacral condition, the conception it expresses of the relation between the micro and the macro, or the individual and the social, is less explanatory than tautological, i.e., building expected conclusions into the structure of the premises.

Coleman understands, or at least, senses the *cul-de-sac* in which he has placed himself. As a result, the great strength of his work comes precisely from his ignoring "theory" and addressing "reality." For example, his constant drawing of attention to the absence of legitimacy as a defining element in totalitarian regimes is a breath of fresh air although it derives not so much from a vision of exchange of actors or demands for effective norms, as from a democratic stand against non-rational authority and against authoritarian systems as such, and perhaps against constraining theories. Therein lies the great strength and lasting value of Coleman's book. He is sound enough in his moral judgments to rise above his own sociological explanations. Its huge size not withstanding, *Foundations* is in the final analysis a simplistic account of social life. There are few people in the text, only "actors," few authoritarians, only "authority systems," few actual nations, only massive, undefined "states and societies," and few corporations in contrast to "corporate structures." When examples are provided, the text comes alive. One delights in comparisons of the Philippines with Afghanistan, not because of any great profundities, but because reference to concrete examples sharpens his points without the heavy boot of fundamental theory.

Where Coleman addresses situations that arise from milieus he is strongest, as in his treatment of the American electoral process as a mediation between individual and social choices. Thinking about primaries as transforming a single-stage process of choosing among multiple alternatives in a multistage process of paired choices is a good way of describing nuances in the democratic process. His explication of how voting preferences determine not only outcomes but also sequences of events is likewise an elaboration on how democratic processes work in advanced societies (pp. 414-415). Albeit, all this is expressed at a level of social abstraction that virtually ignores the Democratic and Republican parties, or, for that matter, liberal and conservative ideologies.

The examination of student rebellions in terms of cost-benefit analysis, estimate of probabilities of victory in the act, the role of the non-participant, how revolutionary movements develop alternative systems of authority and not just a divestiture of authority, all of this extends the Hobbesian world by showing how revocation of authority is a struggle for reestablishment of new lines of authority, a search for legitimacy that is as true of student revolts as of national revolutions (pp. 496-502).

The most interesting and impressive chapters are related to the conduct of social research. But these chapters have little to do with the theses of the book, but have much to do with Coleman's professional and personal battles to make social science the ground for realistic policymaking. Here Coleman is on solid ground as a serious worker in the vineyards of sociology. It is in discussing policy that sociology as a formal construct is raised as a problematic. Coleman examines the place of sociology in a study of how welfare programs operate, of how the American soldier helped determine changing patterns of national integration, why those in authority use social research more than those who hold power. His answer, "in a single word—legitimation" (p. 640), is fair and worthwhile, but hardly begins to exhaust the nuances of the social system. Repeatedly, Coleman lets slip by opportunities to explain the relationship between general theory and concrete application. He properly argues the case that social research is important when it has an effect on social function, and that it is worth pursuing even if it runs a risk of bias. One wishes he had taken the argument further and made the case for reflexive mechanisms that adjust for and overcome biases in the research design, and not just a claim for the rational person pursuing rational models in a rational environment. Throughout the text one feels the presence of an urbane and civil scholar, a principled person who stubbornly pursues the quest for knowledge as a way to inform social policy. But the relationship between the morality of such a social science and the theory of such a social science remains terribly obscure. One feels a recourse to a Smithian "hidden hand" underlying much of the effort at synthesis. The pursuit of self-interest as rational choice somehow makes possible social interests as a rational system. That all the inherited problems of laissez faire economies thus come to the surface does not seem to be disturbing to Coleman.

Coleman states the need to move from sociology to a "new social science"—one that addresses problems of a demand for knowledge irrespective of fields of training and helps realize opportunities in the transformation of society, applied research, and social theory, to form a link "appropriate to the new social structure" (pp. 663-664). However, the specific fault lines of a Baconian *novum organon*, a new social science to go along with the new social theory, is left to the imagination of the reader. The synthesis of new social theory then becomes a restatement of the first section, only not so much in grammar and narrative as in the mathematics of social action. The last third of the book is a relentless recapitulation, in formal and elegant terms and far more condensed as one might imagine, of what the previous two-thirds announce.

The synthesis, the new theory, the new social science, becomes an amalgam of public goods, public choices, organizational frameworks, and individual actors intersecting with corporate goals. While this may represent a triumph of Kenneth Arrow in economics and R. J. Herrnstein in psychology, I see only a return to the problems that plagued economics and psychology at mid-century and led to the breakdown of system-building in the fields of sociology and political science. Coleman's coda and classification of older theory is a synthesis of the civilized person as an abstraction, but it is not a resolution of what ails the social sciences today.

Calling critical attention to the weight of the formal over the historical may appear to be an unfair criticism of a work aiming to provide a general theory that can serve many occasions, peoples, and systems. But I think not. After all, even a master of micro-sociology, such as George C. Homans, could infuse his every page with rich historical examples and a worldliness that Coleman simply does not evidence in this volume. Bringing people back into social research is precisely what Coleman fails to do. To be sure, it is at Parson's weakest point, at the point of subjecting reality to the test of theory, instead of theory to the test of reality, that Coleman comes closest to the individual to whom this book will be repeatedly compared.

One is left with the distinct impression that economics and psychology are the victors, and sociology and political science are the vanquished, or at least vanished. The aura of reductionism is reinforced by the absence of examples from non-Western cultures. It might well be that such an outcome is warranted on the basis of the evidence before us. This does not rest on theory so much as on information retrieval and reliability. It is not enough to ask us to fall back solely upon the strengths of economics and psychology in the shared life of the human race. In the absence of an articulated set of empirical reasons for why this decision should be made, Coleman's case remains unexplained and, in part, inexplicable.

Nothing less than human culture as such is dissolved in Coleman's formal subsystems of corporate life: actors receiving benefits. If social theory can be formalized in such terms, then the book is a success. But if much of social life escapes the net of social theory as civic behavior, if the sum total of generalizable experiences of various societies is more than can be processed by such a consensual model, then the book must be measured as less than satisfactory.

As measured by the criteria outlined by Coleman, this is a successful venture into the organizational known. My own preference would have been for less format elegance and many more forays into the vast disorganized unknown we call society. Such forays alone yield the sort of anomalies and paradoxes that permit the production of new theories and make possible new synthesis. As it stands, *Foundations of Social Theory* tells us much about the state of affairs in the research world of economists and psychologists but precious little about the state of affairs in the messy world of ordinary men and women. It was said of George Bernard Shaw that he was a good socialist fallen among Fabians. One would have to say of James Coleman that he is a good sociologist fallen among economists. What emerges is interesting and provocative, but sad to say, neither entirely convincing nor quite novel.

Works by James S. Coleman

The Asymmetric Society
Foundations of Social Theory
Introduction to Mathematical Sociology
Rational Choice Theory (with Thomas J. Fararo)
Redesigning American Education

9

W.E.B. Du Bois:
Revisiting the Legacy of Atlanta Sociology

I am privileged to offer these remarks into the public discourse at a special moment in personal time: within four days I help you to celebrate the 90th anniversary of the establishment of sociology at Atlanta University, and also the 25th anniversary of Transaction at Rutgers University. Actually, we started at Washington University in St. Louis, but after twenty years at Rutgers I feel it only fair and proper to identify with my present home, rather than with our ancestral place of origins.

These two events, albeit accidental in nature at the temporal level, are very much connected at the professional level. For like Du Bois' early dreams, we continue to believe in the value of exact social research as both sources of policy and a remedy for inequity. And like Du Bois' early practice, Transaction continues to believe that networking social knowledge is at least as much a function of human organization as of clever ideas.

What needs to be understood about Du Bois is his implicit repudiation of a parochial vision of social research. He can be claimed, with equal accuracy, by sociologists, historians, anthropologists, and for that matter, political scientists. From his earliest work on *The Philadelphia Negro*, we can observe an individual whose focus on the practical consequences of theory, and beyond that, the policy requisites of both theory and practice, defined a figure closer to the tendencies of social science in the present period than at the turn of the century. Indeed, in a period noted for the erection of boundaries between sociology, anthropology, political science, and economics, Du Bois intuitively recognized the serious limitations of such thinking, especially its negative consequences for the study of problems on the ground, involving real people. These are sentiments that I share with this extraordinary figure in the founding of modern social science.

Let me then speak at two levels: as professional and as publisher. Again, those of you who followed Du Bois' career will hardly be astonished that one person can have two activities, since in point of fact, Du Bois had more like ten career lines in a single lifetime. Indeed, he was as adroit in history, demography, and economics as in sociology; and his record of public service and political activity has already filled numerous biographical accounts. For however much the concept of society is at the center of our thinking, it is the individual human being who is at the center of society. Du Bois never forgot that simple truth; hopefully, we too will not fall prey to either sociological abstractions or to psychological reductions.

Because of that peculiar individualism in Du Bois, which sometimes manifested itself in an extreme aristocratic personal carriage, and at other times, in his imperial style of writing, he is best seen as a pioneer in communications rather than as an institution builder. It was his deep sense of converting the Negro Project into a well-grounded rage for equity that fueled this interest in the public side of the black experience. Newspapers, magazines, cultural journals, no less than books, indeed, perhaps more so, characterized his forays into the world of communications.

The sociology laboratory that Du Bois established at Atlanta would come to little unless a public forum, a general outlet, could be established. If sociology was to speak to the black people it would need to do so through instruments not in control of established professional organizations or a narrow band of university elites. Thus, while building black institutions of higher education was a value, for Du Bois it would be of importance only if they taught something unique to the racial experience itself. If this approach was fraught with dangers—from extremism in ideology to narrowness of vision—Du Bois sensed that the risk was worth the gamble. In that, I would like to think that the work that my publishing organization and I have been involved with has been carried forth in that grand tradition first made plausible by Du Bois at the start of the twentieth century.

In Hebrew, my two names derive from Ishmael and Isaac: the first born son of Abraham sired by Hagar, the Egyptian (and some claim black) servant of Sarah; and the second son of Abraham sired by Sarah herself rather very late in life—more appropriate for a conference on aging than observations on institution-building. Furthermore, I was born and spent my first thirteen years in black Harlem—at Eighth Avenue and 123rd Street to be specific. So if I am both reticent and honored to speak before such a special gathering, you will understand. The special circumstances of birth and background have always made it difficult for me to speak casually or fatuously about matters of race or religion.

To be sure, in my capacity as a professional sociologist, I have not made race a central category of investigation. Perhaps this is a problem of being too close rather than too remote from the everyday realities of ghetto life. A Jew in a Gentile world, a presumed white in a black world, a malady-ridden child surrounded by muscular and seemingly fearless children. Everywhere I looked I saw anomalies, and every thought I had was to escape from all these damnable sociological categories.

I wanted nothing more than to leave the ghetto, although in later life I have come to think of Harlem more as a Casbah, even a capital, than a ghetto. Above all, I wanted to escape from myself: from being Jewish, from living in Harlem, from being a severely handicapped child. So I went into philosophy at the City College of the City of New York. But its wisdom, and those of my great instructors, taught me that there really is no escape from the worldly cares, much less than from self. To be sure, it was philosophy as such that permitted me to understand and appreciate the religion of my fathers, and it was philosophy as such that sung the praises of Spartan prowess no less than Athenian virtue. And when all was said and done, the City College was smack dab in the center of Harlem. And even if I swore by the *Socialist Anvil*, the newsstands at the subway station at 145th Street stared back at me through the *Amsterdam News*.

This is not intended as autobiography, so I will spare you any more about my travels and travails through adulthood. I just want to make plain the distinction between silence on and indifference to black life in America. After all, what was one to say from the academic heights?: celebration, condemnation, praise, assaults. Everything appeared as posture. It was more important to read Langston Hughes and Ralph Ellison, to listen to Duke Ellington and Count Basie (after all, I grew up only two blocks from the Apollo Theater), and to wonder in amazement at Father Divine's angels, and at the Mother A.M.E. Zion Church. So I grew up with a subjectively rich experience in black life but with no corresponding mode of giving objective expression to such feelings.

Many years later I had an opportunity to resolve that particular contradiction. The transformation of Transaction from a solitary magazine to a broad-based consortium inadvertently and serendipitously came to my rescue. Late in life I could finally make a contribution to racial comity without making a fool of myself, or being untrue to my own sense of the social situation. But even when Transaction was still just a solitary publication, it spoke loud and clear on the burning social questions of the day. It was Transaction that mobilized the support of nearly every major social science professional society for the 1964 March on Washington. It was Transaction that gave in-depth social science coverage to every major urban riot of the 1960s, including those in Los Angeles, Newark, Cleveland, and Detroit. It was Transaction (now *Society*) that carried every major debate on, in, and within black life, from black employment to black empowerment, from black families in America to black troops in Vietnam. I found my voice through others that knew more and better.

As Transaction expanded into new areas, such as book and journal publication, so too did my personal vision of what could be accomplished at these professional levels. Thus, in the 1970s, and even more in the 1980s, when the smart money in publishing left the field of black studies, Transaction enlarged its activities. In the book field, we can boast the publication of many major figures in contemporary black social science: Charles Willie, Anita Waters, Carlos Moore, Jason W. Clay, John Stanfield, Margaret C. Simms, Barbara A.P. Jones, and of course, Atlanta's own Wilbur Watson among many others. And under Professor Watson's stewardship, Transaction began a Black Social Science Classics Series, which now boasts the likes of books by W.E.B. Du Bois, Booker T. Washington, Charles S. Johnson, Abram Harris, St. Clair Drake, again to cite just a few outstanding social scientists.

And as Transaction expanded into the journal area, so too did our coverage and support for black social research at the highest levels. We helped initiate, with Urban League support, the *Urban League Review*, and with its New York division, The State of Black America Series. Our Consortium publishes such major journals as the *Review of Black Political Economy*, edited here in Atlanta; and *TransAfrica Forum* emanating from Washington, which is a major force on the South African question. For ten years, we published the newsmagazine of the Afro-American Institute, *Africa Report. The Journal of African Civilization*, edited and founded by Ivan Van Sertima at Rutgers, and the newly minted *National Political Science Review*, edited by Lucius J. Barker at Washington University, are also central to the Transaction Periodicals Consortium. And this is to say nothing of such publications as the *Annual Review of Jazz Studies* and the *Journal of American Ethnic History* for whom black studies is a central component.

All of this activity has served to enlarge the scope and vision of my own work in the areas of social development, political sociology, and public policy. As an example, I would say that my work, *Taking Lives*, a study of genocide and state power, could not possibly have been written or approached in the same way were it not for this experience with the world of black social science scholarship. And in the same spirit, were it not for the African-American component in our Transaction program I seriously doubt that my writings on international stratification and development could have had a truly global feel. So the work of my publishing side filters into my sociological work, no less than the other way about. And for this, I am deeply grateful. For I am now able to better come to terms with my own past, my own work, through the strange but wondrous set of circumstances just barely touched on in these remarks.

Hopefully, the long march that links *The Crisis* to *Society*, the ninety years of a tradition at one institution with twenty-five years of an allied tradition at another, makes some sense—divine if not empirical. James Weldon Johnson once wrote that taking a stroll in Harlem "was not simply going out for a walk, it is like going out for an adventure." That is very much the way that I feel about social science: it is not simply a bloodless way to describe the world, but a living adventure with many surprises in store for those who dare take the stroll on a sometime wild side. I strongly suspect that Du Bois and the glorious founders of the sociology laboratory at Atlanta felt much the same way. It has been my privilege and pleasure to share with you on this special occasion at least one personal story of what it is like to live a curious life within a cautious academy. Let us now work hard at our appointed tasks so that that when we reconvene this meeting for the centennial celebrations in 1997 we will prove worthy of the moment.

Works by W.E.B. Du Bois

Dusk of Dawn
Negro American Family
The Philadelphia Negro
The Souls of Black Folk
The World and Africa

10

Daniel J. Elazar:
The Covenant Tradition in Politics

The life of Daniel Elazar was intimately tied to his deep affections for that which is best in the United States and Israel. It should be said plainly that his personal allegiances as a Jew and an American were linked to his professional cares and concerns. To extrapolate his interest in the federalist idea, in isolation from the sanctity of the Holy Scriptures of the Hebrew faith for example, is to diminish the life-long intellectual enterprises with which he was linked. Indeed, I would contend that Elazar was driven to prepare the capstone to his life and career, the four-volume work on *The Covenant Tradition in Politics*, by the private and public considerations embodied in his relationships with the United States and Israel.

It is the blessing and perhaps the curse of academic invention that its practitioners constantly combine and recombine traditions that are inherited from the past. So it was with Elazar. One might say that he drew from Moses and Madison in particular in stitching together his unique vision of law and morality, and how they both impact the world of politics. For Elazar, politics did not so much denote parties and elections but rather elements in the social life of a community, state, or nation that actively command the participation of ordinary people—the public if you will. Politics is found when and where a sense of injustice or inequality exists. At its core, politics is the act of removing such injustices or inequalities. In this fashion, normative frameworks that are rooted in politics can be transformed into decent efforts to enhance everyday life.

From Edward Gibbon's *The Decline and Fall of the Roman Empire* to Joseph Needham's *Science and Civilization in China*, multiple-volume works on a single theme define something special, a work of operatic proportions in contrast to, say, a simple song. Of course, not every multi-volume work is successful, and even those that are successful often take a while to penetrate the world of scholarship. Their very magnitude and complexity assure that they will have a cumulative rather than an immediate impact. They often take six years rather than six weeks to penetrate what is euphemistically referred to as the marketplace. Such multi-volume works place a considerable burden on the reader as well as the writer. The reason is rather obvious. Important big ideas, or as Clifford Geertz likes to call them, thick ideas, take a while to penetrate the inherited paradigms of the intellectual class. In this category of thick ideas, we must place Daniel Elazar's quartet of volumes on *The Covenant Tradition in Politics*.

If the truth be told—and this is as good a place as any other to speak the truth—Elazar's multi-volume effort was supposed to be three, not four volumes. Like everything else in the completion of this long-term project, it took some doing to convince Elazar that a work of 2,000 pages is best broken down into edible bites. It is hard enough to get people to read a twenty-page essay, much less a volume of 500 pages. As a result, what started as a three-volume concept mushroomed into four volumes. Even so, this multi-volume work can readily tax the attention span of the most dedicated Talmudist and Federalist alike. Fortunately, Elazar was a man of this world as well as of the past and future. In the battle over length, he prevailed on word count, but I held the line on the number of volumes required to best draw the attention of an already sparse audience. But this is an aside having to do with publishing strategies. Whether *The Covenant Tradition in Politics* is a three- or four-volume work is a small detail. The nature of Elazar's enterprise is significant beyond strategies. This empirical effort attempts to explain actual events as a working out of normative frameworks within the Judeo-Christian traditions.

Like all grand ideas, *The Covenant Tradition in Politics* is elusive and at times a trifle ambiguous (otherwise, what would we have left to debate?). The idea behind the quartet is simple enough: the interpenetration of the polity with theology. Of course, this is the stuff of dozens of books and hundreds of journal articles annually. The more knowledgeable might ask what makes this different from the work of Max Weber on *The Protestant Ethic and the Spirit of Capitalism* or that of R. H. Tawney on *Religion and the Rise of Capitalism*. There is to be sure a connection between Elazar's work and those earlier pioneering efforts at the sociology of religion. But to make a molehill out of a multi-volume mountain, there is a huge difference as well. The difference is that Elazar does not see the political, economic, and religious as separate realms of social togetherness that pass one another as ships in the night, but as a bundle of grounded institutions that emerge over history, presided over by the idea of an Invisible God Almighty. In this sense, Elazar had one foot in the prophetic mold and another in the "postmodern" perspective that considers people shaping history rather than history shaping people. He well understood the centrality of culture in the determination of political behavior, as well as personal actions. The classical sociological paradigm sought to explain the character and functioning of an economy in terms of the religious and political systems found within a nation. Elazar is less concerned with seeing either polity or theology as an explanation for economic change, but as the inherent duality that defines civilization.

In his analysis of "The Bible and the Rule of Law," Lord Acton provided, in a few words, the humanistic inspiration for Elazar's classic effort:

> Liberty is the essential condition and guardian of religion. The government of the Israelites was a federation, held together by no political authority, but by the unity of race and faith, and founded, not on physical force, but on a voluntary covenant. The example of the Hebrew nation laid down the parallel lines on which all freedom has been won—the doctrine of national tradition and the doctrine of higher law; the principle that a constitution grows from a root, by process of development, and not of essential change; and the principle that all political authorities must be tested and reformed according to a code which was not made by man.

The tension between liberty under divine authority and the constraints imposed by human authorities is the proving grounds for Elazar of the covenantal tradition as such. That Lord Acton shared, indeed anticipated, the premises of Elazar's work is a testimonial to the continuing importance of religion in the political life of nations. It is also a warning to avoid boundary maintenance as a test of social scientific analysis.

Summarizing such a large-scale, multi-volume effort in a few brief paragraphs is a daunting task. Perhaps the best way to begin to do so is by noting that for Elazar, the essential universal triad is not Jerusalem, Athens, and Rome, but Jerusalem, Rome, and Washington, D.C. Indeed, in Elazar's worldview, the Greek origins of modern democracy appear as a murky shadow, entering the picture as part of modern constitutionalism. This might be considered a slight to the Athenian democracy of Solon, and for that matter to the American founding fathers Elazar so admired, but my sense is that Elazar viewed Athens as the cultural backdrop of Roman and American politics.

One would also have to note that we are speaking of ancient Rome and contemporary Washington, D.C. Like Judaism itself, in the minds of people, these are less geographical place names or capital cities than grand ideas of political organization and human association.

When Elazar looks at the United States then, it is a special blend of the encounter with politics and religion based on the sum of experiences derived from Jerusalem, Athens, and Rome. America manages not simply to reproduce mechanically but to expand intellectually upon those earlier varieties of the political-religious experience. This, according to Elazar, was made possible by allowing for the many varieties of the Protestant experience linked to the federalist idea of community. Together, they added up to the democratic system. The first new nation is made new by means of the covenant tradition at the secular and clerical levels. Elazar marches with John Dewey in philosophy and Talcott Parsons in sociology, along a path of an America dedicated to multiple varieties of the civil and religious experiences. But he went beyond American nativism in considering the founding fathers as no less influenced by Judaism and the "Old" Testament as by the Christian "New" Testament. Whether such a fusion actually offers a pathway to a modern federalism and a decentralized communitarianism, as Elazar claims, is another matter, for it must be said in frankness that while he was willing to suspend judgment about the federalist future of the United States, he was unshakable in his commitment to the covenantal past as the source of Western civilization.

Other political scientists have appreciated the extent to which the Hebrew Testament and sacred texts issued into the notion of covenant. Of special note in this connection is the pioneering work of Aaron Wildavsky in this same field. The divine sense of law is more than an agreement or a bargain: it is a sacred pact, violated at the risk of the very existence of civil society itself. The creative balance between nation and providence, mediated as it is by law, is the source for Elazar of the covenant tradition. This tradition spins its way through history from Catholic to Protestant sources—and clearly, Elazar is far more comfortable with the latter—to provide continuation of the legal basis of civil society and religious culture alike. In this, Elazar has a far different take on the biblical tradition than did Wildavsky, who saw the dialectic at play more than the architectonic framework at work. Elazar does not see a world of antagonisms within the Jewish prophetic tradition, so much as a world of Jewish transformation, conflicts that may lead to schisms between Judaism and Christianity rather than differences within each faith.

This emphasis on the unity of the religious experience as a cultural formation permits Elazar sometimes to slip into celebration rather than critique of the place of theology or ideology in the formation of modern democracy. There is something almost Hegelian in Elazar's belief that the idea of the covenant contains the seed of the idea of democracy; the latter comes to full flowering in an appreciation of the religious sources of the Western civilization. Is this celebration of democracy as an outcome of the Judeo-Christian religious tradition warranted? This is hard to say. Certainly, the deep ruptures left from World War II, and relative quiescence of Christian people to the fate of Jewish souls, lengthened the hyphen beyond what the covenant or any other shared religious tradition imagined. One is left with the disquieting feeling that the establishment of the American federal system, that holiest of the holy for Elazar, is more cause than consequence of the relative degree of consensus in the covenant tradition. Elazar himself compels such a view in his discussion of even relatively democratic orders such as Canada predicated on British monarchical models. It is given added impetus in his own questioning of the Latin American, Asian, and South African traditions—traditions that had elements of the covenantal tradition but scarcely many elements of the democratic imagination. Many societies had "great frontiers," but few realized their democratic outcomes.

Thus it is, as in all large-scale, multi-tiered efforts, there are interstitial problems. Rather than list personal concerns, large and small, let me rather focus on what I perceive to be the master problem—an elusive one to be sure. The marriage of a sacred political covenant and a secular political entity such as the state strikes me as one less demonstrated by theory rather than by context. Specifically, what might work in one nation may not work in another. I think it quite likely that the federalist ideal of politics and the covenant tradition in religion would work wonders in a small place like Israel. At one fell swoop, it would minimize discord, reduce the friction that derives from innumerable parties and special interests, and fuse the organization and ideology of a nation embattled and embroiled in regional as well as internal struggles.

The same contextual conditions do not obtain in a pluralized and protestantized place like the United States as they do in the more centralized atmosphere of Israeli politics and religion. Under certain conditions, the fusion of the covenantal and federal traditions may increase rather than decrease statism, by imposing a unitary frame of action and consciousness that is more interested in nation-building than in revolution-making. Examining recent issues of *Publius: The Journal of Federalism*, a publication that is close to the heart and soul of Elazar's interests, what one finds is a steady resistance to the drumbeat for greater governmental participation in the affairs of people. However, concerns are repeatedly expressed that various measures of health and welfare can be implemented at sub-governmental units by moral guideposts. But given the stated nature of that publication, what one does not find are Elazar's broader concerns for the religious factor in the affairs of people. While Elazar might argue that he should not be held accountable for ideas other than his own, I see no evidence that the kind of theorizing done in his four volumes will limit the rush to statism or even find unqualified support in the journal he founded. Given the disparate levels at which policymakers and academics alike operate, it would be asking a great deal were the situations to be otherwise. Indeed, one might argue that Elazar's concerns operate at multiple levels as well—and were not necessarily entirely integrated. This is said less in criticism than in recognition of the division of intellectual labors currently in fashion.

Thus, as a guide to policymaking, I find the concept of the covenantal tradition, linked as it is with the idea of federalism, to be more ideal than real. In a political universe in which centralized authority and state power grow exponentially, it is difficult to be entirely optimistic as Elazar was about his covenantal tradition. Too many political figures think of Providence as a partisan ally, than as a phenomenon deserving of respect and at times fear and trembling. It is limited by context even more than content. Of course, Elazar has every right to claim that his four volumes are not intended to be a recipe for policymaking in democratic societies. This is, after all, a study of history and not of policy. However, such a disclaimer should not obscure the problem of secularization as such, as breeding grounds for relativism, subjectivism, and ideology (in place of theology).

Elazar has taken us through an adventure in the history of Western civilization. He has not done so as Arnold Toynbee did, seeing it as a series of challenges and responses unevenly met, or as Oswald

Spengler did, as a series of prescriptions of what is wrong with Western civilization and what moral requisites are needed to combat presumed shortfalls. Rather, Elazar's architectonic framework is an extraordinary effort to show that politics informed by a sense of the marrow of religious beliefs stands on the same platform, perhaps a trifle higher, than political sociology, political psychology, and political anthropology as an explanatory device. Elazar well understood that religion could serve divisive ends of harrowing proportions. He was not so naive as to believe that linking the Ten Commandments to the *Federalist Papers* would solve the evils of the world, but he did believe that political analysis bereft of the religious factor was at least as barren as theology without a sense of politics. The tension in Western civilization is between political systems and religious beliefs, and no less within such systems and beliefs. Overcoming the dualism between politics and religion becomes the task of any society that hopes to achieve perfection, and perfection is the unreachable goal of the Good Society Elazar aimed for.

The covenant quartet is ultimately an effort to demonstrate that the meaning of culture resides in the fusion, after several millennia of struggle, of state and religion, ideology and theology, and above all, covenant and constitution. *The Covenant Tradition in Politics* is an astonishing tour de force—a 2,000-page excursion into social and intellectual history where the drive toward democracy and force of religion meet as in a double-helix system. Even if one can question Elazar's broad assumptions that the covenant tradition can provide us with policy guidelines, its importance in recasting the historical stage of the political culture and its religious attachments cannot be doubted. We are faced with that rare condition in social scientific literature. This is a monumental and unified effort whose prescriptive values can be questioned, but whose scholarly depth and historical sources are exacting. These volumes are a learning experience. Elazar in his final synthesis helped to reshape our personal maps of the political landscape. He did so by emphasizing our common Western heritage in political theology, whatever its originating assumptions. In this way, his study of the past may turn out to be of profound value to the future.

Works by Daniel J. Elazar

American Federalism
Cities of the Prairie (3 volumes)

The Conservative Movement in Judaism
The Covenant Tradition (4 volumes)
The Politics of American Federalism

11

Hans J. Eysenck:
The Liberality of a Social Psychologist

Let me begin my remarks with an admission. Of all the people paying homage to the late Hans Eysenck here this evening, I suspect that I am the least familiar with him in person. Although I had read several of his classic works early on in my professional career, it was not until five years ago that we actually met. In prior correspondence I had suggested that we place back into print several of Hans' major works, in particular, *Dimensions of Personality*, *Uses and Abuses of Psychology*, and *Psychology of Politics*. To my pleasant surprise, he wrote back in full and enthusiastic agreement.

This initiated an intense round of discussions, including several face-to-face visits, in which we enlarged our plans from placing back in print a few of his books to reissuing the essential corpus of his work with new and updated introductions. In addition to the new edition of his splendid autobiography, *A Rebel With a Cause*, published in 1996, there will be approximately a baker's dozen of Hans' major works, including *The Structure of Human Personality* and *Fact and Fiction in Psychology*. I should add that Sybil has been a wonderful person to work with in this multi-year, multi-volume endeavor, as has been his extraordinary administrative assistant, Janet Heath.

In addition to these earlier volumes, Transaction will have the privilege of publishing the last original work of Hans Eysenck—*Intelligence*, completed at the very edge of Hans' life. As one might expect, it is a work uncompromising in intellectual statement and pellucid in its formal design. While Hans has written on this subject before, he has nowhere previously attempted to synthesize the literature, starting with his own experiments and experience. Without delving into the actual substance of the work, it should be appreciated above all that this work exemplifies the liberality of its author. For however widely intelligence may vary, and whatever may be the weight of genetic or environmental factors in accounting for such variation, Hans never lost sight of the fact that ultimately intelligence is lodged in persons. And human beings require a fair starting point if they are to achieve all that they can be.

For Hans, the study of intelligence was not a racial cap on achievement, but a rigorous assessment of what it takes to reach for the stars. He tread a difficult waterway: he appreciated that the new age was such that even the assertion of intelligence as a critical variable in the measure of capability has become a dangerous, even subversive concept. Intelligence somehow conveyed the idea of a genetic inheritance, a position so badly discredited by the racial dogmas of the Nazis that the post-World War Two epoch led to a denial of genetics as such. So much of Eysenck's work was to create a liberal framework in which intelligence could be used as a measure of man, not a labeling device to further stratification and separation. I fear that this middle road, one that recognized inheritance and environment as components in personality development, was not easily understood. It made Eysenck a lonely man—a target for crude environmental theorists and at the same time, not quite the ally of the devotees of racial types the post-Eysenckians were in search of.

This notion of liberality emphasizes the fair and decent treatment of one another, the right to err without incurring the outrage of arbitrary punishment, the right not to engage in ideological polemics. Indeed, to do any of these things would be to violate the spirit of Hans Eysenck. In every single one of Eysenck's major works, his overriding sense of the unity of science and civility is manifest. It is Hans Eysenck's belief that the scientific methods of experiment fuse at some ethical level with the humane goals of experience, and in this fusion even bitter professional controversies can be overcome. It is hardly an accident that among his private heroes one finds Yeats, Montesquieu, Wilde, Montaigne, Nietzsche, Valery, and Diderot—people who read the human heart directly, without benefit of stifling ideologies.

In the Gospel According to St. John we are told that, "In the beginning was the Word" (1:1). A little later this startling revelation is explained when we are notified that "The Word was made flesh, and dwelt among us...full of grace and truth" (1:14). This conversion of the word from the divine to the human is deeply rooted in the Judeo-Christian heritage. It is an article of faith that Hans well appreciated—as is made evident not only by the quality or quantity of his writings, but by the testimonial to their importance as evidenced by the extraordinary number of citations they have received in the professional literature.

This is also another article of faith that I share with Hans. In our publishing efforts at Transaction we have worked hard to identify those figures whose words are of such transcendent value as to become a permanent part of the corpus of learned people wherever they may reside. We have bestowed this honor on: Thorstein Veblen in economics, Walter Lippmann in journalism, Peter Drucker in business and commerce, Aaron Wildavsky in political science, Lewis Feuer in intellectual history, David Riesman in sociology, and Abraham Edel in moral philosophy. It is our high honor to add Hans J. Eysenck in psychology to this august list.

In thinking about paying respect to Hans, I have asked myself if a common core of characteristics links such special figures. I believe there is among them worldliness, that is, a sense of the common culture to which all people of civility aspire to contribute as well as to share; conversely there is an absence of parochialism, of the sort of boundary maintenance that converts professionalism into an ideology. But above all, Hans shares with his fellow "greats" a sense of the public nature of social scientific discourse. He says so plainly and often in his excellent autobiography.

Hans held to a lifelong struggle against totalitarianism of the Right and the Left, against Nazism and Communism. His position was rooted in the profound belief that social science carries within itself the liberal spirit, or better yet, the spirit of free choice informed by the process of learning—not as some insipid middle ground going nowhere, but as a vigorous defense of a free society. Hans had no party save the party of social science. He had no partisanship save the loyalty generated by the shared search for truth. He had no preferences save those dictated by the quality of culture as such. He was a quintessential figure of the best the European culture could offer.

The man we come to honor was a person in whom the purposes of science and the values of liberal culture are easily fused into a seamless whole. This insistence upon conscience and choice infuses everything Hans examined—from weighing the joys against the risks of smoking to the life choices in careers. I submit that this, rather than any particular proposition on the nature of learning or the character of behavior, is his lasting legacy to our times and our culture. Yes indeed, in the end as in the beginning, is the Word. That is why Hans' spirit shall dwell among the living for generations to come.

Works by Hans J. Eysenck

Dimensions of Personality
Intelligence
The Psychology of Politics
Rebel with a Cause
Smoking, Health, and Personality

12

Lewis S. Feuer:
The Unitary Character
of Extremist Ideologies

The work of Lewis Feuer provides a kaleidoscopic view of many tendencies and trends within contemporary social science. Above all, he illustrates the fission-fusion trend in intellectual currents as exemplified in the work of Spinoza, Marx, Freud, and Einstein. He not only writes brilliantly on these figures now appended with "isms," but his work is permeated by socialist, physicalist, and psychoanalytical explanations of political events. In this sense, Feuer is an old-fashioned, arguably Old World, thinker in the best sense. He is someone who combines in his person liberal persuasions with democratic practice in a variety of fields. His work is not so much anti-Communist, as it is anti-totalitarian. He was one of the first major social scientists to appreciate the unitary character of dictatorial behavior—however many dictatorial systems may differ on paper. I daresay he has been singled out as a Soviet *bête noir* precisely because he has so artfully disentangled revolutionary rhetoric from totalitarian reality.

I am struck by the obviousness of this in reexamining his superb body of work on Marx and Engels on politics and philosophy. What emerges is an individual who believes fully and firmly that, even at this late date, the Marxian kernel can be rescued from its Stalinist and Soviet protuberance. He suggests therein that, "American development is out of phase with the rest of the world. America, disenchanted with its own Marxists venture of the thirties, is learning the language of conservatism, and in finding itself ever more removed from the Asian and European worlds." I do not know if Feuer would still adhere to this severe judgment, but I am certain that he would continue to implore us "to re-learn the meaning of Marxism." Feuer well appreciated that as "freedom is reborn in Eastern Europe and Asia, it will speak in the Marxist idiom and try to disenthrall the universal humanist bearing of Marx's ideas from their Stalinist perversion." There was a pugnacious tone to his critique; but then again, given the people and positions that he was critiquing, it is hard to see how an alternative approach would have been convincing.

Given his special background, it is readily apparent how he arrived at this outcome. Indeed, having myself come from the same personal background helped me appreciate the work of Lewis Feuer not so much as an intellectual exercise, but as a personal excursion to some truths about our culture and our discipline. We are both children of immigrant parents, raised in the Jewish cultural tradition and the Hebrew faith. We both went the route of poor Jews: from ghetto public schools, to DeWitt Clinton High School, and then on to the City College of New York. Not that we were unique participants in this long trek that we once had the nerve to call upward mobility. We also had in common the special experience of studying philosophy—Feuer under the tutelage of Morris Raphael Cohen, I under his son, Felix Cohen, and even more important, his younger colleague, Abraham Edel. And we both had early contributions to the Marxist publication of record in those years, *Science & Society*. But the nearly two decades that separated our lives and careers took strongly divergent paths. Among the prewar figures at the City College, Feuer deserves a place at the table no less bright that Irving Howe, Seymour Martin Lipset, Nathan Glazer, or Irving Kristol. That he is not readily mentioned in this light is more a function of splits and fissions within the prewar figures in student Marxist politics than in the quality of their respective works. Most of the other major figures that drifted into sociology found Leon Trotsky and the Fourth International at an early age. Feuer found the Soviet led Third International acceptable. And if the rest of America was a battleground between Democrats and Republicans, the CCNY experience was a far more acrimonious struggle between Trotskyists and Stalinists.

The movement away from such hothouse politics came about in Feuer's case with a deep and early immersion in basic issues in epistemology and language, including a commitment to the unity of science activities then located at the University of Chicago. An early teaching career, interrupted by military service, also liberated Feuer from the rigors of parochial left politics. I suspect too that the discovery of psychoanalysis played a large role in permitting Lewis to see the dark side of the personal life, the role of ambition, avarice, and irrationality in the conduct of public affairs. Indeed, psychiatry mediated Feuer's movement out of philosophical positivism into the world of sociology, and the exciting discovery of struggles among generations, races, religions, and cultures—in short, a range of explanation for human behavior that extended far beyond those of social class. Feuer was probably one of the first people in social science to speak of Soviet imperialism—and do so in unabashed terms. He saw the postwar takeovers in Eastern Europe as devastating evidence that the pattern of territorial annexation and suppression of national and local aspirations was as typical of Communist practice as it was of Nazi and Fascist practice. It was this reconfiguration of postwar European landscape that permitted him to see the unitary character of all totalitarian systems.

What Feuer initiated was to show how this process of perversion and enthrallment across generations has worked its way out as a special variety of the American social idiom. Specifically, the phenomenon of left-wing fascism and imperialism has become one way of accomplishing what Feuer terms a process of acknowledgment of that tremendous segment of reality that the early Marxist philosophy has come closest to grasping. To study the totalitarian phenomenon seriously means to get beyond dogmatism into actual ideological permutations and combinations, which still retain a lively sense of politics. Like others before and after him, Feuer held up the positions of Marx and Engels to show how profound were the corruptions brought on by Lenin and Stalin, no less than Hitler and Mussolini. While such a mirror is now commonplace, and far easier to make public, in the climate of the Vietnam War and student movements against American imperialism, such views were subject to tremendous criticism and in Feuer's case, personal abuse. He moved about university life, for the most part in second tier—but first class institutions, Sarah Lawrence College, the University of Toronto, the University of Virginia. His stay at the University of California in Berkeley was stormy, and indicative of the risks in taking public stands that had become unpopular—to say the least. But in these brief remarks on the occasion of honoring the work of Lewis Feuer, my purpose is simply to make plain the quiet courage with which he set forth the fundamental principles of democratic societies—and their need to understand how they differ in quality from totalitarian societies. For it was this emphasis that brought the wrath of his former allies on the Left down upon his head. His opponents could tolerate a place of Freud at the social science table; they could even accept the role of generational strife as part of the stratification tree in class terms. What they could not accept, what they could not even understand, is the awful simple truth that dictatorships may have different visions of the utopian future, but they have strongly similar practices of the quotidian present.

My own work on this topic was essentially to extend Feuer's work on the subject. I sought to establish in my work on "Left Wing Fascism" the social foundations of totalitarian doctrines in American life and the connection (or lack thereof) with their European counterparts. Essentially, my claim, like that of Feuer's, is that there is a powerful crossover between left and right, between communism and fascism, on American shores. This crossover is blurred by the exaggerated claims to uniqueness on both sides, and often obscured by the different demographic backgrounds of those adhering to left and right forms of totalitarianism. To provide some basis for this serious charge, I examined recent American social history, in particular, those key historical figures who represented left-right linkages—sometimes knowingly, at other times inadvertently—as a function of the political context of American life at its peripheries. In so doing, I sought to explore the roots of political marginality in American political culture. For it is precisely the totalitarian characteristics of both extreme right and extreme left that have not only irrevocably fused them, but have doomed them with respect to any conquest of political power. Much more work will need to be done to prove conclusively the point of view articulated by Feuer, and later expanded by myself. But such research holds open the prospects for resolving long-standing debates not only about why America has had no "socialism" but, no less important, why it has resisted "fascism" at the same time.

Feuer fully appreciated the fact that the twentieth century is polarized into diametrically opposite secular faiths. This dichotomy has taken hold because a century of war and genocide has given expression to competing messianic visions. After class annihilation comes classlessness, after racial annihilation, a triumphal master race. Subordination of the person to the collective is the common denominator. New totalitarian combinations and permutations are dangerous because they move beyond earlier hostility into a shared antagonism toward democratic processes as such. Concepts of evidence and rules of experience give way to historicism and intuition. Comfort with a world of tentative and reversible choices gives way to demands for absolute certainty. In such a climate, the emergence of left-wing fascism is presaged by a rebirth of ideological fanaticism. If the forms of totalitarianism have become simplified so too has the character of the struggle to resist such trends. This awareness offers the greatest potential for democratic survival against totalitarian temptation.

The United States has been singularly prone to look benignly upon the forces of left-wing fascism because it so adroitly managed to escape the real thing, namely, European fascism on one side and Soviet totalitarianism on the other. As a people, Americans are thus more ready to assume the best, not only in people but also in extremist propaganda systems. As a result, the process of intellectual cauterization against such extremism was also an overseas, "foreign" import. The migration phenomenon, with messages delivered by the victims of totalitarian systems, has become the essential source of resistance to the series of insidious and insipid banalities that go under the label of left-wing fascism. The work of Arendt, Halevy, Lichtheim, Reich, and Talmon, however different in intellectual disciplines and cultural backgrounds, spoke the identical message on one key fact: the integral nature of the totalitarian experience and the fusion of left and right sentiments in converting such sentiments into systems. It was, in my opinion, the unique and substantial contribution of Feuer to place this body of literature into a larger theoretical framework that gave political sociology a truly international dimension.

The experiences of the Second World War—when conflict displaced fusion and nationalist ambitions preempted totalitarian tendencies—had the effect of crystallizing differences between regimes, nations, and cultures. However, with the removal of the European wartime experience in space and time came the dismantling of traditional barriers between extremes of left and right. Their capacity to come together in a set of manifest hatreds for minorities, masses, and ultimately for democracy does not signify the end of ideological disputations characteristic of the century, but only a clearer appreciation that such distinctions among the enemies of democracy weaken the chances for the continuing survival, even slight expansion, of new lands and nations, of societies in which every individual counts as one: no more and no less. Feuer was a child of this immense learning process, and also an adult at mastering such a new configuration of factors in our global lives.

Feuer deserves the last word on himself, if only because it combines the deeply moving sense of the personal with the crippling role of the institutional in defining our existence. In his brief "Narrative of Personal Events and Ideas" in a festschrift prepared in his honor, he wrote: "If our human goals and knowledge are limited, partial never total, always edged with uncertainty, we can still cherish the principle of religion, the postulate, perhaps intuitively based, that the human episode is not altogether transient one but reaches somehow into the abiding nature of the universe; and lastly, the principle of humor, that joys are available to every human life, and that those who would maim their experience by superimposing a burden of primary guilt on every human existent are moved both by a self-enmity toward those they would profess to save."

Works by Lewis S. Feuer

Einstein and the Generation of Science
Imperialism and the Anti-Imperialist Mind
The Scientific Intellectual
Spinoza and the Rise of Liberalism
Varieties of Scientific Experience

13

Ronald Fletcher:
Defending Scientific Psychology

Ronald Fletcher died in his seventieth year. He was emeritus professor of sociology at Reading University at the time. He received his early training in philosophy and economics at the University of Bristol, where he graduated with first class honors, and went on to earn his doctorate in sociology at the London School of Economics. It was as visiting professor at the LSE in 1992 that I first met him (where he was spending his semester as Comte Memorial lecturer). He also served as professor of sociology and head of the Department of Sociology at the University of York, and prior to that, was lecturer at Bedford College and Birkbeck College at the University of London.

Fletcher was the author of many books, a number of which have taken their rightful place as works of enduring quality. Among these are *Instinct in Man* (1957); *The Family and Marriage in Britain* (1962); *Human Needs and Social Order* (1965); *August Comte and the Making of Sociology* (1966); *The Science of Society and the Unity of Mankind* (1974); *The Crisis of Industrial Civilization* (1974); *Evolutionary and Developmental Sociology* (1974); and a much reissued trilogy on *The Making of Sociology*. He came out of a tradition in which general sociology and ethical theory were constantly interlinked. In this, his intellectual work well mirrored his personality.

But it was Ronald's lifelong interest in mass communications that led to his involvement in a famous "case" of presumed fraud in psychology—the so-called Cyril Burt affair. He had created several major television series for the BBC, including *In a Country Churchyard* (1977); *The Biography of a Victorian Village* (1976); and *The East Anglians* (1980). This involvement in television made him especially alert to the BBC broadcast in 1981 entitled *The Intelligent Man*, which Fletcher labeled as uncritical, presuming the guilt of Cyril Burt, and which contained many stark errors of fact. Since the program aired five years after Burt's death, and given his familiarity with the world of mass communications, Fletcher decided to write a book that changed the judgment on Burt and led to a reconsideration of opinion even within the official British Psychological Society (BPS).

Thus it is that Fletcher serendipitously had more impact on the science of psychology than on the science of sociology. His manuscript, which was critically reviewed and rejected by several houses, was published by Transaction in 1990. It provided a detailed examination of the charges that Burt falsified data and result with respect to intelligence and inherited characteristics. The work was more than a vindication of Burt. It was also a searching inquiry into the obstacles lying in the way of the effort toward truth and veracity in science, when ideology, in alliance with popular journalism and the sensationalist power of the media, is able to powerfully intrude a particular viewpoint through the whole of the scientific community, and to enter it in a take-for-granted way in the professional decision-makers and general public alike.

By the time of publication of *Science, Ideology and the Media*, passions on Burt had begun to cool. A reconsideration began which, aided and abetted by the very media Fletcher blasted, became easier. Laudatory newspaper reviews, often of a front-page sort, led the BBC to promise a feature story rescinding its earlier docudrama. And the review of the Burt materials by the BPS in which cooler judgments prevailed indicated that Fletcher's lonely crusade was not isolated, nor without broad professional impact.

Fletcher was an unlikely candidate for crusader to a cause. He was a gentle soul, lacking in all guile and bile. His passion was more for the quite and solitude of the English countryside than the rough and tumble of professional organizational affairs. He was at work on an autobiography at the time of his death, which remains completed in manuscript form.

If Fletcher is to be remembered it probably should be less for his views on the Burt affair than for a firm commitment to such old fashioned verities as truth in scholarship and fairness in the treatment of adversaries. In an age of extreme partisanship, righteous convictions about politics, and tunnel vision careerism, Fletcher was indeed a voice of the past; but no less, a light unto the present. He shall be missed—especially in an age when old-fashioned concerns with veracity, evidence, and compassion are in such terribly short supply.

Works by Ronald Fletcher

The Family and Marriage in Britain
Instinct in Man
Science, Ideology and the Media
Sociology: The Study of Social Systems

14

Gino Germani:
Sociologist from the Other America

What follows is an attempt to describe candidly and quickly—as best I can—events that took place forty-plus years ago. Not only does this pose a challenge to one's memory, but to fairness in one's assessments of persons and places long past. The actual weight of someone's influence is hard to measure under the best of circumstances. The tendency in personal recollections is to exaggerate one's own relationships with an important fellow—especially someone deceased like Gino Germani who cannot readily present his own version of events.

This is also a painful exercise. Not only do I have to face the fact that Gino is not among the living, but that many other people near and dear to both of us at the time are also gone from this earth. People like Kalman Silvert, one of the wisest political analysts of Latin America I ever met. Enrique Butelman, the founding director of *Editorial Paidos* and a role model for my later decision to enter publishing. Francisco Romero, the doyen of Argentine philosophy, was kind to me as a student of philosophy even more than a budding sociologist. Even brilliant students I taught in Argentina such as Celia Durruti are no longer with us. Others live but have aged badly. Time does not treat everyone with a sense of fairness and kindness—some people I remember in the 1950s as beautiful are worn and haggard at century's end. All of these considerations make the request for reconstruction a difficult chore. So please take what follows with a grain of salt—perhaps several grains.

I first met Gino in Buenos Aires in early 1958. This was two and a half years after the end of the Peronist Era. Risieri Frondizi (one of three extraordinary brothers who rose to fame and power following the restoration of civil society to Argentina) had been named rector of the University of Buenos Aires. One of his decisions, taken in conjunction with the Faculty of Philosophy and Letters, was to house sociology under its wing, at least during an interim or transitional period. I suspect that Gino shared an anti-fascist commitment with part of Francisco Romero, the doyen of philosophy at the time. Gino's wish to return to the university world may have also played a role in this institutional development. For the truth is that Romero was not especially interested in sociology. On the other hand, Jose Luis Romero, from the history department (no relation to the philosopher), was deeply committed to the restoration of sociology. Another person who supported a new sociology program at the University of Buenos Aires was yet another vigorous anti-fascist, the philosopher of science, Mario Bunge. Mario was a philosopher of science and social science strongly opposed to either theological or political control of the Faculty. Because of his anti-fascist stand, no less than his superb background in physics, he became one of the very first new appointments in the post-Peron epoch at the Faculty of Philosophy and Letters. And in light of subsequent intellectual history in Argentina, he was a sagacious choice at that.

Mario Bunge and I had established an epistolary relationship in previous years. This came about through our both being frequent contributors to the journal *Science & Society*. It was clear from where our work was appearing, and from our stationery, that we were both academic exiles of sorts: he from Peronism and me from McCarthyism. While I managed occasional lecturing, I was working at the time as a researcher for a firm called *J.J. Berliner & Company*, which gathered information and prepared reports on specific industrial developments. I also was involved in a publishing start-up (well before Transaction) known as Paine-Whitman. It was a small activity, but we did manage to produce fourteen titles during the company's brief life. Amazingly, several of our books did well in the marketplace, while others were translated into a variety of foreign languages. (In later years I was pleased to remember how close academic life outside the university and publishing were in actual practice during the decade of the fifties.)

Mario had spoken with Gino about our relationship, and he was asked by Gino to contact me to see if I would come down to Buenos Aires and help launch a new, independent sociology program liberated from justicialist-fascist doctrine. Negotiations went on throughout 1957. But by early 1958 the heavens seemed right for the move. A number of factors influenced my decision—my interest in establishing my academic credentials on a firmer footing, and perhaps not incidentally, a marriage that, while not ready to collapse, was hardly in the best of shape. My responsibility to my two young sons made the move difficult. But I did manage to save enough money to provide for my family for a six-month period of time—which indeed was the time I spent in Buenos Aires in 1958. I returned for brief stints in late 1958, 1959, and 1960. But then, academic life in America became easier for people with my convictions, and I had obtained positions at various junior ranks at Brandeis, Bard, and then as chairman of a combined department of sociology and anthropology at Hobart & William Smith.

These were the "circumstances" faced when I met Gino. He was cordial and supportive in every way. I was given the maximum stipend for a visiting professor, which although modest, enabled me to avoid drawing upon funds left behind for my family to live on. Indeed, I even managed to send some additional funds home. In retrospect, the support I received was amazing. Gino made sure that various junior colleagues took me under their wing. He did everything from helping me learn the Spanish language—at least in a rudimentary fashion, to providing me with living quarters that were comfortable and blessedly rent-free. The student enthusiasm for sociology was so great, so exhilarating, that they saw assisting an overseas professor more as a badge of honor than as a chore.

In retrospect, I suspect Gino probably would have preferred a methodologist to a theorist like myself—and rightly so. The needs of a fledgling department dictated as much. But he made do with limited resources. He brought in Jorgé Graciarena from economics to attend to the basic statistical training needed by sociology students. Indeed, what worried Gino about me was that I reflected the student impulse to theorizing to the detriment of learning the basics of the field. The conflict between Gino and the students that surfaced at a later period derived in some measure from the gap between Gino's increasing emphasis on empirical research and a corresponding rising interest in grand theorizing by many of the students. In that arcane world, Jean-Paul Sartre became a dialectical battering ram against Gino's empiricism. But such issues really did not affect me. Gino was a wise man. He knew how to make use of the resources at hand—and I was such a resource. Beyond that, we became good friends in short order, so that differences in background, age, and orientation did not become too much of an impediment. Indeed, we both knew what had to be done with a "missing generation" of sociologists occasioned by the Peronist dictatorship.

As I recall, Gino spoke little to me about his experiences under fascism—at least not directly. I did raise with him my sense that Italian fascism and German Nazism was operationally and culturally quite different from each other, even if in organizational structure they had some similarities. He agreed, and observed that he had made this point in his own writings. He did speak with me about the Jewish Question, his marriage to a Jewish woman, and the large number of Jewish students who seemed interested in pursuing a career in sociology. An Italian Catholic looking like the stereotypical ghetto Jew did not make Gino's life any easier, or for that matter, spare him from gossip on his "secret" commitments to the Hebrew faith! We did speak about the relationship of totalitarian regimes to the social sciences at some length. By the time we had met, he was well established in Argentine life and letters. I suspect that his knowledge of fascism in Italy was embedded in his larger concerns about totalitarian forms of rule—especially, of course, Peronism. He mentioned being snake-bitten by dictators: first by Benito Mussolini and then his ideological protégé, Juan Domingo Peron.

Gino well understood and expressed appreciation for the irony of going from one form of authoritarian rule in Italy to another similar variety in Argentina. I suspect that this ominous political background influenced the choice of his research topics in the mid-1950s. For example, he was far more interested in the European psychoanalytical tradition than one might have imagined. In part this was attributable to a friendship with wonderful people like Enrique Butelman, but also to a sense that Sigmund Freud, Melanie Klein, Wilhem Reich, Erich Fromm, among others, despite weaknesses in their general *social* theory, had important lessons to teach Argentina and its budding social science community about the totalitarian temptation. So despite reservations, he wrote these intellectual figures into *fechas* for the first-year students.

We spoke somewhat about his intellectual formation and interest in sociology. But what fascinated me is that despite the importance of Italian figures like Roberto Michels and Vilfredo Pareto, these people, whose work he knew, seemed less prominent in his thinking than I would have imagined. He probably was closer to the Germanic tradition of Weber and Mannheim than I would have expected. We spoke of Mannheim—somewhat critically of the problem of relativizing truth in Mannheim—since I undertook to do a major two-volume work on the sociology of knowledge for the University of Buenos Aires Press, whose initial editorial director was the brilliant Jose Boris Spivakow. Indeed, that work did appear in the late 1960s and remains a standard in the Spanish language. Gino placed the full resources of the department behind this effort.

Gino had read very widely in the history of sociology. Indeed, we spoke of a number of figures that merited attention—but again, curiously, the Italian tradition seemed to me to be muted in his thinking. This was not true in music however! Here Vivaldi, Geminiani, Mozart, and Frescobaldi dominated his thinking and listening. I think he loved music far more than sociology! Similarly, in art his favorites seemed to be Paul Klee and Giorgio de Chirico. He liked playful visual images. They reflected a private side of him not easily perceived by those at the Institute who saw only sociology as relevant.

One came to appreciate the fact that Gino had a mission in mind—to move sociology in Argentina from a clerical to an empirical footing. He keenly felt a need to move beyond the ideological debris left behind by Peron and Peronism after the termination of the dictatorship in 1955. So even if he regarded certain European thinkers with great reverence, his emphasis with me—no less than with others—was on North American sociologists—especially the work of the Columbia School, specifically Lazarsfeld, Merton, and Stouffer, among others. In this regard, when I expressed to him my interest in preparing a *Boletin* on Wilhelm Dilthey's Collected Works he gave his assent reluctantly, and only when I assured him that my purpose in writing such a paper was to alert students to the risks in the *Gesiteswinnschaftliche* approach to social concerns. Indeed, he then saw such an effort as worthwhile. He read my study in proofs, making useful suggestions about the transition of Hegelian idealism into sociological theories of culture, and highlighting empirical concerns. Gino was also instrumental in the University Press of Buenos Aires, started under the guidance of an outstanding figure in his own right, Jose Boris Spivakow, contracting with me to prepare a two-volume anthology in the sociology of knowledge. It remains the standard reference work on the subject in the Spanish language to this date.

The practical, organizational tasks that Gino faced in building the Institute of Sociology was, in retrospect, monumental. They ranged from skepticism on the part of the more established program heads in philosophy and history, to presumption on the part of students that they were going to study revolution-making rather than social science. Adding to the troubles was the fact that physical space was extremely confined (until sociology gained its own quarters either in late 1958 or early 1959—I think the latter). There was also an absence of national talent upon which to draw, and hostility from traditional sources within the Argentine cultural elites. In short, his success in building the program was a minor miracle. Gino had a much larger reservoir of patience and organizational understanding than one might have imagined. He met with faculty, administrative personnel, and students constantly. They came to his small office daily, organized teaching programs, research designs, and public relations efforts. Many people helped, but he was the driving force. The public acceptance of sociology was his mission.

Building a faculty was very difficult. In this people like Jorgé Graciarena, Norberto Bustamante, Manuel Sadosky, Torcuato diTella, Jose Luis Romero, the aforementioned Enrique Butelman, and Guido diTella were all very important. But perhaps most important was my fellow American—Kalman H. Silvert. Kal was a godsend. He came to Buenos Aires initially as a member of the American Universities Field Staff, then stayed on with a Ford grant. His knowledge of Spanish was solid, awkward at times, but far better than mine at the time. Above all, he was a political scientist with strong credentials as a field researcher as an empirical sort who could and did work on a national scale—as he did in Venezuela as well Argentina. Gino cared greatly for Kal—although they fought and had differences concerning the direction of the program. Indeed, Gino put Kal "in charge" of socializing me into the ways of Buenos Aires culture, especially that of the University. To my deep dismay, both Kal and Gino died close to one another—both terribly prematurely. Kal came to Buenos Aires with his family, with troubles throughout his stay. (He had a child seriously physically impaired that drained him of every dollar, and a wife Frieda, who was, like Kal, somewhat volatile.) They were "family" to me, and got me through some rough spots in a strange new world. Gino showed good judgment in matching people. Gino also realized the advantages of the North American model by urging a spin-off of an independent institute—part from the department and the university as such. In this, the effort of the DiTellas can hardly be overestimated. But it was Gino's international connections that generated the originating revenues from places like the Ford and Rockefeller Foundations. These grants also provided ammunition for the extreme radicals to denounce Gino as a North American puppet. Nothing could be further from the truth, but appearance ultimately triumphed over reality.

Thinking about my personal experiences in Argentina moves me away from Gino's specific orbit, and is a discussion for another time and venue. I met many students, often only a few years removed in age and outlook from me. Because they had been denied the prospects of a career in sociology under Peronism, there had been roughly a dozen years of build-up for people who wanted such a career but could not pursue it with any assurance in quality. As a result, I had students who were absolutely brilliant—a class full of "sobresalientes"! Even in my later years at elite American universities like Stanford and Princeton I never had such an exhilarating experience. Days melted into nights, and lectures into conversations into dinners. There were confrontations arranged by advanced students and junior faculty to observe my behavior under fire, i.e., as between a moderate Millsian and devoted (rabid) follower of Jean-Paul Sartre.

I lived in several places on my first tour of duty in Buenos Aires. Each room was relatively close to the Viamonte y Reconquista cross section. So I spent many hours at the Institute. Indeed, often after class hours, many of us (younger faculty and older students) went to eat. Especially wonderful in my memories of these evenings was Norberto Bustamante. He was a Falsaffian fellow in size, appetite, but also in talent. He knew the history of philosophy from Hegel to Popper as well as anyone I have met, and his contributions to the Institute were great, despite having to teach in three different schools to make ends meet for a large family. Many of the students—women as well as men—were important to me in social as well as intellectual terms. For example Carlos Slusky, who later migrated to the United States and Silvia Sigal, who also migrated, but to France. Carlos was a psychiatrist who later became a general practitioner. But his help in giving me living quarters and Spanish lessons was Herculean. Speaking of Spanish lessons, Romero's two beautiful daughters, Maria Sol and Maria Luz, were my daytime tutors. Though they laughed at my mistakes (and at me) they actually taught me well. I shall be ever grateful to these young women. I am sure they became hugely successful in whatever they pursued vocationally.

Again it was the hidden hand of Gino in all of this that made my transition successful. He provided the human network and the academic framework for my socializing. In turn, he made sure to gain his measure. I was essentially in charge of the translation program.

And while we violated just about every copyright convention known to mankind, we succeeded in turning out published and mimeographed materials from the masters of American sociology: Merton, Lazarsfeld, Wirth, Goffman, Lipset, and Bendix. These materials from major writings of the masters helped to form and mold the first post-generation of sociologists in Argentina. It was a strange coupling, American empirical sociology with European rational social democracy. The grafting was admittedly partial and at times perverse, but I was proud to be a part of this extraordinary effort to construct legacy as well as a discipline—and to work with Gino in this effort under his tutelage.

There are several guideposts toward a better understanding of Gino Germani as a social scientist. To begin with I do not recollect him ever wanting to "internationalize sociology in Argentina." More to the point, he saw the need for social science to be empirical in character and as a consequence (not an aim) having an international dimension and utility. I found him cool to nationalism of any variety, Latin American, North American, or European. He was a student of stratification—of class, ethnicity, migration, labor, urbanization, etc. He was also skilled at placing in the forefront the social psychology of mass movements, such as fascism. He was a true student of Weber, one who well appreciated the distinction between science as a goal and politics as a vocation. It is not that Gino simply assumed that every form of objectivity translated into high science, but that without a notion of objectivity, even the prospects for sociology would become dimmed. He saw social psychology and social stratification as a linked pairing, one that helped define the interior mission of sociology as a discipline.

To speak of a unique contribution is to come to terms with the raw material of everyday life. Good theory applied to new and unusual circumstances yields important results. In a highly charged ideological context, Gino played a Herculean role in introducing an old subject as a new science. That to me is his outstanding professional contribution. It is hard to measure or know which of Gino's works carried the greatest weight in North America, much less who they influenced. In some ways, I reckon myself Gino's student. That is to say, he helped me appreciate context as well as content in research design. And my life-long interest in Cuba is probably due in part to his own experiences in trying to blend, to meld, the scientific and the democratic.

Let me therefore close by saying that in formal sociological terms, I will stand by my paper written a decade ago that appears as the opening essay in Spanish as "Modernization, Anti-modernization and Social Structure" in *Despues de Germani: Exploraciones Sobre Estructura Social de la Argentina.* I would only add now, a decade later, that I have an even deeper respect for Gino's life-long struggle against totalitarianism. For him, the sort of one-sided, subjective, partisan views represented equally by communism in the Soviet Union, by fascism in Italy, and Nazism in Germany were the united enemy of social science as honest experience and ethnography.

We must not forget that it was less the attraction of Harvard than the politicization and widespread disarray of sociology at Buenos Aires in the mid-1970s that led Gino to shift his venue. Gino confided frankly when we met in Cambridge to discuss one of several book projects that he never acquired much of a taste for the place. We laughed at sociology as it was practiced by the Reverend Parsons, a man of the Protestant persuasion. It was a vision of the field that Gino as a Catholic and I as a Jew frankly could never easily accept. As I indicated earlier, it was the push factors that led Gino to finally leave Argentina. Of course, his connections and roots there were and remained deep. Still, the rupture was plain enough—the know-nothings disguised as radicals won the battle. It was an empty victory, as demonstrated by the continued growth of sociology outside the University by people and institutes like those of Miguel Murmis in survey research and public opinion, Torcuato diTella in international stratification and industrialization, Ruth Sautu and Eliseo Veron in social psychology, Silvia Sigal in Argentine history and stratification, and many other of Gino's colleagues and students. So in the end Gino left behind a double legacy: honest social researchers who possessed decent political values. Surely this is a fine and fit epitaph for one lifetime.

We met quite regularly after Gino migrated to the United States. I found him to have become more candid and sardonic than in Buenos Aires. I do believe he felt quite relieved of the burdens of administration and being in some sort of academic fishbowl in Argentina. He enjoyed big city life, and hence New York and Boston were more of a draw than Cambridge. He came to our Transaction offices on several occasions, and obviously was concerned to see his work widely disseminated in the English language. But I also had the feeling that he came to see me as an old friend from the next generation—a connection with the Buenos Aires past, and a fellow anti-totalitarian. While my experiences with McCarthyism were extremely mild compared with Gino's struggles with fascism, we shared a common consequence of exile from academic pursuits. After all, he came to Argentina in search of the same considerations that made the appointment attractive for me at a much later time. With part of my father's family residing in Buenos Aires since the early 1920s, I had a feeling of family as well as profession—again, much like Gino. We never talked in these ways; there were also private matters better left that way. I suspect that you know about these in any event. I never recollect Gino saying a harsh word about others, what we call in English bad-mouthing was just not part of his make up. Somehow, he did not have to. I think we well understood our mutual likes and dislikes readily enough.

My own role, my own way of repaying a huge debt to this owl-like fellow who not so much looked at you as through you, is to serve as informal literary executor for his works in the English language. Gino knew that his remaining time on earth was short, so he arranged with me to produce just about all of his major papers in several volumes. *Authoritarianism, Fascism and National Populism* (1978); *Marginality* (1979); and *The Sociology of Modernization* (1980). We also took on the distribution of his edited volume on *Modernization, Urbanization and the Urban Crisis* (1973). These remain the primary sources for learning first-hand about Gino's work in the English language. There is also an excellent secondary source on Gino, prepared by a former colleague of mine at Washington University in the 1960s, Joseph A. Kahl. His book, initially published in 1976, was titled *Modernization, Exploitation and Dependency*, and revised and published in 1987 as *Three Latin American Sociologists: Gino Germani, Pablo Gonzalez Casanova, Fernando Henrique Cardoso*. Both editions were published by Transaction.

While many changes have taken place in hemispheric and European affairs, and Argentina is not the same country left behind by Germani, these works still have the capacity to inform and to educate. That Transaction has managed to do this, and that we persist in keeping Germani's books in print and available to a new generation of younger scholars, is perhaps the best way in which we as social scientists transmit culture, honor intellectual labor, and preserve personal memory.

Works by Gino Germani

Authoritarianism, Fascism, and National Populism
Marginality
Modernization, Urbanization, and the Urban Crisis
Politica Sociedad en una Epoca de Transicion
The Sociology of Modernization

15

Eli Ginzberg:
The Economist as a Public Intellectual

The world of Eli Ginzberg can readily be thought of as a triptych—a career in three parts. In his early years, Ginzberg's work was dedicated to understanding the history of economics, from Adam Smith to Wesley Clair Mitchell, and placing that understanding in what might well be thought of as economic ethnography. Ginzberg's earlier efforts took him on travels from Wales in the United Kingdom to California in the United States. His poignant account of Welsh miners in an era of economic depression and technological change is a landmark work. His memories of a cross-country trip during the first year of the New Deal provide insights and evaluations that can scarcely be captured in present-day writings.

The second period, which commenced with Eisenhower's election as president in 1953, corresponds to Ginzberg's increasing involvement in the practice of economics, in issues related to manpower allocation, employment shifts, gender and racial changes in the workforce, and a growing concern for child welfare and education. His work entailed growing interest in the role of federal, state and city governments, and he focused on the question of how the public sector impacts all basic social issues. Ginzberg linked the economics of budgeting to the sociology of stratification. His work sufficiently transcended political ideology that seven American presidents sought and received his advice and participation. One might say that Ginzberg was the father of labor and work allocation studies, and thus he is central to the rise of applied economics both before and after the Second World War.

After receiving well-deserved encomiums and congratulations for intellectual work and policy research well done, Ginzberg went on to spend the next thirty years of his life carving out a position as a preeminent economist of social welfare, health services, and hospital administration. It is this latter portion of his life that is the dominant—but not exclusive—subject of *Eli Ginzberg: Economist as a*

Public Intellectual. What is apparent in his work of this period, as well as that of others, is the growing interaction of all the social sciences—pure and applied—to develop a sense of the whole. The estimable contributors to this *festschrift*, drawn from a wide network of scholarly backgrounds, have come together to provide a portrait of a figure who spans the twentieth century, and yet points the way to changes in the twenty-first century.

Within the triptych is a unified and singular person. Eli Ginzberg from the start possessed a strong sense of social justice and economic equality grounded in a Judaic-Christian tradition. The spirit of public welfare, philanthropic giving, and a commitment to social justice beyond economic equity all play a part in Ginzberg's work. All of these aspects come together in the writings of a person who has transcended parochial beliefs and given substantive content to the often-cloudy phrase *public intellectual.*

The notion of a public intellectual has been ridiculed by op-ed geniuses who see themselves as the clarion callers of the people, and even more by academic figures who feel that going beyond the parameters of research findings constitutes an illicit extension of their qualifications. This is not the place to argue the fact-value dualism, or what constitutes the proper role of the professional economist or sociologist in the larger society. What does need saying is simple enough: there are serious and overriding issues of public concern in any given epoch. These engage a special cluster of unusually talented and courageous scholars for whom such issues demand the infusion of reason into a context of passion. Economists, like other social scientists, have had their share of contributors to policy-laden issues. Some of them indeed are well represented in this volume. None has a higher claim to being a public intellectual than Eli Ginzberg.

The task of a *festschrift* is difficult enough when celebrating talents who reach the ripe age of sixty-five or seventy. But in properly honoring someone who has gone beyond his ninetieth birthday, and who has had multiple career tracks in which he has made unique contributions, such a task becomes close to insurmountable. Since most of the contributors to this volume are considerably younger in years than Eli, they have a far stronger sense of his contribution to the area of health welfare and service than to his earlier work in human resources, economic sociology, and anthropology. In addition, any sense of the world as it was, say, in the New Deal period—

or for that matter during the Great Society—is mired in obscurity and ambiguity. So the participants in this volume can each contribute a sliver of insight into Eli's life, with the hope that the overall effect is to illumine the larger whole.

It is my belief that the volume succeeds in this goal. It does so because the person behind these multiple achievements is correctly perceived as a single individual. The overall thrust of Ginzberg's work is remarkably well captured precisely by intense examination of the specific parts singled out for scrutiny. In addition, several essays make a valiant, and I believe largely successful, effort to treat Ginzberg whole—as a theoretical unity with practical parts. This is not to say that all the bases, or parts, are fully covered. Ginzberg's work in relation to racial and minority rights, his own strong religious convictions, and his place in the pantheon of Columbia University "greats" are really not amply covered. But then again, these blank spots will allow the editor of some further *festschrift* to complete the picture. For one volume, I think the picture is sufficiently complete as to provide a compelling picture of the person being honored.

One very significant element in a *festschrift* is the importance of the contributors as scholars in their own right. The contributors to this volume are master figures in the history of the social and economic sciences—people who merit special recognition in the form of *festschriften*. As a consequence, the essays herein offered are not paeans of praise or adulation, but often-sharp commentaries of a critical nature. If the highest form of friendship is criticism, then this volume is an ample demonstration of just such regard. Without demeaning or dismissive attitudes toward the person who is the subject of this volume, each contributor to a greater or lesser extent uses the essay as a forum to present his or her own contributions as illumined by Ginzberg, and no less, the shortcomings—real or imaginary—in his work that might lead to a different set of results. The area of medicine, health policy, and the social status of health workers is vast, and growing more complex over time. In this, perhaps the highest compliment of all can be paid to this volume: it can be read without a presupposition of foreknowledge of one person's contribution—but as a collective portrait illuminating an area of deep concern.

It has been my good fortune to know Eli reasonably well—at least in his third career period. It has also been my good fortune to have supervised a *Festschriften* Series for Transaction that now includes twenty-four volumes of tribute. Eli fits easily in this list, and perhaps even deserves a special place of honor within it. Throughout the long process of gestation and creation, he has been a tower of support—with a proper sense of when to help and when to let the course of events takes its own turn. The volume concludes with five of Eli's recent essays in lieu of a response. He was given that opportunity, but chose instead—I would say wisely—not to respond to individual points but offer a sense of what a man of ninety can still contribute to the great debates of the time. The secret of Eli, one that reveals itself to those of his friends who have known him over time, is not his age but his youth. That twinkle in his eyes translates into a sense of intellectual adventure that still very much guides his research and his writings. As a result, while the contributors offer comment and tribute to the past efforts of this protean figure in the history of applied social research, he himself shows what it means to remain at least one lively step ahead of his interpreters.

Let me conclude with an acknowledgment to the contributors to this effort. Each and every contribution was uniquely written for this occasion. The authors were asked, and invariably responded, by focusing directly on the impact or implications of the ideas of Eli Ginzberg on their own work. Each individual was asked to write in a manner accessible to an educated (but not necessarily specialist) readership. The results speak for themselves. As in all such endeavors, there were delays in completion, compounded by the usual rewrites and updates. So it is hardly surprising that the work appears one year after the actual event of Eli Ginzberg's ninetieth birthday. But we collectively agreed at the celebration of that occasion that this may be a blessed omen—with but twenty-nine years left to go in order for him to reach the age of the supreme Hebrew prophet, Moses.

Works by Eli Ginzberg

Adam Smith and the Founding of Market Economics
The Eye of Illusion
The Nation's Children (3 volumes)
New Deal Days: 1933-1934
A World without Work

16

César Graña:
The Culture of Sociology and
Sociology of Culture

César Graña was, by any standard employed, both a complex personality and a dedicated social scientist. The first part of this proposition will be evident to the reader of these essays. It was also readily apparent to those who had the benefit of knowing him, even casually. The second part of this proposition, his profound commitment to social science in general and to sociology in particular, is less easy to detect or describe. Graña was such a brilliant literary stylist, so clearly a writer who took every word of his English seriously, that it is all to easy to overlook that throughout his career his subject matter uniformly remained the stuff of social research: human institutions like museums, urban structures like cities, and political artifacts like ideologies. In short, those elements that distinguish and identify society in contrast to behavior or nature.

The volume of essays before you exemplifies a style of doing work that has become increasingly rare in American academic life: the scholar revises and reconsiders a collection of working papers, some are entirely finished, others are in a penultimate stage, and still others are merely stitched together. In the hands of a lesser intellectual craftsman, many of these papers would long since have been published, and its author honored for so doing, with academic promotions and standing emoluments. But it is one of the hallmarks of the late César Graña that he was a perfectionist. And if that meant some doubted his propensity for hard work or creative thought, he could scarcely care less. He knew fully well the power of his mind. And now that his revisions and reconsiderations are perforce complete, that power can now be shared with others. Death puts to an end the anguishing search for the better.

Indeed, before his life was cut short in a highway accident in Spain in late 1986, César Graña was not only completing work on many of his briefer works, but was assembling material for a full-scale study of the role of museums in modern society. In addition, he was developing the working format for a cultural ethnography of Seville—the city in Spain he most loved and best knew. It might well be that were he still alive, César would consider this publication of his later papers a case of sheer "meddling." And while those who knew César will understand that this is a charge that will not readily go quietly into the night, in the final instance we decided that to let these papers languish would have been a far worse decision. Good social research with a human face is too rare a commodity to be squandered or suppressed.

Nonetheless, and in a prima facie sense, sifting the dry bones of another person's literary-sociological remains is certainly a case of meddling. Therefore such a step requires at least a brief explanation. The immense editorial contributions rendered to this project by Marigay Graña, César's life companion and wife, may seem to make such justification superfluous. But I think not. For in the case of these papers, ever absent such powerful and indispensable personal support, a case could and deserves to be made for the publication of *Nationalism and Culture*.

It is hard to say whether Graña had any sort of intellectual master plan. I see scant evidence for this. What he had was the essayist's knack of pursuing a problem in a many-sided way over time. He never quite finished with a problem, since real problems never finish exhausting the moral codebooks that people employ in the conduct of their everyday affairs. So what we have is a lifetime of concern with a series of problems: the relationship of European to American cultural values, social mores and literary manners; the place of art in mass society in contrast to the place of people in traditional society. These themes are the raw materials of his trilogy of works: *Modernity and its Discontents*; *Fact and Symbol*; and now, *Meaning and Authenticity*.

One of Graña's most favored, and favorite, sociologists was Daniel Bell. I suspect that, apart from his great respect for Bell's efforts to link culture and civilization in its advanced industrial setting, there is the fact that Graña also envisioned himself as a figure interested in the same themes, although he looked backward to find the present rather than looking at the present to find the future, as did Bell.

Another, more elusive element, is the parallel respect of both writers for the essay form. As I noted in a review of *The Winding Passage* some years ago, Bell is a premier essayist—as indeed was Graña.

Both understood the criteria which Montaigne long ago established for giving substance to the essay form: it must be well written, precise, with a focused theme, and employ a moral purpose directed to resolving the question: *Que sais-je?* What Graña says of Bell in the opening essay of *Meaning and Authenticity* is no less true of himself: "...a thinker, a thought-man, a *penseur,* a muller over things significant...which has never surrendered its aspiration, at least its ultimate aspiration, to the empirical master of the chosen realm." Such is the essence of this posthumous volume.

Coupled with *Fact and Symbol*, this volume is as close as we can get to a culture of sociology no less than to a sociology of culture. This dialectic stamps each essay, which makes some of them hard going for those in search of finite answers. And yet, in the end this dialectic enriches our understanding of both Western societies writ large, and the lens of classical sociology through which we observe the big picture. Nowhere is this better illustrated than in the essay "On the Aesthetic Prejudices of the Sociology of Art," in which Graña imaginatively lays bare the emptiness of conventional humanistic assaults on sociology, only to find that sociology has its own uninspected conventions, usually bound up with the presentations of inherited traditions and styles.

Graña's assault on a naive aesthetic realism is no less a critique of sociological dogmatism, techniques of analysis that do little to advance the processes of art to "depict" and not simply "record" the world in its own terms. In this finely rained examination of the connection between individual creativity and the everyday life of collectivities, one finds the crucial and oft-repeated key message in Graña's own work: art is liberating, and sociology as a bearer of just such a liberating culture is thus part of that larger world of art. This proposition does not obviate the more conventional converse: that art is very much part of the social world. The tensions between individual creativity and social participation are the meeting place of culture and sociology; for Graña it makes possible the love of the former without sacrificing the use of the latter.

Graña has been described at times as a conservative, even by friends. But this is just plainly not the case, unless one means by conservative the exploration and preservation of a sense of tradition. But by such a broad definition, as Graña himself is at pains to explain, Marx no less than de Tocqueville or Taine was conservative. For any sense of the "long tradition," to use Raymond Williams' phrase (and Graña did just that), involves a sense of tradition. The struggle, if such it be, is in what to keep no less than what to discard. The sociological task at one level is to explain how people decide to discard some ideas, and retain others, while the great majority simply falls into disuse.

"On the Contradictions of Ideas in Marxian Philosophy of History" seeks to understand precisely how defining traditions are retained, i.e., "prey on the human mind" even under new technological conditions and social relations. But this is also a study of how an ideology like Marxism, which denies the autonomous nature of aesthetic production, is trapped by a set of false alternatives: On the one hand is a determinism that deprives the individual of choice no less than tradition; on the other a voluntarism which makes of Marxian claims to be science a shambles, and indeed returns Marxism to the womb of ideology, and its own meager inner resources.

This concern with Marxism was no mere abstraction. Graña had a lifelong disdain for party politics, none more so than communist party politics. Several of these essays strongly condemn notions of a Communist Party that creates the historical conditions of its ideology and the social conditions for who shall live and who shall die. The earliest piece of "public writing" César left behind appeared in *The Dartmouth* of March 24, 1948. Here we find him commenting on the Henry Wallace Campaign thus: "Liberalism is open inquiry and honest critical answers to honest critical questions. What does Wallace do when confronted with communist infiltration in his party and with criticism of the Soviet State? He answers with countercharges about the imperfections of the American system, a substitute for argument well known to the communist press.... Wallace does not understand the nature of dogma. As if the political behavior of the communists were not enough, Soviet scientific pronouncements, literary purges, and artistic dictation have been screaming but one thing: that Stalinism is no longer a part of the Left, but a monolithic dogma, absolute and elusive, which seeks total allegiance and political and intellectual immobility." These were far from commonplace observations in university life of the late 1940s; in fact, they are still muted sentiments, more grudgingly acknowledged than examined.

What prompts recollection of this extract from an article written forty years ago is that throughout his life Graña held firm to the same principles of artistic openness and cultural freedom that have since become the rallying cry not only of dissidents in Eastern Europe, but of its officials in more enlightened areas from Berlin to Beijing. But even this is less significant than the fact that he made the statement at all. In a cultural climate of near-universal rapture with the Left, Graña asserted the principles of liberalism, certainly not of any doctrinaire sort, but those of the open society as discussed and dissected by people like Popper and Polanyi. Graña's concern with Marxism was thus nothing short of a life-long interest in the conditions that forbid individuals in society to be free.

The totalitarian temptation also compelled Graña to examine how intellectuals as a class, a group that is highly favored in bourgeois society, become the purveyors of ideology and willing accomplices to the betrayal of ideals of free expression. His essay "On a Sociology of the Intelligentsia" follows closely the analysis of Karl Mannheim in *Ideology and Utopia*. For it is the very appearance of democracy as a modern social movement that separates the intelligentsia from ordinary citizens. The arrogance, the hubris, the readiness to betray its sacred intellectual trust, derive from a presumption that democracy needs its elite interpreters to properly "feel the popular pulse." Vanguardism on the Left, and Futurism on the Right permit the intellectual to imagine that he is breaking his inherited class isolation. Fault finding is equated with intellectual liberation. Intelligence as a value is betrayed by ideology in search of utopian visions of liberation. Social causes are divested from the very wellspring of creativity: private judgement.

Graña's own work rested far more on a sense and sensibility of national structures than of class contradictions. The organization of culture is national, since the language of a society is often national, with regional and local variations to be sure. In this community of culture, social life is organized by a vast array of sentiments and feelings that pass from generation to generation, through family trees that sometimes turn outward and other times turn inward to enrich and protect themselves. This sort of emphasis on self and family was hardly a fashionable position to take. Indeed, sociology has all but abandoned the search for national meanings, despite the obvious fact that being part of a nation continues to fascinate and inform some of the most important writers and writings of the period. Luigi Barzini on Italians, Ralf Dahrendorf on Germans, George Orwell on the English, to name but a few, reveal the sort of shrewd insights that Graña appreciated and utilized in his own ongoing studies of Spain.

Sociologists of the pedestrian had forgotten the obvious: that world wars are fought between nations. In World War One German and French people all became part of the Axis war effort, starting with the working class. And in the United States, England and other western powers that had similar class systems found the workers forging holy bonds with middle classes to defend the cause of Allied powers. Graña's great strength as a thinker was his love of a people in full-blooded anthropological regalia, and not as a mission of narrow-minded social dogma. His studies of Seville, alas only a fragment of what César had in mind as a long-range project for his retirement, show that the title of the volume, *Meaning and Authenticity*, is especially appropriate. Such abstract terms take place in essentially national contexts, in which the nuance of language no less than the cash nexus define essentially social relationships.

Graña was a dialectical thinker of superb proportions, which are only weakly captured in a book title. For example, "The Bullfight and Spanish National Decadence" can easily be misread. The bullfight is the antitheses of that economic and political decadence through which Spain has labored for so many decades, even centuries. The bullfight provides Spain's "polemical repertory." The folk and popular imagery of the bullfight is the "historical component of the life of the (Spanish) people." God and Bull alike are ever watching, defining the heroic and miraculous, no less than the tawdry and the venal.

Graña's excursion into large-scale systems involves equally large-scale symbols. The victory of the bullfight in Spanish national life coincides with the defeat of Spain's economic preeminence. The panorama of rejoicing is wrapped up with the bullfight, since nationalism itself is so expressed. How is one to give meaning to national integration in an age of decline except through such sentiments? Here then we have a sociology of culture that takes seriously the popular culture, and does not diminish it through the impoverished notion that poverty, even decadence, can only express itself in revolt, or even worse, in empty formulas about rebellion. In this, Graña had sensed that an authentic sociology, like an authentic movement in any sphere of life, must begin with the sentiments of a people—life as a symbolic fusion of language and art, no less than a grinding material poverty. Like the good anthropologist that he was, Graña appreciated that material poverty and spiritual impoverishment are radically different concepts. In his commitment to the everyday cultural practices of a people, of a city, of a community, he was probably truer to the original Marxian idea of cultural continuities amidst economic changes than most of the latter-day revolutionary saints. Indeed, he shares this special feeling for the grandeur of ordinary folk with a contemporary, the late Oscar Lewis.

Graña did not so much write about as live problems of national development. He was a man of three cultures: born in South America, educated in the United States, and dedicated to the culture of Spain, or more exactly, *hispanidad*. These essays provide fascinating points of comparison and contrast between Mediterranean and Central European traditions, essentially the Germanic style that still prevails in most American departments of sociology. Graña was more the bemused outsider looking in, than the presumed insider looking out at the larger world. He took for granted that personal character counts for as much as social standing. And he was less concerned with the cumulative or building block effect of his work than with each piece as a little insight—either worthy or worthless as the case and reader may feel. Perhaps this perspective is part of the aristocratic tradition, in contrast to the bourgeois tradition. But clearly, Graña's method of work shares insights with the reader rather than instructing him in correct thoughts.

In short, César Graña was a fully realized man, a complete person. He possessed a keen sense of the "unity" of academic practice with intellectual theory. His disdain for simplification and vulgarity, for forcing every issue and every theme into a single variable, led him to take the datum of a society as a given. Whether such datum were sentiments or habits at the psychological level; or class, language, or ethnic identification at the stratification level, Graña's concern was description as a rich exercise. Narrative held a fascination unto itself. "Lessons" were derived from the narrative, but by the reader or the observer, not by the writer *for* the reader. As a result, César frequently found himself at odds with other members of the department at the University of California, San Diego, with which he was long affiliated, for whom special concerns or selective variables were more important than the sort of non-directive approach characteristic of his person and temperament.

As gentle and quiet as Graña was in public, in the counsels of departmental affairs he was fierce and uncompromising. Those who came up for tenure with the support of ethnic caucuses or ideological clusters but without intellectual grounds found in Graña a formidable opponent. One such candidate was rejected on the grounds of a "disastrous provincialism of outlook and poverty of scholarship. I realize that these are harsh words; but I can find no others." It is the candidate's "wanton reductionism" that ultimately "irritates" Graña. The grievance of a people should not be allowed to translate into the presumption of being a self-declared spokesperson. Suffering of others does not "justify the abandonment of reasoned and documented analysis, or for the creation of ill-informed, simplistic adversary mythologies." These are not easy utterances to render in an atmosphere of affirmative action.

In one of his many unpublished aphorisms, Graña says that "hypocrisy is the homage that human nature pays to virtue." Graña refused to abide by hypocrisy, and did not pay such homage to the mediocre. When a famous figure was urged upon a sociology department in the University of California system, Graña alone opposed the appointment. He did what few of this candidate's defenders did: he read the entire corpus of the candidate's work. He examined and exhumed, book by book and essay by essay, the contents of this scholar's writings. In short, Graña did what the other members took for granted: he evaluated the quality of the scholarship and the character of the scholar that emerges from the work—and only from the work. His conclusions were measured but uncompromising: The candidate's "enterprise is at an end, the product of an exhausted teleological tradition that has no choice but to try to wring out 'new' perspectives by constantly changing the 'dialectical' grounds." Graña was quick to grant that the presence in the department of this candidate would serve as a stimulus: "a force so to speak, who would cause the intellectual life of the department to jump faster." The problem was that this candidate was not "interested in intellectual coexistence. And thus I was finally convinced, unlike some of my colleagues, that the risk far outweighed the promise."

These are difficult matters to discuss. The judgment of departmental colleagues upon each other is an intimate matter of preferences, not a science of right and wrong. And in this, Graña's views were certainly no more infallible than those of his colleagues. But the reason for daring to introduce in each a discordant note, and in this introduction, is to demonstrate Graña had a certain spine, a dedication to democratic decision-making that was isomorphic and parallel to his sociological analysis. His judgments were uniformly cordial and devoid of bile or guile. The judgments he rendered were based on work performed. Even in troubled circumstances, not a shred of paper exists that would show César to be less than fair or on firm intellectual ground.

Graña's concerns are not restricted to the intramural. He was just as willing to challenge university programs (even those he was asked to head up) and administrative pretenses. He was asked to direct the "The History of Consciousness Program" at one of the branches at the University of California. He did not so much resist this appointment as seek clarification. The automaticity, the given-ness of a concept like "consciousness" gave him pause, if not offense. Was the program interested in comparing the constellation of Marxist ideas of class consciousness or James Joyce's stream of consciousness? Of course, Graña full well knew the answer. But he gave the program's administrator a clinic on James, Flaubert, Byron, Dostoevsky, Dewey, Fitzgerald, Mann, and their ideas on consciousness. Graña then went to the ideological heart of the matter. "Consciousness cannot be made comprehensible unless it is defined within some perceivable historical or social circumstance." Whatever consciousness is or turns out to be, it "cannot be regarded simply as a mood, sense, lift, or even structure of perception in itself. It has to be part of a concrete and desirable act of understanding." Graña was willing to head the program, but only if there were truth in packaging: as a program in comparative cultural studies and history.

There was something quixotic in Graña's arguing with a university administrator, attempting to convince the convinced that the equation of the "political" with the "ideological" was not healthy for the life of social science. But there was nothing dogmatic in his thinking: he nominated Norman Mailer for a visiting professorship, praised Eric Hobsbawm's *Primitive Rebels*, and wrote letters to the San Diego newspapers denouncing Richard Nixon. In this, Graña was a free spirit, practicing the sort of unfettered analysis suggested by these writings. His work offers a sensitizing rather than systematic approach—and in so doing he exemplifies the supple mind and flexible approach that made him special. After all, sensitivities can be refined, whereas systems can just as readily, and with relish, be broken. Graña fought against abstract systems with the "weapon" of concrete cultures. In so doing, he offered sociology a fresh perspective, one as rare as it was required.

In "A Barroom Napkin Anthology," Graña asks, rhetorically to be sure, "Is sociology a vision of the world or is it a sampling of the world?" Graña does not answer his own query. I would suggest that for Graña it is a vision of the world by the act of sampling. His aphoristic style indicates as much. Graña writes of museums as the "disembodied nature of democratic availability." Which is to say, "anyone can look at the dining hall or swimming pools of the Hearst Castle, but no one eats or swims there." Well, this sample permits a vision; and this characterizes Graña's work in general. Again, I take refuge in another of his aphorisms: "The Liberty Bell, now cracked, rings still. It dies as a concrete object. It is reborn as a cultural object." What is one to make of this? Insight and outlook coalesce, the concrete and abstract fuse in the reader's mind. Observations by the author are internalized as the experience of the reader.

What Graña offers his audience in the final analysis is not only moral lessons embodied in the essay form, but the emotional insight embodied in the short story and the intellectual values embraced by the social experience. In this, the second volume of his essays in the sociology of art and literature with which I have been privileged to be involved, I find myself in deep mourning all over again for the loss of this modest, unassuming, and entirely worldly person. He did not publish much in his lifetime, but he thought a good deal. There is little point in bemoaning what Graña did not accomplish in his years on earth. The aristocratic mode was perhaps too much with him. Thus, it is far wiser to soak up what he did leave us. We become better for the experience, as well as sharper analysts in the process. Graña provides us with no small or commonplace combination of skills in this day and age of ideological politics and utopian sociologies. This rich harvest of mature papers makes it abundantly, nay, painfully clear what a fine figure of a man and a solid citizen of sociology we have lost.

Works by César Graña

Fact & Symbol
Meaning and Authenticity
Modernity and Its Discontents
On Bohemia (with Marigay Graña)

17

Scott Greer:
The Dialectic of the Unique and the Universal

It has been my good fortune to know some fine social scientists that were born in Texas. Elwin Powell, Marion J. Levy, Jr., and C. Wright Mills come readily to mind. To this list of special people I am proud to add Scott Greer—who indeed, shared with Mills what Wendell Bell called a "life-long dislike of pretentiousness, snobbery and tyranny." The two also shared in common the city of Waco, Texas—where Wright was born and where Scott went to school at Baylor. Although I was born and raised in Harlem, only blocks away in geography from the building in which we now stand—but light years away in economy and organization from Columbia University—I confess to a similar litany of likes and dislikes as did my Texas friends.

In his fine obituary notice on Greer upon his death in January 1996, Wendell Bell wrote, "Despite his sweet disposition, artistic inclinations, and his complex view of the world, Scott was a hard-headed sociologist." I would change this to read: "because of" rather than "despite." For in the long pull of time, it becomes evident that personality, poetry, and emphasis on the unity of the urban complex are precisely that triptych that makes Scott Greer a unique person as well as universal social scientist. Another good and mutual friend, Raymond W. Mack, caught this sense of the multiple in his introduction to the presidential session of a conference of the Midwest Sociological Society, when he referred to Scott as "an innovative thinker, a loyal friend, and a poet."

It is the relationship between the sociologist and the poet that underwrites the connection between the unique and the universal in Scott's work. This dialectical linkage was already evident in his early work in *Urban Renewal and American Cities*. In that effort he pointed out that "each city is in some respects unique, as is each local public authority and program." But the trick for Scott was to tame the "beast," to tease out the universal aspects of such unbridled diversity. He shrewdly observed that: after all "there is only one federal government, one urban renewal administration, and one current housing act."

Behind the casual narrative mode of address is a tight model of a unified social science approach to urban affairs. He took as the core theorem an emphasis on the coercive impact of the culture, the inherited normative system of the people, and social organization as a set of constraints upon behavior, a powerful tool of control. Taken as a whole, these elements offered a sense of the unique nature and scope of social change, the vast cumulative trends in any society. Such a view was already presaged in his first work of 1955, on *Social Organization* in which the relation of family to corporation inheres in the problem of community as such.

In his maturity, Greer operated in a context of Midwestern sociology, despite his training in California and birth in Texas. In this, the many years at Northwestern and then at Wisconsin imbued him with the spirit of the Chicago School of sociology. It was people like Robert E. Park, Hugh Duncan, and Louis Wirth who were his mentors more than say, Talcott Parsons and Pitirim Sorokin. In a strange way, he aimed at a reversal of the general theory of the Eastern Establishment. Instead of starting with the system he started with the person. Strikingly, when he wrote on social organization he started with the dilemma of the foreman—the individual within organizational life that looked in both directions, above and below, and side to side—in order to get things done. The shift from being a doer to a director of tasks and work assignments becomes the touchstone of social organizations' whole. Again, we see how the unique and the universal come together in a seamless whole.

What is noteworthy in Greer's professional work is his worldliness, his expansive view of the social sciences. Thus he could cite with equal fluidity the economic writings of Selig Perlman and Sumner Slichter as well as the sociologists Herbert Blumer and Ralph Turner. He presages not just the globalization of urban life and other overblown slogans of our day, but no less the utter destruction of barriers and boundaries between social scientists. To do work in the boundaries of urban life is to break the boundaries between social theories. Anthropologists, psychologists, and political scientists all were measured by how they contributed to the understanding of real world phenomena. But early on it was evident that his mentors were drawn from the Middle American fascination with social change rather than the East Coast commitment to social structure. Even when dealing with social systems, one finds a noticeable absence of affirming reference to the work of Talcott Parsons, that is, to individual sociologists who held an imperial view of the field.

One suspects that indeed it was Parsons that Scott had in mind when, in *The Emerging City*, he spoke of "the social scientist as dismayed and a little embittered by the lack of fit between the existing system and any simple powerful and elegant theory." It was Greer's view that the emerging city of the future was loose, but not anarchical. The urban order is not random, just loose. The metropolitan region rather than the city comes to define the postmodern and postindustrial environment. Even without central authority, a sense of order prevails. The emergent technology and communication systems—hardly underway when Greer wrote—created countervailing trends and tendencies: bureaucratization of labor and yet decentralization of lifestyles. Greer was extraordinarily supple in seeing the complex nature of such new characteristics. This preserved him from dogmatism and exaggerations of all sorts in all directions.

The metropolitan community is for Greer the large-scale society in miniature and manageable format. Once again the dialectical of the unique and the universal only transposed from tightly knit cities to loosely organized suburbs, from centralized authority to democratic choice. Scott was not unaware that his views were hardly the stuff of radical critique. Already the voices were being raised that the city was being abandoned, that race would divide city dwellers from suburbanites. But Greer dismissed such rubbish as rubbish. He realized that wealth gravitated to centralized pockets, that the life chance advantages of the cities would provide a centrifugal force. The dialectic of urban life is not reducible to a political ideology, to a demand that people conform to the ideologist cum sociologist.

Greer held out great hope for recentralization of city life, what has come to be called gentrification by some and revitalization by others. But for this to take place with any semblance of rationalization required federal intervention and at least participation. Greer saw the future in terms of a series of tensions that are resolved not by fiat but by history. Announcements of the death of the city were premature. On the other hand, the older city could not be revived since the forces making for diversity and decentralization were linked to growth in the economy. The regional city presaged the regionalization of urban life on a global scale. Greer had a vision that was true to the future as well as the present.

In this regard, the criticisms of Janet Abu-Lughod deserve respect but also commentary. For upon their veracity derives an assessment of Greer as either a minor or major figure. Let me say at once that in my judgment, far from indicating that Greer's vision was limited, the three criticisms leveled underscore how correct his judgment was. Abu-Lughod makes three distinct criticisms. First, that unlike his prediction, Americanization of the American culture did not take place because new forms of immigration flooded American cities with an ethnic diversity. Second, familial solidarity was not in the sociological cards once labor force participation by women left in its wake declining fertility, higher divorce rates, and ideologies of individualism, not familialism. Third, the lack of acknowledgement of racial discrimination and exclusion from the dream of American life, which she finds as "the only deep flaw" in *The Emerging City*.

I would like to take this opportunity to play devil's advocate, or better said, Scott Greer's advocate, and respond to each of these charges. For I genuinely believe that our author had it right and our critic had it wrong.

First, the Americanization of culture has hardly been prevented from going forward by new immigrant groups. Quite the reverse, that process has been accelerated. New groups to American shores, from Cubans in Miami to Koreans in Los Angeles, have accepted with enthusiasm some fundamental canons of the culture. Among them are the right of the individual to choose his or her own profession, the place of private enterprise and initiative in the economic system, the tradition of urban concentration as a mechanism for securing the benefits of the society—especially in areas of educational achievement and health maintenance. It is true that the melting pot idea of culture has long ago given way to the notion of ethnic pluralism and multiple cultural formations. But this is hardly the same as the termination of Americanization of the culture. Indeed, one might well argue that these new formations have strengthened the processes of urban globalization Greer noted.

Second, all polls indicate that family solidarity ranks among the highest of values in present-day America. Indeed, the very penetration of women into the labor force has led to a greater awareness of the place of the family, especially the children, in the complex network of values governing ordinary behavior. This is not to say that changes in the behavior and responsibilities of the nuclear family are the same now as even a half-century ago. But even apart from the growing number of organizations and associations dedicated to the strengthening of family life, the sense of the importance of nuclear families has actually greatly increased in recent years. This is not to deny the extraordinary rise of individual goals becoming central in defining American work roles. But the implication that this in turn somehow is connected to family disintegration is hardly demonstrable.

On the matter of Greer's alleged blindness to the racial factor: this is simply not the case. In *The Emerging City*, Greer makes it plain that segregation served to reinforce older patterns that delayed integration of the urban network. Indeed, even in his first work, *Last Man In*, with the subtitle *Racial Access to Union Power*, Greer showed a deep sensitivity to questions of race. But he saw such older patterns of discrimination as crumbling in the face of the breakup of the differentiation between workspace and living space. But even at the level of African Americans specifically, what is clear is the enormous move toward suburban living, following patterns of class migration to outlying areas of the urban radial axis. To be sure, as the wage differentials between black and white Americans diminish the patterns of urban and suburban living become similar. This is not to deny that discrimination continues and that racial tensions are hardly automatically alleviated by the rise of suburban regions displacing the older cities as the center of metropolitan areas. It is to point out that stereotypical views of racial patterns are a disservice to reality—and that reality was well identified by Greer.

In a perfectly wonderful book entitled *The Logic of Social Inquiry*—dedicated I might add to a student that would become Scott's wife, Ann—Greer puts much of his labors on urban affairs and social life into a larger perspective. It is such a wonderful and poignant book that the impulse to evaluate it anew is hard to resist. But I will draw upon it only to illustrate the fundamental framework within which Scott operated. For it helps illumine the magnitude of his achievement, and no less than the modesty of his person.

But in some larger sense, whether Scott was right or wrong on his predictions is far less important than his willingness to make them, especially to extrapolate from the present into a determinate future in a modest, yet audacious manner. That he was able to do so stems from his vision of *The Logic of Social Inquiry*. In that work he explains that being engaged in a theoretical delineation of a field such as urban affairs raises issues of predictive power. Given the partial nature of theory, one must live with modest results from predictions. "You do not know *a priori*. Your work norms remain open-ended." Greer points to a set of confusions: in the firm, in administration, in personality—"adding them together simply results in confusion raised to a higher power."

In one of Scott's rare critiques of others, he distinguishes his position again from that of Talcott Parsons. "His effort to integrate social, cultural, and personality systems suffers from our very rudimentary achievements in understanding each. Before we can have interdisciplinary approaches we must have discipline." In short, sciences vary by their degree of development, hence results obtained in prediction and explanation vary to a similar degree. This is not a mandate for quiescence, or even silence, but simply a recognition that the results obtained vary in terms of the scientific depth of a field. His is not an argument against interdisciplinarity, but an appreciation that the social sciences are taken as a whole, a discipline unto itself—one that is concerned with human beings—their fates and fortunes. Smuggling in physicalist or biological models may help more at the level of metaphor than explanation.

Greer was concerned that we not simply presume that the social is the same as the human. He sees the social scientists as "craftsmen of social fact," not "charismatic professionals" presuming more than they can deliver. Being right or wrong in this context is less valuable than being good or evil—however those terms are defined. The role of policymaking is to assist in bringing about the good, which for Greer is essentially the reduction of disparities and inequalities by showing their economic and social dysfunctionality. This goal is essentially an ethical one; it cannot be established by empirical research as such, but it remains a consequence of why social science has a public value to begin with.

That brings the empirical level of discourse to a close, and allows a return to the unique and the universal—what Greer calls upon Claude Levi-Strauss to validate as "dialectical reason." Greer interprets this to mean that nobody lives by science and nobody lives without science. By the same token, nobody lives by ethics as such or lives without it. Both are formal creations in the face of nature. Science aims to tame nature. Ethics reflects a faith in what a given society considers its highest aspiration. So at the end of the analytical day, if analysis has a day or night, we are left not so much with science or ethics, but rather aesthetics. For Scott, the design of the world comes to us through art, myth, and poetry. Aesthetics alone makes possible visions of a future better than the present, or at least different from the present. The essence of aesthetics is the act of creation. And "what we have created we can recreate, indefinitely."

It is within that larger holism of the unique and the universal that the work of Greer can best be understood as theory and method. The city—past, present, and future—is a design, a network, a system, a vision, a unique entity within a universal set of parameters. The city was a place in which Greer found places of the heart. He was a worldly aesthete, at home in an imperfect world, in search of a more perfect world. As such, he had no fear of being shown wrong, as long as he was convinced he was engaged in the magical act of genuine creation. Scott represents the best of an American sociology that is no more—a dedication to democratic choice, and no less, opposition to totalitarian rule.

Like his poetics, Scott also took his politics in small, intimate doses. He shied away from grandiose theorizing, and preferred to think of sound politics as that which takes place in community life and local government. Indeed, as he notes in *Governing the Metropolis*, when that sense of community dissolves, the administrative state is waiting in the wings to take command. He wrote his own final epitaph in poetic form, a work he called *Solitudes*. "And here is a man on a darkened veranda/Above the city that has captured his heart/Staring at the purity of lights above the asphalt/The glimmering cosmology of a personal revolt/Creating from stars above the wilderness/His poem, his cry, his embrace and art."

Works by Scott Greer

The Emerging City: Myth and Reality
Governing the Metropolis
The Logic of Social Inquiry
Social Organization
Urban Renewal and American Cities

18

Mason W. Gross:
Philosophy, Science and the Higher Learning

It would seem to be the fate of deceased university presidents to be remembered more by having their names attached to specific buildings and programs than for what they actually accomplished or stood for. It would be nice to report that Mason Welch Gross, president of Rutgers University from 1959 to 1970, and for ten years before that, provost of Rutgers, escaped such a desultory fate. Alas, that cannot be reported. Indeed, a man steeped in the grand philosophical tradition of Alfred North Whitehead is more likely to be known by present-day students of Rutgers as the figure that adorns the School of the Arts, which turns out budding young painters, actors, and musicians. Perhaps the linkage is not all that far-fetched, given Whitehead's own deeply idealistic, albeit liberal, credo of the aesthetic function of education. As he reminds us in *Adventures of Ideas*, "metaphysical understanding guides imagination and justifies purpose. Apart from metaphysical presuppositions there can be no civilization." That this should be the main credo of Gross was a function of his background and belief.

So before we briefly review Rutgers at mid-century from a twenty-first century perch, it is worth mentioning the philosophical formation of Gross's thoughts on the higher learning. He was no cynic steeped in the disdain leveled at American University life, as was Thorstein Veblen. Rather, his philosophy reflected the unabashed optimism of someone educated, if not rooted, in the historic tradition of Cambridge University and the equally compelling, if more recent, Ivy League tradition first at Harvard University, and then at Columbia University, where he became an instructor. Philosophy in these three institutions took seriously what Whitehead called *The Aims of Education*. Whitehead identified the lack of public regard, the inertia about education, as the true source of "the broken lives, the defeated hopes, the national failures," of young people. In modern life, he or she who does "not value trained intelligence is doomed.

Not all your heroism, not all your social charm, not all your wit, not all your victories on land or at sea, can move back the finger of fate. Today we maintain ourselves. Tomorrow science will have moved forward yet one more step, and there will be no appeal from the judgment which will then be pronounced on the uneducated." Since this statement appears in an anthology of Whitehead's works that Mason co-edited, one must presume it was read and imbibed.

Without turning these opening remarks into a discourse on Whitehead's influence on Gross, I would like to cite another passage from *The Aims of Education* that summarizes so much of the educational philosophy of Gross found in his own papers and discourses. "The justification for a university is that it preserves the connection between knowledge and the zest of life, by uniting the young and then old in the imaginative consideration of learning. The university imparts information, but it imparts it imaginatively. At least this is the function it should perform for society. A university that fails in this respect has no reason for existence. This atmosphere of excitement, arising from imaginative consideration, transforms knowledge. A fact is no longer a bare fact: it is invested with all its possibilities. It is no longer a burden on the memory: it is energizing as the poet of our dreams, and as the architect of our purposes." It is with such a vision that Mason served his stewardship at Rutgers. The amazing thing is how he managed to mesh these abstract aims with the specific tasks of running a university.

Mason Gross was such a mild mannered man, the very personification of a thoughtful patrician, that it is little wonder that his years at Rutgers were reported in a rather modest way—even by Richard McCormick, the Rutgers University historian, and genuine friend of Gross. For example, in his *Rutgers: A Bicentennial History*, there are but two mentions to Gross in the entire volume! However, it should be noted that both of them were consequential. McCormick was not a man to pamper those in power, and assuredly not a scholar who would pad the record to make the incumbent (for that is what Gross was in 1966) look bigger for the record than he was in the flesh. Indeed, Richard Schlatter, who wrote the Preface to the original edition of this volume, was likewise noted for his frank talk and sharp views.

Still, the two references and Preface merit the attention of anyone embarking upon the addresses of Mason Gross. For they reveal two moments in time that Gross—by sheer common sense and good judgment—prevented the disintegration of the University. That he did so with force of personality, rather than administration delegation, is a reflection of the last great patriarch of our University. In an interview granted to the *Rutgers Alumni Magazine* in September 1971, he responded rather sharply to a query about what he felt the greatest pride during his twelve-year reign as president. "A president does not do things which bring about transformation. He doesn't. He works with a movement in a certain direction. His main job is to recognize new ideas and encourage them." For I can attest from first hand interaction that Mason was someone for whom a handshake was a binding contract and a word as good as a bond. I suspect that this derived from Gross's special realization of the colonial past, the college present, and the university future—over which he presided. Those who came after him had only a dim awareness of that past, focused as they properly were, on keeping pace with other major state universities—not to mention that enormous presence, Princeton University, fifteen miles to the south of New Brunswick. Without losing track of his obligations to others, he never lost sight of the enjoyment to self that his presidential status afforded him.

The first involvement of Mason Gross in the administrative affairs of Rutgers came as a consequence of considerable discontent among faculty regarding what was felt to be a large number of arbitrary terminations. Students were also involved with the usual menu of complaints from the high price of rooms, lack of parking spaces, and the poor quality of food. Such conventional concerns were enlarged as a result of the failure of an educational bond issue that would have included substantial aid and grants to Rutgers. With the end of the post-World War Two boom in college enrollment, and the normalization of competition, Rutgers was not faring well in the educational wars of the time. In addition, the then-president, Robert C. Clothier, was seriously ill. But he did put in motion a series of reforms through a Committee on Personnel Procedures that brought Mason Gross to the forefront of Rutgers' affairs.

Gross came to Rutgers from Columbia in 1946 as a professor of philosophy. He also served as an assistant dean of the College of Arts and Sciences. But as a consequence of the report and recommendations of the aforementioned Committee on Personnel Procedures, Gross was appointed as the first provost in 1949. McCormick succinctly summarizes what was to be a ten-year period of tranquility in the following terms: "Possessing in an unusual degree the confidence of the faculty and the student body, Dr. Gross by his personal tact and his boundless energy infused a new spirit into the University administration." In effect, the presidency had become a "two-man job"—filled by a rapidly failing Robert Clarkson Clothier and a rapidly rising Mason W. Gross. Perhaps the most significant concern of the period was ushering in the transition from a college with the appearance of a private institution to a university that represented state interests and a broad-based citizen constituency. While Gross retained a highly personalist style, he understood, if not quite appreciative of, the requirements of an administrative apparatus responsive to such broader public issues underwitten by tax payer revenues and statewide bond issues.

While the growth of the University continued between 1949 and 1959 under the new president, Lewis Webster Jones, it was a period still marked by uncertainty as to its direction. On one hand there was the growth of professional schools, the reorganization of the governing body, and the sheer physical expansion of Rutgers. Each of these were elements in a larger Rutgers that Gross was very much connected with bringing about—there was also the by now classical discord between those who saw the University primarily in economic terms and those who held out for loftier cultural goals. In this context, Mason Gross turned out to be a near perfect solution to a near insoluble set of dilemmas. Having served as provost, he knew the economic context in which Rutgers operated, and no less the cultural content of what made for a great university. He had the support of administrative, faculty, and student bodies, and he had the background in training and temperament to implement decisions already well underway by the time he took office in 1959. Indeed, Dean Boocock indicated that Mason was ready for the role of President *before* the appointment of Jones. One reason for his being passed over by the Board of Trustees is revealed in the following "side slant" revealed in the *Rutgers Alumni Magazine* of 1971. "On one occasion he [Mason] talked too much at a social gathering in New Brunswick and said in a joking way: 'Nobody but a goddamned fool would be a Republican!' That little *bon mot* was on Governor Driscoll's desk the next morning, and so Mason had seven more years as provost to live through."

The next decade, when Mason assumed his duties as University head, was one of great implementation and organization: from bond issues, which allowed for enormous expansion in the sciences and engineering. Enrollment doubled in a five-year period between 1959 and 1964. And while the undergraduate opportunities of in-state residence expanded, so too did the graduate and professional schools, especially in areas ranging from medicine to law. It was also a decade of growing student unrest as a result of an undeclared war in Vietnam and violence in the ghettoes of America. In this climate, one in which universities came to be seen as knowledge factories, Mason Gross proved to be adroit at managing polar opposite needs and aspirations. Primarily, he did so by avoiding the notion of polarity altogether, in favor of a spirit of reconciliation and liberality. In retrospect, it is not an exaggeration to say that of the various presidents of Rutgers in the second half of the twentieth century, he was unique as a consensus builder. That he did so without compromising the goals of the University or the instruments to bring about such goals remains perhaps the hardest balancing act for a university president to accomplish—one he achieved in a seemingly effortless manner.

Mason was a relatively tall man, neatly dressed, but never ostentatious. He had an avuncular quality—perhaps derived from his training in philosophy, or from his years at Cambridge and then Columbia. Such a posture is not exactly unknown among people in high places. Still, he remained accessible to the Rutgers community throughout his years at the University. He ate regularly at the faculty-administration dining hall, so he was often seen interacting with people at the University. He made himself available to all, and yet managed to conduct an active correspondence. After Mason's tenure at Rutgers, and I daresay throughout American university life generally, one notes among university presidents a decreasing involvement with everyday campus affairs and an increasing participation in, or at least supervision of, fundraising campaigns.

The landmarks of Mason's tenure as president are the trademarks of the present era. He engineered the University's acquisition of the land on which Livingston Campus and Busch Campus now reside. He brought the University to a major-league position with respect to specialist schools and research support. He maintained a principled approach to academic freedom and tenure in critical cases such as that of the historian Eugene Genovese and the classicist M.I. Finley. This was not a simple task in a period that still suffered from the hysteria of witch hunting in a state that lagged behind New York in coming to terms with the changing times and circumstances. A hint of Mason's essential liberality comes through an appreciation of his early affection for, and relation to, F.S.C. Northrop, the author of *The Meeting of East and West*. It was perhaps the landmark text that put the xenophobia and exaggerations of the Asian theatre of World War Two to an end. For in that major work of the late 1940s, Northrop reminded his readers of the unique aesthetic contributions of Asian or Eastern civilizations to American and European societies. That plea for mutual understanding by Mason's good friend was translated into an effort to make Rutgers a place in which international studies was a primary emphasis. Indeed, the University was arguably the first to open the West to Japanese students in the late nineteenth century, and so a tradition of tolerance was alive and extended during Mason's watch.

Less apparent was a spirit of tolerance toward youngsters of African American ancestry. The presence of Paul Robeson at Rutgers in the twenties notwithstanding, it was on Mason's watch that the gates of racial and religious exclusion came tumbling down. Today, Rutgers ranks as a major public university with one of the largest enrollments of black and Hispanic students. That Rutgers avoided the type of racial confrontations that gripped major universities from Cornell to Stanford (and more immediately inflamed New Jersey from Newark to Plainfield to Camden) is perhaps due in no small part to Gross's style of personal diplomacy. Mason's invitation to students staging "sit-ins" to join him in a cup of coffee helped avoid direct confrontations that might otherwise have involved law enforcement agencies. Whether this was a function of common sense or a recollection of the lessons learned from Whitehead and Northrop, the results were an orderly transition process in disorderly times. Another explanation that offers itself is that Gross built up a sufficient reservoir of goodwill among the student body so as to invite their understanding, if not outright support. He expressed his liberal persuasion best in commenting on student unrest. "By all odds, the biggest outbursts against the universities take place when either students or faculty or staff take it upon themselves to express strong opinions on matters of public concern. Protest against the war in Indochina, like marches in Selma, Alabama, brings violent kickbacks. Faculty members are then accused of being communists, and all kinds of vituperation are poured on the heads of students. But even more than these personal attacks are the attack upon the university itself. Here it is clear that the university must do all it can to protect the civil rights and the academic freedom of all its members."

There is little doubt that the transition process from Mason Gross to Edward J. Bloustein was traumatic—not so much for Mason himself as for those who waited but were never called to the possible "beruf" of the Rutgers presidency. Mason well understood that a radical change was required for a new era—one in which the legal superstructure of the University was tightened and its national mission sharpened. In going outside for a new head, the University saw the need for a figure who continued the tradition of intellectual eminence and civic conscience, but who added a larger dose of administrative sobriety. The era of administrative and bureaucratic direction was not an option, but a necessity for anyone hoping to supervise the growth of a major university with goals—perhaps more longed for than realized in the waning years of the final quarter of the twentieth century.

That caveat registered, Mason left a remarkable legacy that endures at Rutgers: a strong classical liberal arts tradition, and a University in which the autonomy of the parts endures—sometimes more as anarchic satrapy than systematic individuality. His was an appreciation of the university as a community, and in turn a community of learning as a democratic assemblage. An advisory committee or a vice-dean for public relations does not produce these lectures and papers. They are the products of Mason's singular mind. They emanated from a tradition honed in Whitehead's sense of philosophy as applied wisdom. They no less derived from Northrop's sense of politics and economics as rooted in the common core of aesthetic culture. Above all, they represent an effort to fuse the aims of education with the actualities of institutions that lay claim to such lofty missions.

Works by Mason W. Gross

An Anthology by Alfred North Whitehead (F.S.C. Northrop and Mason W. Gross, eds.)

Philosophy, Science and Higher Education (Richard P. McCormick and Richard Schlatter, eds.)

The Selected Speeches of Mason Welch Gross (Richard P. McCormick and Richard Schlatter, eds.)

19

George Caspar Homans:
Bringing the Individual Back
into a Collectivist Discipline

On an occasion when we come together at Harvard to honor publication by Transaction of *Behavioral Theory in Sociology: Essays in Honor of George C. Homans*, I think it fair to say that the work of Robert Hamblin and John H. Kunkel are also paying respects to probably the single-most decisive force in the creation of social psychology. Homans did so many things well that it is not too early to assess at least a few of his contributions.

To start with, he bridged the wide gap between psychological and sociological visions of the field of behavioral research. This is another way of saying that he took the role of the individual in society and the place of society in individual emergence as a problematic, not as a struggle between disciplines for mastery. By insisting on taking the individual seriously within the social role, Homans allowed psychologists to take seriously aspects of behavior they tend to be dismissive of. Everything from collective behavior in confined environments to the place of class and custom in national formations became fair game for the social psychologists. But the price for this was to insist that sociologists take seriously that they often downgrade: that individuals and their behavior can be, to be sure, must be, seen as more than the sum total of pattern variables in the social system.

For Homans, the great scientific breakthrough comes not with the ability to extract human behavior from the hard kernel of idiosyncrasy and personality, but precisely to study how such idiosyncrasies and personalities themselves come to form a pattern. His oft-recited differences with Talcott Parsons and what might be called the higher functionalists resided not in matters of etiquette or even ideology. Rather, it came down to the bedrock issue of whether the very idea of science is itself a determination of specific behavior of observed people or a mosaic that permits extrapolation from such

125

cases to form a general system. That Homans was suspicious of, nay held in contempt, a social science that aped the physical sciences is hardly a secret. But what made Homans special was his familiarity with scientific canons of investigation and experimentation as such. In method, he was closer to the marrow of science than those who insisted on a foreknowledge of its general principles. That this very fact irritated his intellectual enemies only delighted Homans.

The Marxians shared with the Parsonians a belief that if we could only determine the role of the individual in society and history we would be well on our way to a pure theory of human behavior. But for Homans this was less a search for science than a faith in meta-science, or more bluntly, metaphysics. All general systems theorists, whatever their political persuasions or professional backgrounds, suffered the same fallacy: that science must somehow explain the behavior of individuals—especially, how they manage to gum up the sense of history or the worth of systems. Homans had no such problem. He took for granted a commonsense pragmatism—and in this he was true to the William James in whose memory this edifice is named—that the task of the social scientists like that of the philosopher was to come to terms with the mind of the person. In so doing, the principles of sociology no less than of psychology will fall into place.

In thinking of Homans, the author of *The Human Group* and *English Villagers of the Thirteen Century*, there is a tendency to believe that he failed in his own efforts at a unified sociology. I think this estimate is incorrect. It was precisely what superficially appeared discordant in Homans that established him as a master. For what is important in the work on the English villagers is precisely the fact that they represent a human group! It is a group that endured over time, stamped a people with a special culture, grand at times, quixotic at other times, but unique at all times. The human group is writ small at times and larger at other times. But how else is one to establish the notion of national character? It is spoken of so often and feared so widely. National character can indeed become the rhetoric of the bigot, no less than the tool of the social scientist. And one must be frank and admit that Homans did not always make the distinction as sharply and as clearly as he might have. Still, if character traits persist over time, indeed over centuries, they must be explained as a good chunk of what we call behavior. To drown such specific character and personality traits in a sea of variables called race, gender, class, or what have you, is to simultaneously weaken the bases of social investigation, of ethnography, and worse, to cheapen the meaning of individual life. In years to come, I think that Homans will be understood as the unique person who was capable of seeing through the fog of abstractions in twentieth-century sociology.

Homans aroused great feelings of collegial animus (if that oxymoron of a term can be allowed) precisely because of this emphasis on the person as something that extended beyond the corpus of scientific study, into the study of social action. There can be little doubt that his emphasis on the will, on the moral code, on the capacity for the act, for Homans defined the special people of this world. It was the source of his participation in the Henderson Group at Harvard in the early 1930s, a group that elevated Vilfredo Pareto to iconic highs that gave credence to claims of elitism. It certainly fueled the hatred on the part of the self-declared radical elements that were powerful if not outright dominant in the heady days of the Popular Front against Fascism. But while it was doubtless the case that Homans' preferences were for those who upheld the tradition of his own Protestant ancestry, and for the Italian School of power and elite studies, it was not true that this ever extended into any sort of animus along racial or sexual lines. At least those close to him in the department insist this absence of malice in critical decision-making to be uniformly and always the case.

Indeed, as we know from an autobiographical work in progress, Homans took the place of the powerful or influential individual to be an obligation, or a series of obligations, to one's fellow humans, and not a divine right. He was after all an American patriot, and not a British subject—however much he might have admired the culture of England. I daresay that this emphasis on the obligation to assist the less fortunate, its patronizing element not to be discounted, formed the essential core of Homans' view of American politics. It was not so much a Republicanism of substance as it was of manners—or to be more polite, of tradition. Homans' individualism traced back to the Adams family of pre-Revolutionary times. It was not something he could avoid taking pride in, nor for that matter, what the bulk of his colleagues and professional associates could begin to take pride in. He was so far removed from the battleground of post-World War Two America that he gave off the appearance of being a fossil, some antiquarian aristocrat still roaming the intellectual forest of academe. I knew George well enough and long enough to know that such characterizations disturbed him. Had he behaved in a less bellicose and combative manner, he might have been forgiven his positions as eccentric. As it was, forgiving him was not something his opponents could do easily or lightly.

In death, such squabbles tend to diminish in importance. The voting preferences of those who pass into the next life hardly matter to those of us still living in this one. What does persist is the body of work, reflected in this *festschrift*, that provided the social sciences with a way to discourse on individual behavior in the social system with precision and predictability. The curious element for me is that in the very act of defining the contours of a social psychology—a micro-social psychology at least—it turns out that while the experiments and the contests can be replicated, the genius behind those efforts are less easily reproducible in others. I am not entirely sure I know why it is, but it is nonetheless a fact, that such peculiar traits of intuition and imagination play a role in making George Homans himself a special individual rather than simply an exemplar of a method of research. Perhaps it is the irony of this dichotomy that drove Homans from the laboratory to the field, from the group to the history of groups, and finally, from sociology to biography. For "coming to my senses" meant for him at one level the uses of empirical research to create a truly social psychology, but at a quite different level, and later in life, it signified an appreciation of the limits of the senses—common or rarefied.

Works by George Caspar Homans

Certainties and Doubts
Coming to My Senses
English Villagers of the Thirteenth Century
The Human Group
Sentiments and Activities

20

Laud Humphreys:
A Pioneer in the Practice of Fugitive
Social Science

Laud Humphreys died on August 23, 1988 after a lengthy battle with lung cancer. This essay, authored by three who knew him well, is devoted to examining the life of Laud Humphreys and his effect on colleagues and on various aspects of American sociology. While some of the material is based on personal recollection and thus subject to the always precarious vagaries of memory, we have attempted to portray as accurately as possible Laud's biography and work and the intersections between both. Thus, we accomplish here the central task and promise of our collective sociological imagination as articulated by Mills: "...to grasp history and biography and the relations between the two within society." In addition, we attempt to remain true to the tradition of the sociology of knowledge whereby it is defined as the discipline concerned with the social and existential origins of thought and, along the way, to proffer a sociology of sociology.

Born in Chickasha, Oklahoma, Robert Allan (Laud) Humphreys graduated from Colorado College, Colorado Springs in 1952. He received his Master of Divinity degree from Seabury Western Theological Seminary, Evanston, Illinois in 1955 and that same year was ordained in the Episcopal priesthood in the Diocese of Oklahoma. He went on to serve churches in Oklahoma, Colorado, and Kansas prior to entering graduate school. Laud Humphreys later earned M.A. and Ph.D. degrees in sociology and criminology from Washington University, St. Louis in 1967 and 1968, respectively. Prior to joining the faculty at Pitzer College and Claremont Graduate School in 1972, Laud was on the faculty at Southern Illinois University and the School of Criminal Justice at SUNY, Albany. Upon becoming a California Licensed Psychotherapist in 1980, Laud developed a private counseling practice in Los Angeles.

The Early Years: Washington University

Laud arrived at Washington University in 1965 dressed in the gray and white garb of the Episcopal Church—nothing unusual since Washington University had begun to attract a substantial number of theology students from nearby St. Louis University. These students' interests in social science were kindled by the excitement generated at Washington University in particular and the field of sociology as it was practiced in the mid-1960s. It is worthwhile noting that the crossover of theology and sociology, hardly unique in the history of sociology, was especially fruitful at a time when moral concerns and empirical investigations cross-fertilized with such fierce potency. In this sense, the form of such cross-fertilization was quite different from the turn of the century, when the interest in sociology was essentially a concern for social work, a way of helping good-bad boys and bad-good girls keep out of institutions for the indigent and the delinquent. This new in-migration was a flintier group of religious students and a "tougher" period in sociological history. In short, Laud was clearly part of a social force, and not simply an individual who randomly dropped out of the sky.

During his first term at Washington University Laud enrolled in Horowitz's seminar on sociological theory. The course was essentially classical, oriented to the historical problems and figures, covering Marx, Durkheim, Weber, and a less typical emphasis on Sorel, Pareto, Michels, and Mosca. Laud was an apt pupil, indeed excellent in his grasp of materials, though it was evident that his love of sociology was rooted in ethnographic encounters rather than theoretical disputation. It was the works of Becker, Goffman, Garfinkel, and Rainwater that clearly gripped Laud's interests. But it was a measure of his worth that Laud constantly related their work to the classical tradition; his class presentations and term paper reflected this sense of sociological continuity. Even the chapters of Humphreys' dissertation, *Tearoom Trade: Impersonal Sex in Public Places*, reflect as much; the chapter on "The Public Settings of 'Private' Encounters" was clearly a play on the familiar Mills theme and the chapter on "Patterns of Collective Action" owed as much to Durkheim and Simmel as to Erving Goffman or Marvin Scott.

Tearoom Trade was Laud's most significant book and in view of the fact that it has become as much a part of the folklore of sociology as it is central to the literature of the discipline, it serves us well here to recall aspects of its genesis and development. The dissertation evolved out of a pre-doctoral research assistantship provided by NIMH and was allied to the work in central St. Louis to which Lee Rainwater and David Pittman were especially linked. Horowitz's involvement with the dissertation was as a "second-in-command"; Rainwater was clearly the principal advisor, and the "Chicago" characteristics of the dissertation were amplified by Howard S. Becker's support for this research effort from start to finish. Horowitz's role essentially came into play when the first draft of the dissertation was complete, after the data had been collected.

In reviewing the data it became increasingly and painfully evident that homosexual men in the mid-1960s were touched by a variety of emotions, fear and doubt no less than joy and pleasure. Now it should be remembered that prior to the contemporary development of gay studies and before the rapid growth in scholarly research on gay issues, there were few scholarly publications about gay people written by gay people, and the psychoanalytic literature had done much to perpetuate negative and harmful analyses of homosexuality. Humphreys' data challenged these taken-for-granted assumptions, making it evident that the sources of the sentiments experienced by gay men were rooted much more in stratification than in psychosis.

In his dissertation Humphreys had created a profound sample of social stratification of homosexual participants and this effort went far beyond the canons of psychoanalytical doctrine which sought to explain behavior but rarely investigated structures. The "Tearoom" participants were drawn from a wide network of people, more often than not married, more often than not middle class, more often than not church-goers, and most intriguingly, more often than not conservative in political persuasions and voting practices. On close inspection, the totalistic models of the inherited literature on deviance had little value; the religious imagery of a homosexual fallen from grace into a life of sin had even less relevance. Thus, Laud began to appreciate with a life-long insight that deviance was not an ambiguous "blob" or thing, but a carefully filtered and self-selective process. It was this insight into "deviant" behavior and its investigation that motivated Laud to later write:

> Sociologists engage in the study of deviant behavior because man reveals himself best in his back alleys. It is there that we may see the raw undergirding of the social structure—and, perhaps, observe our own weaknesses reflected in the behavior we fear and berate the most.

What emerged in this ground-breaking research was a sociological portrait of conservative and tormented lives: married men, family men, conservative men, business men, whose personal proclivities and preferences were powerful enough, institutionally grounded enough, to break through the conventions of social life. And Laud was careful not to confuse the fundamental accidental; he simply took as the given in any situation the complexities of social or public life as it intertwined with the private life and, in doing so, unobtrusively exemplified Mills' classic declaration that "It is the…task of the social scientist—as of any liberal educator—continually to translate personal troubles into public issues, and public issues into the terms of their human meaning for a variety of individuals." This aspect of Laud's work well exemplified the sort of fusion of social stratification and psychology that characterized a considerable body of work being done at the time in the Washington University sociology department.

Processing the dissertation became something of a minor scandal unto itself. It was bitterly opposed by Alvin Gouldner on the grounds of Humphreys' presumed violations of fundamental canons of ethical research, including the use of disguises, active participant observation in deviant, criminal behavior, and use of police information to track down participants for study at a later date. This is not the place to review these charges, nor the rebuttals, which for Laud included the immense wealth of information gleaned about homosexual communities, the positive uses to which such information could be put in the gay communities, and the inability to do research at macroscopic levels in any other feasible way. Suffice it to only repeat here what Horowitz and Rainwater wrote in a "Retrospect" added to a later edition of *Tearoom Trade*:

> Laud Humphreys has gone beyond the existing literature in sexual behavior and has proven once again…that ethnographic research is a powerful tool for social understanding and policymaking. And these are the criteria by which the research should finally be evaluated professionally.

At this late stage, with the exact meaning of old wars lost, and a quarter century removed from the scene of the initial moral battles over the research techniques Laud employed, it is helpful to offer commentary on the deep well of belief in the discipline engendered by both sides of the debate and by Washington University's sociologists.

I was on sabbatical leave at Stanford during the time of the much-heralded encounter between Gouldner and Humphreys in January

1968, so I lack firsthand knowledge of the fisticuffs. Whether their fight was fair or foul, occasioned by remarks made by Gouldner or Humphreys, or by personal fears and concerns of either party, is now of little moment. The key factor is that two strong-willed people felt the issues were such as to merit physical combat. For people to risk careers, or at least ridicule by their peers in combat, suggests that the work, the discipline, means a great deal. The intensity of emotions over this dissertation, the issues raised by Laud in such a vivid, descriptive manner, the need to rethink fundamental moral premises about the way in which useful social research takes place, and finally, the risks one runs to do such research gave a characteristic special imprint to the department at Washington University.

More serious than the altercation was the attempt at suppression of Humphreys' work: a university administration all too willing to void the decision of a department to grant the degree to Laud for *Tearoom Trade*, a desire to keep the dissertation under lock and key once the decision to cancel a departmentally approved dissertation became impossible, and finally, a tacit agreement to withhold publication of the dissertation for at least a two-year period once approval for the degree and right of interested researchers to read the results were granted. For here, a basic issue of science and not just social science was at stake: the right, even the obligation of scholars to read and review the results of a dissertation. The attacks leveled at Laud's work by Nicholas von Hoffman and others were answered by Horowitz and Rainwater, and by Humphreys. The issues were summed up nicely by Humphreys in the 1975 edition of *Tearoom Trade*: "What began as a relatively uncomplicated ethnography of the gay community grew in complexity as the logic of the research took hold, and ended as much in a quest for justice as for knowledge alone." Twenty years may not be long enough to solve problems, but it does cool passions. It is fair to say that issues of such far-reaching consequence are not readily resolved by a single example.

To his credit, Humphreys never shied away from the implications of his work. Yet, it is correct to say there was something of the Alfred Dreyfuss about Laud. He did not seem at the time entirely aware of the moral implications of his work, though the brief four-page question of ethics in the published version of the text did make some effort to come to grips with the issues swirling around the dissertation itself. But it was perhaps too soon after the fact for Laud to come to full grips with the intellectual issues this work raised and the way in which his work was introduced into the sociological literature.

In 1970, the Aldine Publishing Company published Laud's revised dissertation, *Tearoom Trade: Impersonal Sex in Public Places*, and in that same year the Society for the Study of Social Problems (SSSP) announced the book won the coveted C. Wright Mills award. It was shortly after the SSSP announcement in 1971, while Laud was on the faculty at SUNY, Albany, that Humphreys was first approached about joining the faculty at Pitzer College.

The story of the negotiating and signing of Laud's contract with Pitzer College is itself a comment on the turbulent early 1970s and on the prevailing *Weltanschauung* of sociology at that time. Always the civil rights activist, never really being able to escape the Oklahoma populism that seemed almost generic to him, Laud arrived at Pitzer fresh from serving a three-month jail term for a draft board demonstration. Laud negotiated his contract with Pitzer's dean of faculty (also a sociologist) from a prison pay phone and his wife, Nancy, smuggled the contract into the prison for his signature. It was his groundbreaking research accomplishments, coupled with Laud's sense of courage in standing fast for principles he believed in and his clerical sense of decency and kindness toward colleagues, students, and friends, that the College found so attractive in Laud. The sociology faculty, at that time well aware of and subscribing to Mannheim's dictum that all sociological inquiry is "...bound up with social existence" and that "...all thought processes themselves are influenced by the participation of the thinker in the life of society," found Laud's professional accomplishments and involvement in civil rights causes very appealing. It was to be a marriage that for the most part would be happy and mutually fulfilling.

Tearoom Trade continued to stir up much controversy in the 1970s about its findings concerning a form of behavior rarely acknowledged and because of its unique methodology. Indeed, to this day textbooks in introductory sociology and in research methods continue to debate the ethics of the methods Laud utilized. What is often lost in these discussions is the importance of *Tearoom Trade* to the early years of gay studies. Although Laud demonstrated that impersonal public sex was often engaged in by heterosexuals and married men, the research opened the doors in the 1970s for others to begin studying marginal groups, especially gay men and lesbians. With the publication in 1972 of *Out of the Closets: The Sociology of Ho-*

mosexual Liberation, the study of gay subcultures was advanced, though it must be said in all candor that the tendentiousness and partisanship in a follow-up work like *Out of the Closets* worked less well than the cool analytical properties of the dissertation. It did appear, however, that sociologists and other social scientists could now legitimately research the visibly growing gay movement and sexuality in general, and the continuing research efforts initiated by Laud in the 1970s helped to proliferate the positive aspects of coming out of the closet. His later work would establish empirically, for example, that the "movement of homosexual marginals into openly gay lifestyles appears to decrease their vulnerability to violent crime."

C. Wright Mills wrote that "...the most admirable thinkers in the scholarly community...do not split their work from their lives...they...take both too seriously to allow such dissociation...." Nowhere in his life and work did Laud personify Mills' words more dramatically than in 1974 at the annual meetings of the American Sociological Association in Montreal. Laud stood up at a crowded session and accused Edward Sagarin of homophobia and revealed Sagarin's identity as Donald Webster Cory, author of the 1951 book *The Homosexual in America*. This controversial and contentious interaction continues to be seen as one of the episodes marking the beginning of the Sociologists' Gay and Lesbian Caucus and, equally important for the matter at hand, Laud's personal acknowledgement of his own gay identity. Mills, in discussing the relationship between knowledge and power, tells us: "What knowledge does to a man (in clarifying what he is, and setting it free)—that is the personal ideal of knowledge." It was at that session in Montreal, as Laud later confided, that he defined who he was and set himself "free." To use the Biblical phrase (Ephesians 6:14) that Laud had borrowed and developed in *Tearoom Trade*, the "breastplate of righteousness" had been torn from sociology and from Humphreys' own life.

While Laud's pronouncement signaled a quality of personal liberation, becoming involved in gay research was still stigmatizing; structures are required to fully implement the fruits of such liberation. Accordingly, in 1974 at the ASA meetings, several sociologists, including Laud, formed the Sociologists' Gay Caucus (SGC) to provide a forum for those studying gay issues, to lobby ASA and SSSP to include more sessions on gay themes, and to bring gay sociologists together to form a social network and professional support group. From that time, Laud, married and with two children, began to open his life and explore his gay identity, exemplifying once again in his life and work Wirth's classical insight of the sociology of knowledge: the recognition that "...we are not merely conditioned by the events that go on in our world but are at the same time an instrument for shaping them."

The 1970s marked a period of rapid growth for the gay liberation movement. By the mid-1970s certain neighborhoods in several large cities, notably New York, San Francisco, and Los Angeles, emerged as social, economic, and political enclaves of openly gay and lesbian people. During this time, Laud, who in 1972 had arrived at Pitzer College in Claremont, increasingly became involved in the life of the developing Los Angeles gay communities. His political and religious commitments, continuing research on violence and marginal men in homosexual lifestyles, and his own personal growth as an openly gay man are nicely summarized in a line from an article he co-authored at that time: "Evidence indicates that personal happiness and social adjustment increase in a social context of which one may be proud."

It is clear that this social context has been strengthened because of Laud's involvement. His early research and the risks he took doing it have opened the way to almost all sociological research on gay topics that followed. His contributions to the founding of the Sociologists' Lesbian and Gay Caucus have helped make it a visible and active force in our professional associations. Laud's participation in Los Angeles' gay communities during the late 1970s and 1980s clearly left its mark on many gay political, social, and health care organizations. Seventeen years ago Laud Humphreys predicted that "...gay liberation will not leave untouched the society that brought it into being." In a very real sense his own life and work helped make this prediction a self-fulfilling prophecy.

Although Laud's research contributions to the sociology of gay subculture waned after 1981, he remained an active participant in counseling gay people, working with gay alcoholics and drug abusers, and, in his final years, returned to the Episcopal ministry, performing services for those who died from AIDS. Humphreys was present at the beginning of the gay movement, grew with it during the 1970s, and continued to serve the gay community even while personally combating the ravages of lung cancer. Mills suggested that "it is now the social scientist's foremost political and intellectual task—for here the two coincide—to make clear the elements of contemporary uneasiness and indifference." The life and work of Laud Humphreys presents a vivid exemplar of such.

Works by Laud Humphreys

Tearoom Trade: Impersonal Sex in Public Places
Out of the Closets: The Sociology of Homosexual Liberation

21

Jeremiah Kaplan:
The Publisher as Social Vanguard

I would like to introduce Jeremiah Kaplan to you with a proverbial "true" story, albeit one that took place nearly thirty years ago. When I first started to teach at the University of Buenos Aires in Argentina, I remember asking a group of students after class what first came to mind when they thought about the United States. One very intense woman (her name was Celia Durruti, and is sadly no longer with us) answered unambiguously, almost defiantly, that for her the United States meant The Free Press, not as a concept, but as an actual publisher. And for emphasis, she added: "The Free Press is more important to me than the Statue of Liberty."

When I overcame my initial surprise, I understood that her answer made perfect sense. After years of an authoritarian regime in which General Juan D. Peron had been the only authorized sociologist, the students and their professors alike craved untrammeled thought and the latest thought. Robert Merton, Talcott Parsons, and Paul Lazarsfeld in sociology; Harold Lasswell, Daniel Lerner, Karl Deutsch, and Leo Strauss in political science were at the forefront of analysis. I confess that not a small amount of time at the University was spent in supervising translations of key essays and portions of books written by these pioneer figures, in clear violation of copyright regulations, for plain old-fashioned pirate editions.

That nearly all, or a huge majority of titles, deemed important for us in those days were published by The Free Press was not lost on me. Indeed, I take it as a central mission of Transaction that we perform, or at least try to perform, a similar role of presenting the full range of social science and political speculation on a world scale in this day and age.

In the hubris of self-congratulation that attends academic fetes, scholars may easily forget the critical role of those who facilitate the dissemination and distribution of ideas. It is at this level that Jeremiah Kaplan has excelled and taught us much for these last forty years.

He has throughout his distinguished career identified what is important in the social sciences with uncanny accuracy; and he has marketed important social research with unparalleled skill. Indeed, it is to Kaplan that we largely owe the concept of social science as a unique market offering a special product, no small achievement unto itself.

This year is not simply the 25th anniversary of Transaction, but no less, the 40th anniversary of The Free Press, which Jeremiah Kaplan founded. What better occasion then to acknowledge his special legacy? Today, The Free Press remains a great arm of the social sciences. It has been joined by other superb publishing programs, like those of Basic Books, Academic Press, Methuen/Routledge, to mention but a few. Indeed, the durability and expansion of social research as a definable market, despite substantial adversity, is part of a larger phenomenon: the redefinition of the intellectual and academic world in the second half of our century. Here again, Jeremiah Kaplan, through his concept of professional programs and multivolumed compendia on everything from bioethics to comparative religions, has kept faith with the past while emphasizing the tradition of the new.

In short, Jeremiah Kaplan should be viewed as considerably more than a publishing mogul, although he is that. He is better understood as a key contributor to the redefinition of social research: one that is ample enough to embrace the 19th-century ideal of the great and isolated scholar with a vision to match, and no less extending to a 21st-century ambition of serious people working in tandem and cooperation, whose aims are to address if not always resolve major policy issues set forth by complex societies.

Richard S. Snyder, the chairman and chief executive officer of Simon & Schuster, praised Kaplan as possessing "a rare combination of talent and vision. He is knowledgeable in all facets of the book publishing business, has unparalleled understanding of every major market, and embodies a remarkable strength of character." To which one might add that he is a person as modest in his demeanor as he is extraordinary in his achievements. It gives me great pleasure then to introduce to you Jeremiah Kaplan: a pioneer in the delivery of social scientific information and knowledge, and in publishing, not as an accidental but as a necessary profession of a special sort. All honor to he who, in the words of the Common Book of Prayer, has brought forth "the kindly fruits of the earth."

Work by Jeremiah Kaplan

"This Urgent Need to Publish." *Society*, March/April 1988, Vol. 25, No. 3

22

Russell Kirk:
Revolutionary of the Past

My relationship to Russell Kirk exists in two distinct and discrete parts: as a young critic in the mid-1950s of *The Conservative Mind*; and as an aging publisher of Transaction issuing works in the tradition of that classic text. We bill ourselves as "the publisher of record in international social science." As part of that "billing" we publish one series of books on conservative thought and another on liberal thought. I have never felt that mindless denunciations of opponents, or dismissive approaches to those with different persuasions serve the common culture. Indeed, the spirit of fanaticism is, or at least ought to be, alien to honest social thought. And I believe the same is true for honest cultural analysis.

While I still believe my critiques of the new conservatism made nearly forty years ago remain essentially valid, I must also be frank and say that the liberal bastions from which those criticisms were launched seem far more vulnerable now than in the past. Indeed, both conservatism and liberalism are under assault from the forces of fanaticism. The neo-liberalism that would substitute assurances that we end up in the same place, however different people are in talent and interests, undermines precisely the classical ideal of every person counting as one. By the same token, the neo-conservatism that would demand allegiance to evangelical and or fundamentalist persuasions deprives the conservative tradition precisely of the individual, anti-statist credo that has sustained it over time.

It is the infusion of "neo" that has done much to confound traditions of conservatism and liberalism alike. I suspect that both Russell and I now feel more comfortable in each other's company precisely because what is new, what is neo, is what is so ersatz, transparent, and fanatic. In short, these new credos do violence to the spirit of learning to which all people of the book are, in their nature, dedicated.

I would like to think that my relationship with Russell has not simply been one-sided. For while I readily confess to being pro-

foundly influenced by his emphasis on the moral grounding of political life, I also have a sneaking suspicion that he would modify his
earlier assaults on the social sciences profoundly. He now appears
to recognize that the great traditions he represents are just as readily
serviced by honest social science as by honest classical humanities.
Russell knows better now than in the past that the key term in normative outlook is *honesty* of effort, not background discipline, or
area of training.

Under the impact of Russell's thinking I have become more critical of established trends and tendencies in present day social research as the title of my next work, *The Decomposition of Sociology*, should make quite clear. He in turn has begun to incorporate
solid social and political science into his approaches. Consider, for
example, some new titles for The Library of Conservative Thought:
The Politics of the Center by Vincent Starzinger, *The Italian Fascist
Party in Power* by Dante Germino, *The Phantom Public* by Walter
Lippmann, and *We The People: The Economic Origins of the Constitution* by Forrest McDonald. To be sure, these are hardly "mainline"
efforts. But they do indicate ways in which social science studies
and classical conservative traditions meet. It is to Russell's lasting
credit that he can put aside old fears and incorporate the best of
scholarship, whatever its professional sources.

Russell needs no further encomiums. He has received enough of
these to last ten ordinary lifetimes. Indeed, I consider it one of his
great virtues that his head is not easily turned by praise. He has as a
result never rested on his oars, but continues to turn out work at a
feverish pace, albeit with elegant results. And while he rarely forgets
or ignores the long view, the long tradition as it were, he has a secret
love affair with the present. He responds to the immediate with a far
greater sense of urgency than might be imagined by casual readers.

In a world of assaults on American ties to Europe, under the ru-
bric of Eurocentricism or multiculturalism, he can fashion a book on
America's *British* Culture. During the celebrations of the American
Constitutional Tradition of 1989, he wrote major position papers on
the character of that tradition, including the sort of acute analysis of
the Bill of Rights that helps put in deep perspective the first ten amend-
ments to the American Constitution. He has also spoken frankly in
relation to presidential candidates and global matters such as the
United States involvement in the Iraqi takeover of Kuwait. It would
be less than candid to say that I share his positions on all practical or

contingent matters. Clearly I do not. Just as clearly, I think that his views on practical issues do not necessarily issue from his general proposals on the nature of the political culture. Politics may have rich philosophical implications, but it is also a craft practiced on an everyday ad hoc basis. This double-edged nature of the polity is well understood by Russell.

But that said, we have in our midst a special sort of person—one who constantly fine tunes the relationship of the general and the particular, the universal and the personal. His commitment is not now and never was to an economic system. Rather Russell's faith is in a cultural order. Indeed, one suspects that capitalism may be as much an anathema for Russell as it is for hard-bitten socialists. It is rather that Russell sees the present economic arrangement as far better than the utopian promises by the communists (and who could argue with that!). But it is the struggle for a culture, for a tradition of shared values, for a world in which religion is linked to practice at one level and morality at another, that characterizes Russell.

And I would say that at the very end of the rainbow, it is the cement of ethics rather than the grist of law that gives meaning to Russell's idea of justice. Without a morally centered world, Russell sees the contentions and conflicts engendered by the spirit of the laws as the last, but not the best, hope for survival. With a morally centered world, and one lodged especially in the Judeo-Christian tradition (especially Anglo-Catholicism if one places a fine point on this element) there is hope for the future because there is a prospect for social consensus.

Whether this sort of approach can actually resolve deep rifts and divisions within American or Western culture is a topic for a much fuller paper. It would require a reanalysis of my earlier critique of 1955 of the New Conservatism, and a reevaluation in 1993 of what passed for old liberalism of the sort I represented in the past—and yes, still do. We may have shared values, but not necessarily shared heroes. I prefer to remain in a world of Leonard Schapiro, Morris Raphael Cohen, and Jacob L. Talmon, to name a few. This is a world of unfulfilled prophesies to be sure, but one which raised the same warnings about totalitarian potentials in politics and culture that emanated from the writings of Russell's favorites: Irving Babbitt, Edmund Burke, and David Hume. But curiously, I think our decade-long relationship, close in every way, indicates that people of good will and good faith can live and work together in suspension of ultimate judgment whatever the sources of cultural inspiration. Those lacking good will cannot so endure.

There is an area of common enterprise that has been possible because both Russell and I believe in and practice the arts and crafts of publishing no less than professing. Over the years we have published not only our own works, but those of others. The idea of scholarship is not simply that of self-promotion or vanity. Collegial relations are feasible because a sense of the other is so real, so necessary. Russell and I have come to share what another colleague calls a conspiracy of excellence. This is not said in the spirit of snobbish righteousness, but simply in recognition that the act of publishing the works of others, no less than of ourselves, constitutes a statement of what is important, what is enduring. This has become a most powerful, if admittedly unstated, bond between us. This appeal to the majesty of the Word transcends differences in philosophies, ideologies, and even cultural backgrounds.

Perhaps we find a common bond at Michael Oakeshott's supper table: a place where dialogues replace daggers, and good wine does not have to be spiked with deadly potions. My faith in reason and Russell's faith in tradition, after all, derive from a common belief in persuasion not power, the authority of tradition and not the authoritarianism of raw force, and the evidence of the senses not the fear of the truncheon. These we hope will ultimately determine the fate of people, nations, and civilizations.

In his farewell from American shores to the late Christopher Dawson, one of Russell's favorite figures, Richard Cardinal Cushing noted that he "is one of those rare human spirits who stands back from the world in which he lives and takes the true measure of time and man." Since I cannot advance a proposition that is more appropriate to a summary of the life and work of Russell Kirk, I dare appropriate the Cardinal's words and place him in the special pantheon of people who has taken the true measure of our age and our people.

Works by Russell Kirk

America's British Culture
The Conservative Mind
Orestes Brownson
The Roots of American Order
The Sword of Imagination

23

Jeane J. Kirkpatrick:
Legitimacy, Force and Morality

Hopefully, both the Ambassador and the invited guests will permit me to confine my remarks to the meaning of this publication and leave to each of you the right to interpret for yourselves the contents of this pair of volumes. Needless to say, as both a social scientist and a publisher of social science books and journals, I view this as a solid, even path-breaking, addition to our list of roughly 2000 published volumes in the past quarter century. But it ill befits a person with an obvious vested interest to beat the drums, even lightly, for a work with which he has been intimately linked since the start.

Rather, I would like to address the paradox that the author of *Legitimacy and Force* could at one and the same time be properly viewed as a moving force in the making of American foreign policy in the 1980s, and in the shaping of a broad perception of the United States as a nation of moral probity as well as political force in the world at large; while at the same time remain an academic outsider. Posing the issue in such stark terms, while subject to modification, raises a thorny question about the underside in the life of American letters no less than politics: How can it be that an individual who, perhaps more than any other single person, is responsible for giving philosophical shape and structure to American foreign policy in the current decade could be subject to a continuing barrage of academic fire from university fortresses?

On several occasions, Dr. Kirkpatrick and I have discussed the existence of this paradox, this anomaly, between an acclaimed political role and a marginalized professional condition. This is not to say that Jeane Kirkpatrick lacks for offers and engagements. Indeed, I can think of very few social or political scientists who can command her extraordinary lecture fees since leaving the United Nations ambassadorial post, or who are in greater demand at every social function of the many voluntary associations and societies in America, or for that matter, who became the object of intense bidding amongst publishers, usually reserved for novelists, for the preparation of her political memoirs.

At the same time, I cannot think of another figure other than Jeane Kirkpatrick who would have a harder time obtaining a tenured position in a major department of political science in this country. And political science, mind you, is a field of social science that has remained relatively balanced, stubbornly so, in the face of challenges from the new ideologists that permeate other fields of social science and social policy. Indeed, the issuance of *Legitimacy and Force* has subjected Transaction to a level of academic critique unusual in its volume and vehemence.

Once upon a time, there was a widely accepted belief that public service is itself a public good. And that those scholars engaged in the making or execution of American policy, foreign or domestic, were entitled to special consideration. But Vietnam changed this. In part, this was the inevitable consequence of a losers syndrome: to have been involved in American foreign policy was to be party to vilification not so much because the cause fought for was wrong, but because the cause fought for was lost—at least in a temporary sense. But what compounds the paradox of broad public support and equally widespread academic opposition to Jeane Kirkpatrick is that she was not part of a losing effort, but rather a winning effort. She managed, in her years at the United Nations, to redirect its very fault lines. Under her leadership there was a new perception of the United States as very much a leader of freedom in the world, and a resolute opponent of totalitarian regimes in that world, whatever ideological garb their heads of state wear.

In many of these papers, lectures, and speeches, one senses that Dr. Kirkpatrick is less concerned with instructing diplomats at the world body on the rights and wrongs, truths and falsities, of a given issue, than with informing her fellow Americans that the United States stands for principles which are at once universal and flexible. In this she is numbered in a relatively short list that includes Ralph Bunche, Adlai Stevenson, Arthur J. Goldberg, and Daniel Patrick Moynihan, for whom the United Nations became an element of American foreign policy, and who searched out ways to implement the basic principles of the Charter, rather than wheeling and dealing from a position of presumed weakness and a posture of guilt.

Earlier figures seeking a return to academic life were perceived as being connected to losing policy efforts. In the post-Vietnam syndrome, the new ideologists believe that the United States should not be connected with victorious moods much less pursue a course of national strength. I would suggest that the academic opposition to Ambassador Kirkpatrick is thus of a new type, one predicated on the belief that America should be defeated or at least enfeebled as part restitution for imagined past colonial sins and imperial transgressions.

Academic affairs are not reducible to popularity contests. I am not suggesting that Dr. Kirkpatrick's premier place in politics necessarily entitles her to a similar place in letters. On the other hand, neither should such a policy role send her to professional Coventry. The risks of ideological conformism far outweigh those of intellectual controversy. Yet, it is the former mode that too often characterizes the halls of higher learning. If I make much of this matter it is not for fear that Dr. Kirkpatrick will lack for work, but that academic life will lack for vigor. The prevailing mood of a surly dissensus from the American mainstream in the name of global metaphysics is curiously not unlike the situation one finds at the United Nations itself, in which decisions are made and votes tallied with small regard for empirical realities and democratic values alike.

Jeane Kirkpatrick became the symbol, the lightning rod, of a new proud self-image of the United States as a democratic world leader, one at the helm of the several dozen other nation-states in the world that correlate political freedom and economic well-being. It was precisely this new American optimism, this aura of inspired self-confidence, that she helped restore that so infuriated her opponents— especially those in the academic environment for whom feelings of guilt became a psychoanalytical substitute for the study of actual political processes and systems.

Publication of these two extraordinary volumes, largely derived from Kirkpatrick's United Nations years, is thus important in a double sense: They confirm the public perception of her as a major force in the political redefinition of America during the course of this decade. No less, they disconfirm an academic perception of her as a digressive force in the intellectual and moral redefinition of America.

In these two volumes, Jeane Kirkpatrick does what was characteristic of the great British statesman of centuries gone by. As with Burke, Disraeli, and Churchill, so too with Kirkpatrick, we find a combination of intellect, moral force, and political instinct. I am not suggesting that historical judgment will be identical in all these instances. I am suggesting that *Legitimacy and Force is* significant in that special way given to few and dreamt of by many: the volumes embody the linkage of sound theory and solid achievement.

Under the circumstances, for Transaction to be the vessel carrying such a mighty cargo is both a large responsibility as well as substantial honor. We shall do our best to discharge the responsibility and merit the honor of publishing this effort by Jeane Kirkpatrick in the best way possible.

Works by Jeane J. Kirkpatrick

Dictatorships and Double Standards
Legitimacy and Force (2 volumes)
The New Presidential Elite
The Strategy of Deception
The Withering Away of the Totalitarian State

24

Milton Konvitz:
The Moral Bases of Legal Theory

On the "Statement of Purpose" page of each issue of *Midstream* rises the name Milton R. Konvitz. He is listed as "Chairman Emeritus." But I know from personal experience and association that this title is anything but gratuitous. Milton may be slender of frame and short in height, but for all his mid-ninety years he remains a fearsome and exacting editor. His devotion to the Jewish Project, and specifically to the purposes of this publication, is known to those who edit and to a few who write. I suspect that every article of each issue is scrutinized far more with the dedication of an editorial eye than the calm repose of a retired chairman.

But I would like to draw attention to Milton as a giant in the legal profession and the political science field. Last year, I had occasion to deliver a speech on the convocation of Milton's years at Cornell University. The audience was a stellar cast of major figures—from New York City Schools Chancellor Harold Levy to Commissioner of the National Hockey League, Gary Bettman. They all came to pay respects to their beloved teacher. I never had that opportunity study under Milton, but as publisher of three going on four of his books at Transaction, I have managed to imbibe his wisdom, shrewdness, and above all, his humanity. What follows then will hopefully throw light on the special house of Zion called *Midstream*.

It is a transparent absurdity to summarize the career of a 94-year-old scholar—especially one whose writings in his current period matches that of work done in previous decades in quality as well as quantity. For it is an extraordinary fact of Milton Konvitz that his recent work still remains at the cutting edge of the intersection between law, political science, and social philosophy. And so it is that however implausible the task, it remains a charge to summarize—reduce would be a more honest term—a lifetime into a matter of minutes.

But before making this attempt, it is important to note that this is a celebration of a life and not a remembrance at a wake. Milton Konvitz continues to be a sharp-eyed observer of careers and events. Yes. It is true that his hearing is not what it once was, and his sight is hardly perfect. It is also the case, that a certain frailty is evident in his movement. But these are infirmities often the case for individuals half his age, and twice his athletic prowess. So the toast *le'chaim*, to life, is very much in order this day.

In thinking hard about Milton, one must place him in the context of what I choose to call the "Cornell School." For as assuredly as there is a Frankfurt School in sociology or a Chicago School in economics, one can speak with confidence about a Cornell School of legal theory. The dorsal spine of that school goes back to several great scholars from an earlier period in the twentieth century. First, there was the late Carl Becker, whose skepticism about the French Revolution and in equal measure, enthusiasm for the American "experiment" as he called it, set the tone for much normative theory in politics and law alike. It was Becker who provided a sense of distinction between the lawful compassion of the American founders in contrast to the lawless passion of the French Revolution as it spun out of control that was a lesson Konvitz learned well. Then there was the great George H. Sabine, whose writings in the history of political theory set the comparativist tone for Milton's department. Sabine's writings remain a benchmark of present-day political theory. This linkage of law and politics continued to gain in gravity with the scholarship of the late Clinton Rossiter, whose work in the constitutional sources of government use and abuse also gains in status as the years of his preeminence recede. Milton Konvitz was the last, but by no means the least, of that era and of that group. He also provided a bridge between the "private" Cornell University, and the "public" School of Industrial and Labor Relations, and no less between conservative values and liberal policies that dominated the epoch as a whole.

But it would be wrong to think that the Cornell tradition simply ceased with his retirement. With scholars like William Whyte, Andrew Hacker, and now Theodore Lowi, the tradition continues to bear intellectual fruit. What then is the essence of that tradition? Assuredly, it is not ideology—since Whyte, Hacker, and Lowi offer a commitment to the liberal ethos no less clear and assuredly as fervent than the earlier commitment of Rossiter and Konvitz to a more traditional vision of American society. I rather suspect that the unity that these figures expressed is in the linkage of politics as a process to law as a normative system. At any rate, that is how an admitted outsider like me sees the Cornell School of political science.

Within that general context, one must point to the special contribution of Professor Konvitz. What others tended to state in whispers, he made loud and clear: the unity of Jerusalem and Washington—more specifically, the covenantal tradition of that which binds human beings to the divine authority. While this is neither the time nor place to review his last three works, and even less the entire corpus of his writings, together they form a mosaic of the special person who stitches together his political, legal, and religious beliefs to form a unified whole. *Fundamental Rights* is a theoretical breakthrough. Using case law materials, Konvitz shows that there are different layers of significance to the written law and even tacit acknowledgment of the unwritten law—all responsive to changes in custom and practice. As a consequence, some rights are more fundamental than others are. And in that tacit recognition, the legal system adapts to change rather than breaks under the strain of change.

The other two titles are indicative of a lifelong commitment to and affection for the Jewish tradition in law, philosophy, and social affairs. *Nine American Jewish Thinkers* is, however, no mere celebration of major figures. It is like the Hebrew Biblical tradition itself, a dialogue with God and at times a critique of Man. Konvitz knows that being great and being right are rarely perfect coordinates. As a result, this work avoids the hagiographic and becomes truly an impressive account of the Jewish factor in the American political tradition.

Judaism and Human Rights is a new edition of an earlier work. But this version is especially important in bringing the story up to date, that is, by a careful examination of Jewish law as it operates in a nation-state context of modern Israel. The continuing struggles in the Middle East are far beyond those between Palestinians and Israelis, or even Islam and Judaism. They involve practical decisions of when to use force, when to retaliate against enemies, when to conciliate, and when to resist. Beyond all else, Jewish tradition in human rights involves empirical thresholds to violations of rights, whatever may be the provocation. So in this work, one senses a unified construct linking all of the elements that make Konvitz's work unique and resistant to fanaticism of all persuasions.

At this moment of celebration of a special scholar, one must not ignore the social any less than intellectual context of Cornell. For if there is a Cornell School of law and political science, there is a tragic side of a rebellion against that tradition by extremists, fanatics, and activists for whom the very notion of science and the very notion of law are anathema. In place of theory we are offered action. In place of objective analysis we are offered subjective sentiment. In place of social science we are offered social utopia for the future and political ideology for the present. That revolt against reason was largely successful in the late 1960s. The center did not hold and neither did the Cornell School of Politics as an integrated entity. It is not unwarranted to note that this was also the fate of the Vienna Circle and the Frankfurt School—both of which were decimated by Nazism in the 1930s. Irrationality also claimed as a victim the various experimental schools of culture and philosophy that flourished in the USSR in the 1920s. Stalinism took its toll in human life and in intellectual careers from genetics to physiology. The asking price of fervent extremism is nothing else than the life of the mind. That such a price is sometimes exacted even within democratic societies should caution us about being unduly optimistic that repression can't happen here.

But good thinking, in contrast to correct thought, has a way of reviving itself. So it has been with the Cornell group. The work and life of Milton Konvitz, the man whom we have come to honor on this occasion, is a warning as well as a lesson. The warning is that the life of the mind is a fragile as well as beautiful thing. The lesson is that decent, honest analysis does not perish—at least not easily and not willingly. The three books of Milton Konvitz published in the past several years by Transaction offer a testimonial to the resilience of a great scholar, but also offer a message of hope to the young, to those uncorrupted by slogans and easy generalizations. That hope ultimately resides in the self-criticisms inherent in the promise of higher education itself—a promise that Milton Konvitz like Emerson, Thoreau, and James before him, delivered in full measure.

Works by Milton Konvitz

Fundamental Liberties of a Free People
Fundamental Rights
Judaism and Human Rights
Nine American Jewish Thinkers

25

Walter Laqueur:
Tribune of Political Theory

Walter Laqueur is both unique as an individual and as part of a collectivity of special intellectuals with a strong identification with, no less than background in, German-Jewish culture. That he should be granted the Aufbau Prize at the Goethe Institute in his eightieth year is no more than a proper, if belated, recognition for a lifetime of service. But one might ask, a lifetime of service to what and to whom?

Here we come upon the magic of Walter and the tradition he so ably represents. For there are certain peculiarities that define the person and the scholar. They deserve mention in a straightforward way. First, is his catholicity of interests—from problems of terrorism to prospects for democratic societies. Second, is his ability to weave such diverse subjects into a whole cloth, to give to his audience a sense of linkage between subjects and insight into objects. Third, is that rare capacity to distinguish the critical from the trivial, and thus making international affairs a matter of intimate concern.

The sense of context is not to be overlooked. For Walter, while very much part of the American policy scene at CSIS, remains part of the European intellectual tradition as well. One can mention such figures as George Mosse, with whom he functioned as co-editor of the *Journal of Contemporary History*, and also George Lichtheim, Melvin J. Lasky, and Elie Kedouri, just to mention a few, who sustained his European connections. Indeed, his American and Israeli cohorts also have strong ties to Europe. Charles Maier, Stanley Payne, Gordon Craig, and Bernard Lewis all come readily to mind. Whether that amazing blend and amalgam of German, Israeli, and American scholars for whom the fate of the West matters can survive this generation is something that remains to be seen. But its capacity to produce stunning intellectual breakthroughs is not in question.

I have known Walter in a variety of contexts. As a contributor to the early years of *The Washington Quarterly* at his end, and as a contributor to *Society* at mine, we interacted on academic questions bathed in political realities. But these were never simply mechanical juxtapositions, not just "one hand washing the other" or simply being kind to each other for mutual gratification. Neither of us needed nor would have much appreciated back scratching. I also contributed the lead article to a *festschrift* honoring Walter's 70th birthday—with a special emphasis on the double theme of democracy and development, or if you will, real alternatives to totalitarian styles of mass mobilization.

But I suspect that the most important ways in which we have interacted was through his contributions over the years to Transaction Publishers, of which I serve as editorial director and board chairman. We consider our house as "publisher of record in international social science. And if we are entitled to such an appellation, it is assuredly because of people like Walter who give rich meaning to such a phrase. Over the years, Transaction has published eleven of Walter's works. Even so, I suspect that we probably have not touched more than a fraction of his total output. But like European houses, more than American ones, we assess the importance of the author and not just the value of any one specific title.

Walter is the only scholar I know who, at least until recently, issued a monthly report of his writings. These usually arrived in English, Hebrew, German, and Russian. And while a certain repetition was inevitable, I was always impressed by his extraordinary skill in addressing concrete national psychology in the language in which his work appeared. I suspect that his early training as a journalist on *The Jerusalem Post* sensitized him to such differences in cultures as expressed through languages. But whatever the reasons, it is evident to even casual readers that he invests each article, each review, each op-ed piece with an insight not readily found in either pure journalists or for that matter, pure academics.

In navigating the worlds of journalism and scholarship, Walter also brought something special to the table, what might be called a Montaigne- or Pascal-like quality of aphorisms with a moral edge. Indeed, the genius of Walter is to deal with ethically charged issues in a subtle way, so that the reader is lead to consider alternatives and options—not simply as strategic or policy considerations, but as moral standards of judgment. It is rare indeed for Walter to write in anger. Rather, his anger is modulated and controlled. It becomes part of the texture of thought itself.

Larger and wealthier commercial publishers initially published a number of works by Walter that Transaction issued. But as they quickly tire of works that do not possess the "blockbuster" capacity to titillate, they also quickly release rights to authors. Happily, we were often seemingly in the right place at the right time. And so it is that what was written for a specific place and time became part of the general culture and part of the timeless workload that typified the best of scholarly writing for a decent audience.

Of the eleven titles that Transaction has published, I am proudest of the four volumes of Walter's papers, the shorter, briefer works. For it is in collections such as *Fin de Siècle and Other Essays on America and Europe*, *The Political Psychology of Appeasement*, *Soviet Realities: Culture and Politics from Stalin to Gorbachev*, and *America, Europe and the Soviet Union* that the heart and soul of Walter become apparent. Better yet, it is in these less well-known essays that the crossing points of politics, history, and ethics become apparent.

There are times when differences of opinion between Walter and myself became clear, as in our respective writings on public policy questions. The historical view, the longitudinal view that Walter brings to questions of decision-making in foreign policy when they first appeared, seemed to me to endow the policy apparatus with less intelligence than it deserved. But the fact is that over time, my own emphasis on choice and decision in matters of national interests and political ambitions seem less persuasive, or at least less full as an explanatory device than did his more skeptical view of events.

What we share is overwhelmingly more significant than the matters over which we disagree. I would say that first and foremost, avoiding an equation between explanation and prediction. There is a need for both. The good analyst will permit the thoughtful person to arrive at predictions by his or her own extrapolations from the available evidence. Walter has the wonderful habit of a cultivated mind—of not bludgeoning his readers into submission, but rather carrying them along where the evidence dictates one should travel. In philosophy, I suspect that Walter is more of a Kantian than either a Hegelian or a Nietzschean. He is attracted by the search for universals as embedded in specific events, rather than the abstracted dialectic of mind in or out of historical focus.

It is difficult to think of Walter as old or even aging. There is that ever-present twinkle of a young man in his eyes and movement, and that wondrous curiosity about the world that prevents a hardening of intellectual arteries. Walter seeks no followers, has no acolytes, and I suspect is repelled by hero worshippers. He does solicit collegial approbation, but does not unduly concern himself with the opinion of others. He comes before us as a worldly combatant; or as Goethe declared in *Buch des Paradies*: "I have been a man and that means to have been a fighter."

So I conclude neither in a funereal mode, nor in a celebratory style—but in recognition that having a colleague such as Walter is what enriches my own life and gives shape to my own goals. Walter must tolerate such self-interested appraisals, for I suspect that there is a sly utilitarian component in his own response to friends and enemies, crusaders and critics. And now, onwards to the final quartile of this righteous Jewish life bathed in the national cultures of Europe, Israel, and America. Provincial ideologues notwithstanding, Walter has given cosmopolitanism the good name that it deserves.

Works by Walter Laqueur

Fin de Siècle and Other Essays on America and Europe
Guerrilla Warfare
A History of Terrorism
Russia and Germany
The Uses and Limits of Intelligence

26

Melvin J. Lasky:
An American Voice of the
European Conscience

Too readily, it is forgotten or, better, ignored that the restoration of democracy in Germany came at the barrel of a gun and the point of a bayonet. Quite simply, the Nazi regime of 1933-1945 did not fold its tent in Hobbesian style as a consequence of internal upheaval but as a result of the might provided by the armies of the West at one end and Russia from the East. In an impassioned moment, I said to Lasky that the idea of regime change was not quite as innovative or contemporary, as President Bush would have us believe, but was a result of George Patton and his Third Army. And he replied in his sometime sly Pickwickian way, "Oh no, Irving, it was General Lucius Clay, the commander of military government in Germany." Whatever the military force, the point remains the same: regime change, whether in political systems or in economic policies, are sometimes due to internal strains and at other times to external explosions. Winning battles and signing peace accords are not matters of universal law or regulation.

Mel Lasky was a soldier in that war. He served with General Patch on the Southern Front, which liberated Dachau and conquered Hitler's Munich. More pointedly, he was able to play an extraordinary role in postwar reconstruction of Nazi Germany, and no less, a deepening consciousness of postwar retrogression of Stalinist Russia. In his editorial role on *Der Monat* he marshaled the intellectual forces that gave backbone to the revival of the democratic traditions of Weimar Germany, and in his editorial performance as long-standing editor of *Encounter*, he gave voice to those who saw communism as the betrayal not simply of a democratic Russian tradition, but of the socialist ideals that motivated Lasky as a young man. The intellectual performance was stunning enough, but that it should have been accomplished by an American Jew, educated at City College of New

York along with such other luminaries as Seymour Martin Lipset, Irving Kristol, Irving Howe, Philip Selznick, Daniel Bell, and Nathan Glazer, is the measure of how wars change cultural no less than material conditions. Educated in one of the last graduating classes in the pre-World War Two epoch, these young people helped shape the cultural milieu of the early postwar era. But it must be said in frankness that while the "Cold War" was something most New York intellectuals fought out at Union Square, for Lasky the battleline was located at the Berlin Wall. However, that distinction on the ground notwithstanding, Lasky was very much a part of the New York intellectual tradition of the 1930s.

There have been many fine journalists who have performed literary acts of a memorable sort—Eric Sevareid, Edward R. Murrow, and the immortal Ernie Pyle—the foot soldier's chronicler. But in truth, none of them rose to the level of fundamental thinkers, however pretentious that phrase must sound to jaundiced ears. One might point to an older editorial tradition, such as that established by Walter Lippmann or H. L. Mencken. But it must be noted that these people came from earlier generations when the gap between journalism as an occupation and social research as a profession was far narrower. And at the risk of inviting derisive anger, it could be said that with several rare exceptions such as *The American Language* by Mencken and *Public Opinion* by Walter Lippmann, the tradition of staying close to the story made explorations into general theory, theories beyond the experienced range—rare events. Melvin Lasky was unique as a journalist in reaching the heights of social theory and intellectual history. And in *Utopia and Revolution* those heights were profoundly scaled.

In discussing the reproduction of a new edition of *Utopia and Revolution* with Lasky, I mentioned to him my belief that it probably was the best sociological study of the subject of ideology and utopia since the work by that name by Karl Mannheim. This is so despite the fact that the Frankfurt doyen of the early 1930s was hardly mentioned in his work. His oral response to the idea of this linkage was enthusiastic. "I tried to close the circle on a problem bequeathed to us by Mannheim—namely the conundrum of an exposé of ideology that lurked behind so much that passed for political and social theory, and the relativism that this sort of sociology of knowledge left us with."

Lasky's informal summation is, I believe, quite correct. For left as a pure methodology, the sociology of knowledge provides us with an anti-science, a way to uncover the sources of error, rather than a new way of gathering and presenting modes of establishing truth. For if every particular of information we have is tinged with ideological self-deception and utopian longings, then what grounds remain for a science of society? The task then Lasky set for himself is to examine not only the ideological rubble left behind by totalitarian systems but also the historical grounds that made extremism so widely embraced by the intellectual classes. Behind the close reading of seventeenth-century English radical theology, eighteenth-century French Enlightenment scientism, and nineteenth-century German philosophies of history is the story of that experience that Lasky was closest to in his own background: the Second World War and postwar reconstruction in the mid-twentieth century.

There is a sense in which the radical analysis of revolution and utopianism is less a study of real world events than of the linguistic management of such events. In that way, for Lasky, the sociology of knowledge shades off by degrees into the history of ideas. The effort is fulfilled by a discourse into the politics of language. And Lasky has always been more comfortable in that latter realm. It is one touched by his sense of writers of quality—of George Orwell, Luigi Barzini, George Steiner, Ignazio Silone, Aleksandr Solzhenitsyn, and a host of Europerans whose sensibility was forged in the struggle to expose the debasement of language by offering an option predicated on its grandeur. One might say that this is the positive outcome of the European cultural experience: of some notion that reason is reflected in expressions of truth-telling rather than any single vocabulary of reason as some pure entity unto itself.

Utopia and Revolution can be understood as turning classical political theory on its head, or better, inside out. Instead of the usual patois of how English radical theologies contributed to the revolutionary process, Lasky shows how instead such political theology of the mid-seventeenth century became the backbone of the natural history of revolutionary disasters. In looking at the Leveller tradition, for example, Lasky draws attention to following stages in John Lilburne's much-admired writings dedicated to the Cause at least as it appeared in 1649. Rather than take a tradition at face value as it was from George H. Sabine to Edward P. Thompson, Lasky pulls the plug on radical theology as simply a codebook for revolutionary fanaticism. It does not take much to infer that such thinking three hundred years ago is the forerunner of liberation theology.

There is a natural history to utopian belief systems. First, there is the dedication to death in the maintenance of Truth, Justice, and Righteousness. Second, the monolithic Unity of single-minded action—including armed struggle. Third, the turn to Force and Violence as a mechanism for eliminating the tyrants. Fourth, the Fury against a revolution betrayed the charge of nominal changes even as the monarchy changes into a republic. While the players change and the turf is different, the same natural history of revolution was to play itself out in eighteenth-century France and in late nineteenth-century Russia. Indeed, from "The Politics of Paradise" to the "sweet dreams" of present-day fanaticisms the same pattern occurs. Each age evolves new types of reasoning and conclusions, although dwelling on the same inherited problems.

With Simone deBeauvoir, Jean-Paul Sartre, and Marx and Lenin before them, there is the much-despised tendency by the masses to accept reform as a goal. Lasky's work ends as it begins: with the ways in which utopia and revolution conflate into each other with devastating consequences. "Clever, versatile, excitable, volatile, never reforming, always transforming—have come full turn. In their end is their beginning." And in a searing final departing goal, one that recalls Vico more than Burke, these "intellectuals of utopian and revolution" end up "guiltless and without conscience, they embrace an anonymous future in the name of invented but undisclosed values. The sweet dream has become inviolable dogma. The revolution remains their utopia." There is a precision in this line of analysis that has escaped many of the finest social scientists of the age. I suspect the reason is only a few could match Lasky's sense of the common culture from Shakespeare to Milton to Dante and Camus.

Such words can only be written by those who have passed through these "stages" of history as a personal odyssey. They belong to Arthur Koestler, Albert Camus, and of course, to Melvin Lasky. Like the novel of ideas, *Utopia and Revolution* does not follow a chronological ordering; it is not a history of political theory so much as a phenomenology of political movements—sometimes cloaked as religion, other times as secular partisan politics. The work proceeds from Nietzsche, Proudhon, and Marx and their various views of salvation, to the millenarian visions of today. In one epoch after another the same sort of tendencies drive revolutionaries and utopians: the dream of the universal, the total transforming properties of intelligence, the mythologizing of "the people," the reality of the elites.

A. O. Lovejoy's Great Chain of Being hangs like a noose over the heads of the revolutionary impulse. This is, after all, a work on the great struggle of reform versus revolution. An ordinary world of incremental change pitted against an exciting world of cataclysmic change. This dialectic comes up in plays, novels, historical essays, and religious tracts.

Like the subject matter itself, the book *Utopia and Revolution* has no beginning or ending. The work can be viewed as a revolving door of the risks of false options provided by the escape hatches of pure reason and unbridled passion in a modern context. Lasky's own growth, his own transformation, was to move away from the dialectical polarities and toward the continuities of culture. In a touching moment, he shares with his readers and listeners the discussion he had with Bertolt Brecht. The great dawning came after the Hungarian uprising of 1956: "I began to feel more and more that what had been called 'bourgeois democracy' was not a thing of the past and that the Bolshevik Revolution did not represent humanity's inevitable, progressive step forward." Quite the contrary, freedom was "not the forlorn ideal of a handful of intellectuals but a popular and dynamic force." The irony was that Lasky's break with socialism enabled him to view with measured optimism the worth of populism. It may be commonplace to now speak in broad generalities about the failure of revolutionary socialism, but it was less so in 1965, when the lectures were first delivered.

The end of the Cold War signaled the collapse of the Soviet Empire but hardly of the communist idea and its practices beyond the pale of Europe. It was a collapse that Lasky celebrated in his own way by calling a conference in Berlin in 1992 on "Last Encounter with the Cold War," a subject that was intended to put closure on this chapter of history. But beyond that celebration of a denouement came a question: what becomes of the core theory of *Utopia and Revolution* in an age that had wearied of both words and the concepts that underlay them? For Lasky, the answer lay in the trek from *Utopia and Revolution* to the *Language of Journalism*. This latter-day ambitious project, of which two of three promised volumes are complete, offer insights into the person, but also how expressions of political opinion have become pervasive acts unto themselves. The positivist residue, for all of its narrowing down of the realm of meaning, has made the study of language synonymous with the examination of political culture. Lasky's work in this area has done just that.

The first volume had as its title *Newspaper Culture* whilst the second volume is titled *Profanity, Obscenity and the Media*. He documents how the issue of formerly forbidden language is a triumph of sinuous semantics. The torturous struggle of a once puritanical literary culture writing to break free of censorship is examined against a background of the transformation of the news culture into comic texts. Language itself becomes a battleground, a place in which the realm of ideas is fought out. The struggle against censorship and curbs on free speech becomes enmeshed with a struggle for a mode of expression that converts such freedom into license. Language can barely move beyond the politically correct, the embrace of banality, in the form of jargon, slang, patois, and varieties of grunts and groans in print.

In this way, Lasky's earlier politics of anti-totalitarianism was transformed into the cultural struggle for a democratic culture. His has not been a simple trek, and certainly not a linear movement. Rather it is the effort of a post-Orwellian exile to maintain a radical thrust in a situation in which radicalism itself has become a debased coin of the realm. This sort of writing is a guaranteed way not to make friends and influence people. But it does make possible a sense of connection and even participation by those of us impacted by quotidian culture to appreciate just how difficult, perhaps even self-contradictory, is the trek toward personal freedom in advanced societies. For what started out as a trek in understanding how, within the bowels of Marxism, the "straightforward issue" of reform or revolution worked its way through party history, became the master theme in the twentieth-century world at large.

Without a doubt, the most painful aspect of Melvin Lasky's career is his association, and that of *Encounter* magazine, with The Congress of Cultural Freedom. This major global agency based in Paris and dedicated to the freedom of intellect in the arts and sciences enlisted Lasky's deepest passions. Indeed, from its formation in 1950 to its termination in 1979, it served as a virtual "shadow" UNESCO, doing precisely what the United Nations agency was organized to achieve, but failed at so thoroughly: to guard and expand the free expression and exchange of ideas and creative peoples. Under its banner, the work of dissident scholars, journalists, and exiled or imprisoned political figures found a home. Arguably, it was the most effective instrument of opposition to Soviet-sponsored international peace conferences aimed at weakening, if not destroying, the democratic West. While The Congress of Cultural Freedom had supporters in the United States, it is the case that its core base was in Western Europe. Lasky was one of its principal founders and architects.

The problem was that the funding for The Congress of Cultural Freedom was essentially funneled through the CIA, the United States Central Information Agency that in the imaginary world of poor fiction and cheap films became synonymous with American covert operations. By extension, The Congress of Cultural Freedom became tarred as little else than an intellectual fraud—ideas bought and paid for by Cold War struggles. However, the influence of *Encounter* did not dissolve. It is the case that several critical editors, including Stephen Spender and Frank Kermode, resigned from the editorial board. But for the most part, the editors stood firm, and these included Hugh Trevor-Roper, Max Beloff, Colin MacInness, and Denis Brogan, among others. Without laboring the point, the key problem was not the source of the funding, but its covert nature. Many less than perfect foundations and philanthropies support ideological products that are less pure in their scientific pronouncements. But the audience of the intellectual product has the right and ability to measure the sponsor's ultimate intentions no less than the actual product. An organization dedicated to achieve democratic reforms in science and culture is obligated to accept the consequences of openness no less than the penalties of secrecy.

That said, I know of not a single serious intellectual product produced during this period, whether it be Milovan Djilas' electrifying work on *The New Class* or Melvin Lasky's *Utopia and Revolution*, that was written to CIA specifications—or for that matter, any other sponsoring agency of The Congress of Cultural Freedom. Doubtless, we would prefer an intellectual battlefield predicated on pure moral premises, good democrats and bad dictators. We have come to believe that accepting salaries from universities is acceptable, but receiving stipends from governments is abominable. The actual moral condition of intellectual life in an age in which even the concept of the freewheeling intellectual is an anachronism was muddied and even warped by the intensity of the Cold War struggles. The consequences of the relationship between the sources of funding and the character of the product is not a subject we enjoy entertaining. To be sure, few academics relish looking into the system of grants and awards that convert public universities into private satrapies, and private universities into public charges. Fewer still are willing to entertain the idea of the corruption of ideas as a result of such a system of emoluments.

Perhaps Lasky himself had the last word on the subject when, in private correspondence, he noted with great vigor that "it is a contradiction in terms to indict a Statist cultural system for its *Gleichschaltung* and itself be state-funded. But since no one ever persuasively impugned the integrity of *Encounter*'s various and variegated writers, nor the absolute independence of the magazine's course, the general shrug of the shoulders was the mainstream reaction. Indeed, it could have been argued that we were substantially freer at *Encounter* than the journalists and copy editors of *The New York Times* and *The London Times*. There they were always looking over their shoulders at their owners or proprietors. We did not decline. But we did have periodic nose-bleeds." This piece of biographical sketch might appear excessive for reintroducing *Utopia and Revolution*. But I think not. Quite the contrary, it serves to remind us that the world of ideology is rooted in the larger world of everyday decision-making.

The gray area of shifting premises and different lines in the moral sand is the essential property of serious scholarship no less than accurate biography. In looking back at *Utopia and Revolution* from a perch in the present it is clear that the very impurities of human actions and motivations give the book its essential fascination. Such imperfections as we live with every day preserve us from the far worse sins of fanaticism, dogmatism, and irrationalism. The latter triad leads directly to the *Gulag*; to the death of victims in the search of moral perfection itself. If the resulting universe is less attractive, even more skeptical about the joys of long-run solutions to immediate problems, it is also more readily inhabitable by human beings. That lesson is nowhere better outlined than in *Utopia and Revolution*. It may not have been the express purposes of the lectures when he started out, but it was the clear judgment by the end. Few figures in the twentieth century were more skillful in plumbing the political mindset of the human heart than Melvin J. Lasky.

Works by Melvin J. Lasky

The Language of Journalism
On the Barricades and Off
Utopia and Revolution
Voices in a Revolution

27

Harold Lasswell:
Garrison States and Good Societies

When I accepted the responsibility of writing a preface to Harold Lasswell's prescient papers on *The Garrison State*, I had every intention of providing a basic overview of this critical concept and milestone in his work. But when I read the brilliant introduction by Jay Stanley, who also serves as the editor and inspiration for this volume, I realized soon enough that my intention would be terribly redundant. I would have ended up repeating what Professor Stanley had already said, and probably not nearly as convincingly or thoroughly.

I was faced with a difficult choice telling Professor Stanley I had little to add to his fine remarks, and simply sending through a few encomiums that might be little more than a press release; or writing something original, that might even be of interest to Lasswell scholars, no less than students of political and military sociology. I chose the latter course, and I beg the indulgence of Professor Stanley for using this space, not to deflect from his own expert analysis of Lasswell, but rather to provide personal insight into a private man.

Many people have had a far lengthier and closer relationship to Harold Lasswell than I did. Indeed, I entered his world only in the final decade of Harold's life—a period marked by a certain quiet bitterness that peeked through the calm and reserve he allowed the outside world to see. He was such a private person that it must remain a mystery to his colleagues why his enormous intellectual output was so heavily focused on the destructive and constructive aspects of personality factors. For a man sometimes described as the father of political psychology it does seem somewhat curious how few people he allowed into his inner circle.

There is little purpose to repeating the rumors that were rampant about Harold during his life. Anyone so private necessarily invites speculation about what qualities "really" moved him. Rather than add to that sort of rubbish, I should simply like to record three special occasions—at least they were special for me—on which we met, talked, argued, smiled, and walked away with a heightened sense of respect. Again, at least this was the case for me. I can only suggest that Harold's correspondence confirms the mutuality of this regard.

Our first major contact related to his manuscript *The Signature of Power*. This extraordinary work, yet to receive its proper due, attempted to show how the architecture of public places can be viewed as the physical representation of power. For reasons not altogether made clear by Harold, neither of his two major publishers of an earlier period—the University of Chicago Press and Yale University Press—were interested in publication of this book. Both claimed that the market was limited for such a crossover book, and the use of a large number of half tones would make it an inordinately expensive undertaking.

Harold did not dispute the matter of costs, but he was sardonic bordering on the sarcastic in noting that neither of his major publishers balanced at earlier works in which profits were high and royalties low. He first contacted Transaction, and this was in 1977, when our book program was still in its infancy, about the publication of two works with which Harold was identified as a co-editor: the first was *Patterns of Policy: Comparative and Longitudinal Studies of Population Events*, in which he joined John D. Montgomery and Joel S. Migdal in a Harvard-sponsored activity that attempted to show possible linkages between demography and policymaking.

The second Transaction title with which he was linked was a volume he participated in as contributing editor, John McHale and Magda Cordell McHale's *Basic Human Needs*. The human needs approach had emerged in the decade of the seventies as a response to abstract, general notions of development that disguised political agendas behind economic systems theories. Anyone who knew Harold or his work can appreciate how he looked with disdain on abstractions that serve elite agendas rather than human needs. In short, even before we met in person, we had established a literary bond that made our initial meeting pleasant and easy going.

We met in Harold's New York apartment, and the manuscript was laid out on the coffee table with the precision and neatness that those who knew him well understood was characteristic of the man. I read the book over the course of the next several hours, then simply pronounced our willingness to publish the work. I realized that the cost of photographic materials would be high, but the opportunity of publishing what, alas, turned out to be Harold's last full-scale manuscript was hardly an opportunity a relatively new mission-oriented social science publisher like Transaction could easily turn away. In any event, the book was so well written that we were spared the usual extra cost of copyediting.

After we agreed with a handshake—and that was a bond for us both—he went on to explain how the idea of the garrison state helped underscore the message of the book To be sure, many of the images in *The Signature of Power* relate to military installations, court houses, and maximum security prisons. For if the garrison state is real it must have a physical representation of itself. Harold observed that although most of the images in his book pertained to buildings in the West, the relationship of power to architecture was even more apparent in the dictatorial regimes of Stalin's Russia, Hitler's new Berlin, and the Roman city of the future in Mussolini's Italy. He could not understand why so few political scientists had appreciated the obvious symbiosis of power and buildings in their efforts to identify the sources of state authority.

What I found interesting is how, as in his essays on the Garrison State as such, Lasswell paid scant attention to distinctions between East and West, totalitarian and democratic regimes. It might be argued that this indifference is a weakness in Lasswell's thinking, a failure to distinguish systems and ideologies one from the other. On the other hand, it might also be argued that it was his way of cutting through the sticky glue of ideology, to reveal how regimes actually work—and how they enhance or mitigate their authority in the physical world. Indeed, one might argue that for Lowell, such hardheaded considerations always weighed far more heavily in his analysis than broad theoretical frameworks. I do not mean to suggest that Lasswell harbored authoritarian instincts. He definitely did not! He did harbor a deep suspicion that underlying systemic differences was a thick layer of stratification that distinguished those at the top from those at the bottom. In this, notwithstanding his reservations for the European style as a whole, Harold was probably closer to the Franco-Italian School of power than the German-Austrian emphasis on authority.

We corresponded about the manuscript but in an essentially perfunctory manner. *The Signature of Power* appeared, but for reasons still not clear, to me at least, the book failed to take off, even in professional circles. The reviews at the time were on the positive side, but they were written by individuals singularly out of touch with Lasswell's essential premises. It might well be that Lasswell himself is at fault, since the book was far more schematic and his ideas were less developed than in his classical writings. He never does explain how different strategies dictated different sort of institutional buildings, and worse, he does not offer a model of democratic architecture in the style of Hugh Dalziel Duncan's study of Louis Sullivan and the Chicago School. Probably some of the responsibility for the book's weaknesses fall on my own shoulders, since I failed to convey my doubts about it, for fear either of losing the prize altogether or seeing it delayed in an era when topflight new manuscripts by senior authors did often come to Transaction.

Lasswell and I had an opportunity to meet soon thereafter in Washington, D.C., since we were both members of the publications committee of the American Political Science Association in about 1980. In an emergency meeting convened by the late Evron Kirkpatrick, who at the time was executive director of the American Political Science Association, Harold came up with the solution to what had been a thorny problem. It seems that far too many manuscripts submitted to the *American Political Science Review* had been accepted— so that delays in publication has become interminable. The option of a rejection after acceptance was considered and tossed out as potentially volatile, while, the other option of publishing oversized issues was also considered and rejected—first on the grounds of costs and second on the grounds that the journal already was far too large and bulky for any practical purposes.

In those circumstances, Harold proposed what appeared to be a sensible alternative: to tell the authors of the accepted manuscripts that their work could be published earlier and with greater fanfare in any number of regional or professionally specific political science journals. That if an author should elect such a route, the editor of the *APSR* (I believe it was Nelson Polsby or Charles Jones) would write a special commendation, indicating that the article in question had already been satisfying to the board of the *APSR*. This seemed like a perfectly sensible solution, one the committee was quick to adopt. Alas, the plan did not work, since very few authors were willing to surrender publication in the periodical of record of the profession, and all the pleading in the world would not convince nor console most that what was lost in prestige could be gained by more rapid publication. In short, Harold had an excellent idea for solving a problem created by editorial enthusiasms, but his thinking turned sour to the taste, especially among younger scholars who believed that publication in the *APSR* was tantamount to entering paradise.

But it was lunch on that fateful day in Washington that I recollect best. I had received a promotion piece from the Reverend Sun Myung Moon's Unification Church. Harold was listed as an advisory editor for the Reverend Moon's intellectual front, The Unity of the Sciences Movement of the Unification Church. Since I was hard at work on the subject, with a book in the works of the MIT Press, I used this unusual opportunity to speak candidly about the Reverend Moon, his church, and the role of senior American scholars in that outfit.

Harold knew I was in the process of putting together a volume for MIT Press on the politics of the Unification Church. He also knew of my critical stance on the organization. As a result, he was perhaps a bit more edgy and abrasive in his response than he might otherwise have been. In response to my queries as to Reverend Moon's various quasi-legal activities, Harold said simply, "Show me a smoking gun, and I will leave the organization." I responded that we are not in a court of law, but in a court of public opinion. Harold was singularly impressed by my line of reasoning.

As academics are apt to do when the dialogue gets rough and there seems to be no way out, we became polite. I changed the discussion and asked what attracted him to the Unity of Sciences movement as such. Keep in mind that our dialogue was taking place with at least a dozen people in attendance from the APSA committee reviewing publication options. This was not something that Harold appreciated, but there was no place to hide, so the discussion continued. Lasswell confided to the group that he had a sense of being cast off by the profession since his retirement, except on ceremonial occasions. The Unification Church, with its emphasis on value theory, allowed him to express himself without impediment. I think it must also be said with candor that Lasswell also had strong negative feelings about the Communist movement, and the Unification Church, an outlet for anti-Communist sentiment at the ideological level, seemed a harmless enough vehicle for expressing his philosophical dispositions.

The luncheon ended on an indecisive note. There was no hostility expressed then or later, although I always suspected that Harold thought my raising such issues over a luncheon was more an example of poor manners than of poor thinking. We never again spoke of the Unification Church; but at the same time, I suspect that his involvement declined from that point forward. Certainly it did after *Science, Sin and Scholarship* appeared.

Our next meeting was far more pleasant. I spoke with colleagues inside Rutgers political science department, who conducted a monthly colloquium with outside speakers. They agreed that Lasswell would be an excellent choice for a speaker, and I (they?) extended an invitation. I was given to understand that, despite the proximity of Rutgers to New York City, Lasswell had never visited our campus. The department was kind enough to ask that I make the opening remarks—which I was pleased to do. I felt it was an opportunity to erase the bad taste from the Washington luncheon, and, get back to the era of good feelings engendered by our publication of Harold's last works.

I pointed to the elements in Harold's work that had the greatest impact on me. Obviously, they were not necessarily what others might have emphasized. In this regard, I pointed out that Harold had done such a wide range of work that it was easy to see him as an intellectual dilettante instead of what he was, an innovator in a variety of areas. He introduced the psychoanalytical dimension into political science—not through a theory of crowd like LeBon, but through a theory of how personality intersects with power to define the character of political elites. I also pointed out no one better combined the microscopic and macroscopic, the intimate structure of local organization and the pandemic character of international movements. And finally, I observed it was hard to overestimate his role in placing policy research on a scientific basis.

Indeed, Lasswell's emphasis on policy might have led him to neglect or minimize the role of ideas in the political process, but nothing could be further from the truth. His work with Abraham Kaplan in *Power and Society* was indeed a veritable catalogue of sociology of knowledge potential in the world of real politics. The evolution of the idea of a garrison state was more than a mechanical view of the role of the armed forces. It was his writing in this area that spawned a whole raft of followers and imitators for whom military determinism was a critical variable in its own right. From Samuel Huntington at one end of the political spectrum to myself at the other, it became clear that international and national political analysis could never be pushed back into the bottle of diplomatic history. The armed forces had become an independent actor in their own right. That is the essence of Lasswell's garrison state—its consequence in world politics as it were.

After making my statement, I sat down with an air of self-satisfaction. Harold then took the podium and in his finest sardonic mode said, "Well Irving, that is the best obituary notice I am likely to receive for a long time to come. But it is best that I talk about things I am now working on." He then proceeded to speak about his work in nonpolitical contexts—from demography to urban research. I am not certain that the audience, lacking much knowledge of Lasswell's major contributions, could quite appreciate his encyclopedic review. Nonetheless, it was a pleasant evening—and one that gave Harold a good feeling about his profession, or at least his colleagues across the Hudson.

Alas, Harold's quip about a funeral oration proved curiously prophetic. Within a few months of his appearance at Rutgers, he suffered a massive stroke that left him paralyzed and hospitalized for the short balance of his life. I visited him at a New York hospital, where he was alert but unable to communicate very well. I quipped that it was pleasant to have the floor to myself and have the great man lay back in a bed and either nod or frown. I spoke perfunctorily of his work, offering to help in any way possible. But it was clear that all arrangements had already been made by his colleagues, especially at Yale. As he approached the end, one was impressed by the sense of the natural history of life, the sense of organization in death as in life. To the end he was a private man, a reserved man, a civil man.

Having said this, however, one is still left with an uneasy feeling that the essence of the man eludes easy analysis. I suspect that this is the case with all figures who stand mighty and tall. Still, the effort at summary judgment needs to be made. To me, Harold Lasswell is best seen as an American Original. I do not mean by this anything chauvinistic; simply that he brought to all analysis a special combination of that Jamesian tough-mindedness and tender-heartedness easier to observe than to explain.

One could draw a straight line from Lasswell's pointing out the emergence of the garrison state—as a mentality no less than military reality—to C. Wright Mills' expressions of alarm concerning a military-industrial complex. True enough, there is less stridency and urgency in Lasswell than in Mills. But for both figures, however different their personal and political proclivities, the need to link analysis to policy is transparent. The source of that linkage is a belief that the mission of social research is fulfilled in the support of democratic institutions.

Lasswell did indeed have a fascination with power. But unlike many of his European counterparts with the same concerns, he did not have a fixation with power. Whether studying the formation of radical cells at the Chicago level or the formation of military cabals in Tokyo, Lasswell was smart enough to know that power does not define the limits of morality. Rather, it was the porous nature of morality that permitted the expansion of the instruments of war, revolution, and aggression throughout the twentieth century.

Having had the privilege of knowing Lasswell as a latter-day colleague and sometime publisher of his work, I also had the advantage of knowing that he spoke in private as he wrote in public: a practitioner of social research and a believer in political democracy.

Works by Harold Lasswell

Essays on the Garrison State
Politics: Who Gets What, When and How
Psychopathology and Politics
The Signature of Power
World Revolutionary Elites

28

Peter Lengyel:
The Anti-Bureaucratic Bureaucrat

Peter Lengyel was born in Hungary, raised in Australia, educated in England (the University of London) and the United States (Harvard University), and lived beautifully in France. This condition, sometimes described as "half-packed, will travel," was the fate of numerous Jews in a Central Europe gone mad who became an easy prey for fascism. In his own life, Peter Lengyel illustrated the benefits of democratic institutions: the right to be left alone by authorities in charge. I have long believed that the immense currents that buffeted those who came to play a role in postwar reconstruction of academic as well as social institutions also shaped Peter's beliefs, and intellectuals like him.

Because of his worldliness, and his ability to navigate a variety of languages with remarkable ease and fluency, Peter Lengyel was a natural candidate to serve as editor of the *International Social Science Journal*—a UN publication. He held this post for thirty years. The journal was started in 1949, four years after the establishment of UNESCO (United Nations Educational, Scientific, and Cultural Organization) which itself was one of the very first offshoots of the United Nations. Both the United Nations and UNESCO were launched in 1945. Lengyel's first wife was an American. The marriage ended in divorce. His second wife was German, and she survives him. Although Peter was an editor, it would be improper to view him as an entrepreneur. Throughout his life he was a paid functionary, a bureaucrat if you will, of the United Nations, or at least an agency devised by the UN to disburse findings and identify issues that made the world one. If such a mission was farfetched in terms of achievable goals, then at least it put on display an appreciation of the shared nature of human concerns. Peter was in the forefront of a cluster of fine social scientists within the French and European UNESCO commissions. They included English critic of contemporary mores and manners Richard Hoggart, Elizabeth Crawford of the International

Social Science Council, and Jean-Jacques Salomon of the European Council of Economic Advisors.

Since so much of Peter's life was coincidental with the final stages of Soviet dominance of East Europe, and the continuing belief in Marxist-Leninist teaching as the inevitable replacement for, rather than an integrated portion of, the social sciences, his tasks as editor of UNESCO's premier journal were hardly simple. Squaring the best of western social science with the worst of communist dogma was not exactly an easy trick. But there they were—Claude Levi-Strauss, Simon Kuznets, Jan Tinbergen, Paul Lazarsfeld, Peter Wilmott, and hosts of others, rubbing shoulders with Soviet apparatchiks writing on command. As an observer of Peter, as well a contributor to his journal, I always felt that Peter's most challenging task was to make the Soviets a lot better through judicious weeding and avoidance of risky subject areas, while making Western social science a little bit less so by the same process of selective editing and ideological avoidance.

By a blend of bile and guile, Peter and his journal managed to raise many large-scale global issues. These ranged from communication to crime, and he presented them in a way that enhanced the reputation of the social sciences overall. It took special talent and skill to accomplish such extraordinary ends. And I suspect that his effectiveness was enhanced by the unique circumstances of Peter's upbringing. He was a child of two world wars—and thus a witness to European history. He accomplished his tasks by a public display of civility and courtesy that, while not easily fitting into Peter's feisty temperament, enabled the social science show to go on—and also helped him acquire new recruits in dangerous areas. In an atmosphere of "unipolarity" it might be hard to appreciate just how complex was his understanding of UNESCO. After all, Lengyel had to factor into consideration radical revolutionary regimes in China, Cuba, and Vietnam, no less than those of Russia and Eastern Europe did. And if suspicions were neither quelled nor erased by his judicious work, then at least they were mitigated in part by the efforts of this amazingly adroit figure.

Lengyel was an advocate of globalism when that term was still very much in fashion with the Left. He was involved with the World Society Foundation. The linkage between political movements and technological evolution throughout intrigued him. A key to his later thinking was his belief that the resurgence of religious values was often connected with the legitimization of private property. At the same time, the centrality of human rights legitimated pluralistic, democratic societies. Lengyel saw things in a Giambattista Vico-like manner, as a series of recurrent cycles of economic and political systems, each taking place at different times in the technological transformations of an age. In this way, waves of open and closed societies, stagnation and innovation were explained by technological breakthroughs. In a somewhat modified materialist conception of history, he held that not the genius of intellectuals but the everyday discoveries of ordinary people served as the motor of human history.

Lengyel saw the role of the international social scientist as an extension of the role of the United Nations as such. Diplomacy rather than confrontation were the hallmark of this style of work. But his work involved placating or quieting political regimes that were rightly suspicious of the consequences of open research, much less open societies as such. The challenge for people like Lengyel was to work with repugnant anti-democratic regimes while at the same time preaching the values of open and democratic approaches to problem solving. How Lengyel and others achieved this became a task unto itself: the search for large-scale concerns that would not threaten the power base of regimes, while advancing the concerns of an international organization grounded in democratic theory.

The near insuperable charge of Lengyel and others was to stand for social science and against restrictive political regimes. One way he performed his task was to raise the issues covered to such a general level that even the most backward of regimes would feel advantaged rather than menaced. On the presumption that all systems are concerned with the threat of war, famine, and crime he treated these large-scale issues with broad, impressionistic strokes, and some statistical embellishments where possible. The central difficulty of the social science as bureaucrat was that at the level of explanation. Large-scale abstractions like war, crime, and oppression broke down in the trench warfare of ideology. The radical wing saw war, famine, and crime as a function of imperialism and capitalism in advanced stages, whereas democratic societies had middle-range or at least far less global explanations for events.

Ultimately, even the hint of a scientific consensus collapsed in Lengyel's journal. And he knew as much. For instance, issues arose concerning the freedom of the press. Totalitarian regimes insisted that social science reporters observe decent standards of class values and regime sensibilities. For the most part those in the communications field within regimes in the democratic societies rightly perceived and understood such constraints on reporters not to be an effort to instill a higher type of ethics, but to allow for a lower level of empirical results. Interestingly the breakup of the Soviet Empire sharpened rather than weakened such debates on "ethic of responsibility." The emissaries of the so-called Third World took up the concerns of the Soviets and their allies as their own. It was far simpler to blame the old long-departed colonial powers for poverty, child slavery, and ethnic disenfranchisement than the contemporary despots in charge of these regimes. Increasingly, far from being able to serve as an agent of healing, Peter was forced into a combative role, into a forthright break with the bureaucratic administrative apparatus of that tiny sector of the world organization he had worked for so tirelessly and in the end so helplessly.

Over and against the pleasant fictions of "dependency theory," a credo adopted by UNESCO as its own, Lengyel began a review of the administrative apparatus of UNESCO itself. He understood the rise of ideology within the organization as an effort to disguise its growing antipathy to western values, and especially to the United States. While Lengyel was no great admirer of the American way of life, neither was he fool enough to see all problems of the Third World emanating from Washington DC. He was torn between his own anti-Americanism and his firm loyalty to the principles and premises of social science, nowhere better practiced than in the United States. Under such strains, the need for intellectual choice finally overrode his efforts to find a consensus. Peter's final years were thus tumultuous. He made a clear break with his stewardship of the UNESCO journal of social science, and finally with the UN organization as such.

His break, which took place in 1984, was framed not in political terms, but in the breakdown of professionalism with the organization. As he puts it in the Preface to his memoir on *The Unesco Experience*, "The organization had been despoiled by breaching the bulwark of functionalism, and by the destruction of professionalism at both the level of programming and that of project execution." He went on to say that, "I write more often in sorrow than in anger, having been witness to the virtual collapse of an undertaking to which I devoted most of my professional energies. And I uphold UNESCO's own constitution where it refers to the 'unrestricted pursuit of objective truth' and to the 'free exchange of ideas and knowledge as a means for the purposes of mutual understanding.'"

Peter's book on "the UNESCO experience" gave expression to his strong side. At the end, it was an appeal to thew the Weberian notion of science as a vocation in its own right, apart from politics. His was a belief that social science was best when seen as an objective or scientific expression, rather than as a handmaiden of any particular regime. That his own break coincided with the United States' break with UNESCO did not exactly serve Peter well. Indeed, he was at great pains to distinguish his position from that of the administration in Washington that refused to honor its dues commitments to the organization. But the fact was that on a personal level the split was seen as an extension of the larger struggle between those who saw UNESCO as an ideological extension of developing areas, and those who viewed it as a focus for the intellectual coming together of all peoples.

What was delivered in hortatory style, with abstract slogans as the frontispiece, disguised realm, long-smoldering struggles defining the nature of scientific and cultural struggles as such. UNESCO rivalries were simply a microcosm in a struggle already well underway in the United States between the social sciences as an ideological expression of the search for equity, and an older view of social research as an attempt to understand rather than to influence the main currents in the social world. In such a world, championing the cause of the American Indians, the Brazilian natives of the Amazon, the peace loving peoples of Vietnam, flew in the face of a social science tradition in which good and evil is less an attribute of systems than of individuals. Lengyel made the choice for science—and in so doing, he lost an UNESCO platform that he had long viewed as sacred. In one fell swoop, Lengyel lost a career and a constituency.

What is fascinating about Lengyel is his "premature," indeed cautious, repudiation of left totalitarianism. He may well have been one of the very first French or European Left intellectuals to begin the long and painful march away from socialism as a dictatorship of the political class toward a classical liberalism that made room for the private sector and opposition parties. The fashionable world of Jean Paul Sartre, Maurice Merlau-Ponty, and *Les Temps Modernes* circle had already shown some serious cracks—with the absence of anything more than repression from China to Cuba. But the events of

1989 were at least the equivalent of those of 1789 in announcing closure to dynastic regimes—whether based on monarchy or family. The winds of doctrinal change did not easily reach UNESCO— which had become captive to an anti-Americanism that bordered on the ludicrous. Under the pressure of corrupt Third World states, even failed attacks on the American Indians by General George Custer became the source of concerns and celebrations.

In such a world, Lengyel witnessed firsthand the subversion of UNESCO's mission, its capitulation to militarists and despots of all types. Affirmative action at UNESCO meant filling posts with questionably qualified individuals from new nations that had barely established institutions of higher learning, rather than the Euro-centered traditions of its founding period. The work of then UNESCO Director-General, Amadou-Mahtar M'Bow (1974-1987), also involved a none too subtle critique of Israel, as some sort of cultural and scientific outpost of Europe without a legitimacy of its own. This fissure was one of many that came to light when the United States officially quit UNESCO in 1983. UNESCO's transformation from an agency of social science to one of social ideology had become evident. Even so, it took a lot for the United States to take such a precipitous step, particularly because the Cold War was in decline. In such an environment, Lengyel's days at UNESCO and its journal of social science were numbered. He was a man deprived of an ideological base to start with, and a career to end with.

Reflecting on his life and career is less a study in success, than one in personal courage. Peter Lengyel elected to resign not with a whimper, but with a *cri de couer*. His is also a lesson in the values of that medieval institution known as the University—a place in which tenure means the exercise of control by those who teach, one in which different voices are not simply tolerated, but necessary to fulfill the terms of its ultimate goals. In agencies of government, in policy instruments of international organizations, such safeguards do not exist. One is left with individuals being either carried on the winds of doctrine, or leaving the scene of battle in confusion or worse. Lengyel was no simple victim. He neither sought nor received sympathy for the honorable performance of his duties. He was, for all of his marginality to academic agencies, a central actor in the century of social science. But to his lasting credit, he was proved to be much more—a courageous contributor to that creative period in social science.

Works by Peter Lengyel

Conflicts and New Departures in World Society (edited with Volker Bornschier)
International Social Science: The UNESCO Experience
Waves, Formation and Values in the World System (edited with Volker Bornschier)

29

Max Lerner:
Journalist as Political Educator

Of all the individuals invited to the dais, I probably have the least claim on your attention. For my personal knowledge of Max was slight and essentially confined to the final decade of his life. That said, I am honored to speak briefly on the meaning of Max Lerner's life—as the "youngster" of this august group. Max was of the generation of my parents, and like them, was born in Russia. In his case, it was Minsk. Also like them, his family, prior to emigration, was close to the socialist Bund. Then again, Jews had a choice: orthodoxy and traditionalism, or radicalism and modernism. It is hardly unexpected that being only five years old when he arrived in the United States, he acquired a taste for the Western Enlightenment tradition. In some sense, the mix of family values and a new national outlook gave him a cosmopolitan outlook—one that embraced being liberal in ideology, anti-statist in politics, and deeply Jewish in religion.

Transaction Publishers, the firm I have directed for the past thirty years, has embarked on a series of reissuances of twentieth-century American masters of thought. They include publication in new editions of the complete or in some instances extensive work of such figures as Walter Lippmann, Thorstein Veblen, Walter Laqueur, Peter Drucker, and Lewis Feuer, to name some of its more prominent figures. Having published five of Max's classic works already, I believe that he very much belongs in the company of these special people. Like the others, he managed by dint of energy, effort, and raw talent to transcend all sorts of parochialisms and reach audiences from many and diverse spheres of social life in order to achieve a new universalism.

But what exactly is it that gives special meaning to Max's contribution; or more bluntly, what is it that permits one to wager with confidence that his work will endure beyond the present moment, or even beyond the end of the century? I think that the answer is to be found in Max's enduring faith in the law. Writing in a period and in a culture where raw power was elevated to a special status, he uniquely focused on those classical figures from Alexis de Tocqueville to Oliver Wendell Holmes that sought to define both American national character and American political legitimacy. Coming from a Czarist world in which the rule of law was more observed in the breach than the practice, and this followed by a Leninist-Stalinist world in which the law even as myth was a function of partisan party politics, the sense of law as justice was especially critical. Lerner's formal training at Yale University and then at Washington University—two schools at which a legal education was prominent—gave intellectual substance to his instincts.

From all quarters, left and right, from Mills to Burnham, the emphasis of the American Century was on a reconciliation of democracy with power. The problem became how to curb no less than exercise power as either executive or legislative privilege and even excess. But it was Lerner's special talent to appreciate the limits of power as defining the American Civilization. Those limits were located in the law, in the delicate web of rights and obligations that American people are dedicated to preserve and enlarge. Lerner may have learned much from radical and conservative traditions, but he was suspicious of extremism. He understood its harsh consequences for the Jewish people, for minorities in general. And this suspicion of extremism also moved him to a high regard for the law as a source of political legitimacy as well as decision-making, something that both radical and reactionary theorists tend to minimize if not altogether disregard.

It is not simply the legal or juridical edifice that Max uniquely understood, it is the special compassion of a people capable of transforming law into justice. For without justice, the law is a punitive tool externally imposed. With justice, the law is the internal expression of a tradition, and of a good people. Max was acutely aware of the extent to which the law was a touchstone for doing good or evil. Even the worst of authoritarian regimes cloaked themselves in legal garments. As a result, and not unlike the tradition he imbibed from Aristotle to Dewey, legal theory was seen to be alive only when embedded in ethical practice.

In this special concern with justice, Max was able to fuse with remarkable ease a Jewish covenantal faith, an American pragmatic credo, and a European conscience of history. He gave meaning to the notion of the liberal imagination far beyond arguments about benefits and welfare nets. He did this in a variety of guises: as a scholar of American civilization, as a newspaper columnist for *The New York Post*, and as a voice for a liberalism divested of totalitarian dross. In the performance of these multiple roles, Max was subject to withering criticisms: he was denounced as a "celebrationist" of American society without seeing its faults, as a liberal who saw little need for affirmative responses to historic injustices, and as a popularizer without intellectual depth. The actual body of work that Max has left behind gives the lie for much of this criticism. Because of the historic crossroads of liberalism, from a theory of equity to the practice of pluralism and cultural difference, I believe this to be less a memorial service honoring Max Lerner's life than a gathering of friends and colleagues. We are all seeking to become wiser and more worthy in our own lives in remembering that liberalism is a view of the world in which we all have a place at the starting gate, but finishing at different places. The option of converting liberalism into a doctrine of state power in which we all end up at the same place is a view of social life that Lerner vigorously opposed. His work helps to ease what appears to be an endless task in our choice of values and goals.

Works by Max Lerner

Ideas are Weapons
Magisterial Imagination
The Mind and Faith of Justice Holmes
Thomas Jefferson: America's Philosopher-King
Tocqueville and American Civilization

30

Marion J. Levy, Jr.:
Modernizing International Relations

Contrary to unpopular belief, Marion J. Levy, Jr. did not arrive at
Princeton University some 250 years ago when the school was first
given its charter. That is not to say that Marion had any disrespect
for his University. Quite the contrary, he was fond of saying how at
home he was in Princeton as a town no less than as a University. In
quieter moments he would confess that not too many institutions of
higher learning would have found him an easy pill to swallow. He
displayed an admixture of pride in his home University and displea-
sure with other institutions, noting that invitations to other institutions came to him far more sparsely than his quality of work warranted. In this judgment, made without a trace of vanity, he was
entirely correct.

A key to understanding Marion was his background in Texas. He
shared outsider status with his colleague of student days at the University of Texas, C. Wright Mills, an important compatriot. It is hard
to say who was the rarer bird: Wright, the Catholic choirboy from
Waco whose father was an insurance agent, or Marion, the Jewish
son of a quite prestigious lawyer in Galveston. But the experience of
Texas gave to both men a sense of looking at a world with which
neither was entirely comfortable. In my biography of Mills, I also
noted that "the late 1930s produced figures who went on to make
substantial contributions to sociology. Marion J. Levy, Jr. was a student in the economics department. William J. Goode came from the
sociology department. Each went on to become a significant figure
in the development of American sociology."

His background in Texas and its major university also gave Marion
training ground in grass-roots American liberalism at its authentic
best. The Chicago-trained Clarence E. Ayres in economics, George
V. Gentry in sociology, and David Miller in philosophy, made Texas
an oasis of free and unfettered thought. To this day Texas as a learning place stands apart from most Southern institutions. It is impor-

tant to take note of this since not a few of Marion's colleagues in later life confused his sophistication with some sort of hidebound conservatism, presumably stemming from his Texas roots. Nothing could be further from the truth. Marion was a deep-seated liberal, whose career choices and intellectual pursuits revealed as much. His study of modernization, especially in the contexts of China and Japan, derived not so much from a regard for traditionalism, but rather his interest in how deeply rooted religious and cultural norms are transcended in the forging of modern nations. He was especially interested because this took place in contexts that were far removed from New England visions of the Protestant Ethic.

Marion's Texas roots were mediated by post-graduate work at Harvard, where he went after graduating from Texas. The two schools shared an early passion for interdisciplinary work in social research— but the cast of characters differed immensely. The bridge for Marion was institutional economics; it connected Clarence Ayres with Talcott Parsons. And if such general theory had more political bite with Ayres, it also had far more compelling features with Parsons. Unlike others who came under Parsons' powerful influence, Marion did not especially take to heart the formalization procedures and the pattern variables. Rather, he absorbed the more subtle art of Parsons: of connecting general theory with the full range of psychological experience and anthropological exploration. Similar claims could be made by other senior figures at Harvard such as Sorokin, Henderson, and Homans. But it was Parsons' ability to link the specific to large-scale theorizing, devoid of extrinsic, ideological agendas that was especially attractive to Marion and deepened his interest in theory construction in social life.

Both the various institutes of area studies at Harvard and the receptivity to such worldly concerns at the Woodrow Wilson School of Public and International Affairs at Princeton offered an environment that encouraged Marion to think big about large subjects. The Woodrow Wilson School is a major center of policy studies, which has encouraged many younger scholars to move beyond departmental parochialism. And there are few subjects less parochial than China and Japan. In the process of modernization of these giant polar forces, Marion saw the best prospects for the realization of democratic order. And where so-called dependency theorists saw only imperialist connivance and conspiracy, Marion in a far more accurate appraisal, saw western developmental patterns as the key to escape from poverty, want, and oppression. That vision also allowed Marion to avoid the drumbeat of communist declarations of power to the people through long marches, hard labor, and ideological indoctrination. Needless to say, as the Cold War dragged its way to a weary end, those acolytes of the Left subjected Marion to endless charges of being a reactionary and even worse.

But Marion lived long enough to have the last laugh—perhaps many laughs. Japan emerged as a Western-style, modern industrial state, admittedly force-fed by American military might. Then came the collapse of Soviet communism in Russia to be replaced in fits and starts by a free-market economy with a nascent democratic political system. Finally, and above all, China emerged from a quiet post-Maoist revolution, in which the four pillars of modernization were replaced by the hundred flowers with the same distinct totalitarian odor. Each of these vindicated Marion's faith in Asian capacities, but not incidentally, his considerable belief in his own two-volume magisterial work on *Modernization*. As a proper Veblenian, as filtered through his beloved master, Clarence E. Ayres, Marion liked what he saw: nations moving into the modern era, but without the trappings of opulence and excess that he felt characterized recent development patterns in Europe and especially the United States. In the end Marion reduced the neo-Leninist dependency theorists to a shadow. Modernization theory emerged triumphant, not as another school of dogmatic thought, but as the work of serious people who combined a sense of economic history with appreciation of ethnographic research.

Let me conclude on a more personal note. What I most admired about Marion is that in contrast to most post-Parsonians, he was a high-risk taker. Marion's intellectual risk could get him in hot water. In the teeth of pedestrian radical feminist readings, he asserted in *Maternal Influence: The Search for Social Universals*, originally published as *Our Mother-Tempers*, that men and women do indeed have real differences—biological and sociological. That he argued within the unity of the human species that these differences weigh heavily on the side of the superiority of the female over the male seems to have been overlooked by his fulminating ever on-guard critics, who could not distinguish the idea of difference from inequity. Perhaps his preference for the female was grounded in respect for the key woman in his life—Joy, his partner in life and especially the world of the Komondan, his daughter Dore, and earlier, his mother, and other strong Texas women.

That essentially quotidian observations on stratification would bring down on Marion's head an outpouring or criticism is a sad reflection of how the world of male and female has been reduced to ill-disguised preferences and personal choices. Marion knew full well that declaring human beings to be below angels, and closer to animals, was something that many did not care to hear. Furthermore, his assertion that human beings are thus subject to the laws of science was also something not everyone was delighted to admit. As a result, Marion earned the wrath of non-believing extremists and believing moderates alike.

In his work on Asian development, *Modernization and the Structure of Societies*, Marion avoided reductionism of differences to some mythical meeting of East and West in some abstracted cultural realm. He uniquely appreciated the extent to which Asia's drive to modernization was a result of how deeply its societies knew that their defeats in the prior century and a half were the result of economic backwardness—not cultural differences. East or West, a price must be paid for catching up. That is the essential driving spirit behind Marion's emphasis on modernization. His vision was well understood by Asian elites, if only dimly appreciated by Western intellectuals. Marion thought of his work as a contribution to science and not to policy. Indeed, his closing words in the Epilogue to this classic work indicate a deeply Hobbesian streak—what might be called a plague on both the houses of policy and ideology in the development literature. In his own words, "Life under modern conditions and under conditions moving in that direction is not likely to become solitary, poor, nasty, brutish and short. It is far more likely to become crowded, affluent, nasty, brutish, and long." These are words of someone who, right or wrong, never bothered with pandering to the crowd—public or professional.

I have chosen to speak of Marion's work since what goes into the word is still what lasts. It is also my way of saying to Marion, somewhat belatedly, that my criticisms of him in 1965 were arguably correct on the frills of presentation, or on form as it were. Emulating Parsons' substantive work was one thing, emulating his literary manners (or lack thereof) was something else again. But Marion was right and I was wrong on matters of substance. The fact of the matter is that the world is a far more unitary place than I understood it to be at that time. My Second World of socialism has shriveled into "third stream" styles of free-market capitalism, while the Third World never did settle on options that made possible full development. As a result, the nations of Asia, Africa, and Latin America moved either into the free-market orbit, or into statist regimes that viewed the economy as a plaything subject to management from above.

Globalization may be a slogan for those who hold placards aloft, but it is the essential content of the structure of societies for people with Marion Levy's vision. And while we may still speak of three *styles* of social and political development, it is of utmost importance to recognize that there is but one unitary *substance* of economic development—and the modernization process captures that distinction better than any other analytic framework. So at the end of the day, Marion—and it is indeed the end of the day and the start of the long journey into the eternal night—I stand before your family, friends, and our colleagues, to admit the error of my ways. More importantly, I celebrate the accuracy of your way. You can rest easy now. Our debate is finally at an end. You won this round on development, even as the battle continues.

Works by Marion J. Levy, Jr.

The Family Revolution in Modern China
Maternal Influence
Modernization and the Structure of Societies (2 volumes)
Modernization: Latecomers and Survivors
The Structure of Society

31

Seymour Martin Lipset:
The Social Uses of Anomaly

Let me preface my remarks by saying that we are here to honor a living, breathing colleague. My great concern, and in this I am sure that I speak for my colleagues as well, is that any imputation of a post-mortem be avoided. Indeed, I would like to believe that Marty will review these various contributions and make his own assessments—critical or approvingly. The fact that he is not present in this conference hall should not deter us from speaking frankly and forthrightly. Marty merits nothing less. What binds us all is the sure knowledge that the work of Lipset speaks to us in personal as well as professional ways. That he has touched so many of us in both the private and public realms is itself a testimonial of the magnitude of his contribution to the field of political sociology. So it is in that spirit of a collegial dialogue that I offer these remarks. Let us hope that one year from now a session of one person can be held, at which S. M. Lipset, will provide rebuttals and responses to those of us herein gathered.

As the twentieth century moved from a clerical to a secular society, at least we thought it was moving in that direction, certain changes in celebratory patterns became evident. Memorial services, retirement benefits, and international festschriften have become the norm. We shift in offering our respect from overtly religious rituals to supposedly a humanist homage, or what a colleague of mine from the "Chicago School" persuasion artlessly refers to as performance ceremonies. Given the nature of sociology, the trick is not to emphasize the obvious secular role of the discipline in human affairs, but to the contrary, to return to basics, to locate the need for a spiritual place in the hearts and minds of secularists. That is what I should like to attempt in this tribute to our colleague, Seymour Martin Lipset.

My own iron rule in this business of growing old and giving homage is first, to remember the time-honored belief that one should speak well of the person retiring and being celebrated; at the very least to tender him the benefit of our intellectual doubts. Second, to be certain that one knows whereof one speaks—a simple-minded *Who's Who* recitation of the diplomas one holds or institutions at which a person taught is not exactly the same as a clear-eyed statement of the belief of the generalized other. Finally, public occasions should never be used to toot one's own horn, or institute one's own importance at a time for celebrating another person's achievement.

Through thick and thin, I have adhered strictly to these self-imposed guidelines. However even the best of rules come up short in relation to real life people. And in the case of Seymour Martin Lipset— a scholar and a social scientist with whom it has been my honor to be associated for the past forty years—these guidelines must yield to existential reality. These realities are that we two were from the outset and remain, as theologians like to say, in eternal dialogue.

To speak of Seymour Martin Lipset and his work requires that I speak of my own work as well. It is not simply that we both pioneered the world of political sociology, but that we did so while often diverging in the sharpest possible ways: over the nature of the evidence, and no less, the adequacy of the theory. In one area after another this was the case. But I must note that Marty Lipset was uniformly in the vanguard. For the most part, I found myself saddled with the proverbial battering ram trying to slow down if not derail the vanguard.

The one time that Lipset and I had the opportunity to hook up and lock horns in a two-day face-off resulted in a less than memorable work called *Dialogues on American Politics*. I suspect that several reviews that think of American politics as a series of op-ed comments did not exactly help the book along. Differences were expressed as to the nature of the developmental process inside and beyond the democratic system, but the work revealed too little of the depth of the dialogue actually raging between us. From my perspective, and I suppose his as well, it was almost as if a private war was going on for the minds of the social science community, while the public statements resulting from that war were couched in conventional terms of polite academic debate.

Perhaps this politesse was due to the obvious fact that by the time the 1970s were winding down, we were bound to each other not only in dialogue, but also in deep commitment to the democratic order of things that made dialogue possible in the first place. The fissures within American society that surfaced with the catastrophic failure of the Vietnam War only heightened a shared realization that the legitimacy of the system was not quite invulnerable after all. Ours was less a world of victor or vanquished, but of two old prize-fighters displaying their wares for a sometimes jaded and bored public. But the choice, the decision on who was correct—indeed if either of us was—lay with the publics we serviced. Despite self-declared appeals to rules of evidence, Marty and I were heirs to an older humanistic and renaissance tradition, rather than the experimental tradition in which truth disposes of error, while learning is a building block of facts leading to truths that in turn make possible further experimentation and explanation.

I suspect that our early shared encounter with socialism, and a consequent rejection of a then fashionable psychologism as an explanatory device, allowed both of us to roam the social universe for meaningful topics. In sharp contradistinction to current emphases on precisely defined areas of research and expertise, where reputations are made in exact, bounded areas, and not incidentally where risks are avoided in exact proportion to such specialties, Lipset and I both took on major themes and concerns. We did so with scarcely a look back at professional boundaries. While the patina of work supported by evidence was also a shared premise for us both, neither of us permitted the lack of evidence to rationalize a lack of opinion! Or to put the matter more tactfully, we each drew sustenance from a body of evidence that was likely to support our respective views.

What made Lipset's work so fascinating and endlessly interesting to me—and still does—is his keen sense of the anomalies of social life. He has an uncanny knack for looking at the obvious and delving into why the obvious does not take place. This is a giant leap beyond the "Dahrendorf Principle" that sociology begins with asking the question why. Rather, Lipset examines the reasons for asking questions in the first place. So whether it is why the United States failed to go down the socialist roads of Europe, or why Canada shows such distinctive cultural differences from the United States, or many other like-minded considerations—Lipset works hard to turn over the stones on which so many who came before him stubbed their toes. In this way, Lipset sets the parameters for discourse, for determining whether what appears obvious is indeed the case or is not the case. If at times this means sitting atop the shoulders or shooting at the feet of the giant, then at least it takes us to an operational guideline of what constitutes greatness—and in our discipline Lipset merits that term. Let me now turn to putting some meat on the dry bones of these observations.

Revolution and Counter-Revolution (Lipset). For Lipset, the differences between Canada and the United States can best be explained by what has come to be called the Imperial Connection. That is to say, the relatively high degree of acceptance of the Church of England, the strict sense of hierarchical stratification, the more homogeneous racial characteristics, and the continued sense of being a British colony, all helped set the tone for the counter-revolution. This led to sharp differences in levels of criminality (low), degrees of divorce (low), and state-mandated social services (high). For the most part, Lipset's Canadian mosaic paradigm is based on the dominant Anglophone areas, and not the French-speaking province of Quebec.

"The Hemispheric Connection" (Horowitz). For Horowitz, differences between Canada and the United States are greatly exaggerated. They are more a function of space and place, that is, in less friendly physical terrain, than of cultural ties to the British Commonwealth. This position emphasizes the Continental connection, the proximity of Canada to the United States. Thus, levels of criminality are getting closer over time, degrees of divorce are similar over time, and state-mandated services are becoming similar as the United States expands such services. Differences between the two nations remain real, but are functions of policy rather than tradition. Essentially, modernization draws the Anglophone and Francophone clusters in Canada closer, causing cultural hegemony and political differentiation at the same time.

Elites in Latin America (Lipset). The essential driving force of development in Latin America has been its elites, both civil and military. The relative deprivation of such elites, their frustration by populist and pseudo-populist forces, has thwarted the course of normal capital formation and development. There has been an absence of rewards, or opportunity structures the culture of work, i.e., the Protestant Ethic. As a result, high educational achievement translated into economic frustration instead of integration. Thus to examine both the successes and failures of the hemisphere is to study the formation of elites and modes of stratification inherited from European societies.

Masses in Latin America (Horowitz). The essential characteristic of Latin American development is more a function of mass instead of class, and more a consequence of interests than of values. The level of dispossession of large groups from the financial system, the protracted strength of rural poverty and absence of life chances, and the consequent gap between urban capitalism and rural feudalism has frustrated autonomous development in the region. At the same time, elites, instead of investing in national economic development, became part of an international network of advanced systems. Latin America displayed the result of the absence of risk taking by its elites and the presence of fatalism as a culture in its masses.

Rebellion in the University (Lipset-Altbach). The changing character of university life is a function of extending to the classroom the liberal values of the larger society. The radicalization of student life, the emergence of activism, is essentially an effort to extend to the recipients of education the largesse of the educational establishment itself. It is an effort to create a larger pie and a culture of inclusiveness in the liberal society. As a consequence, it is best to see the student movements as part of a tradition of rebellion within essentially legal frameworks, with a corresponding attempt to extend the revolution of rising expectations to new groups. The location of rebellion in students of social science and humanities and the absence of such tendencies in students of business, engineering, and the hard sciences underscores for Lipset the shallow grounds of such rebellion.

The Knowledge Factory (Horowitz-Friedland). The changing character of university life is a function of its transformation from a feudal to a capitalist base. The student, far from being integrated into a system of liberal values, becomes alienated from the new university emphasis on bottom-line thinking and an emphasis on industrial innovation requirements. The demands of mass education, in contrast to class education in European lands, leads to demands for rapid processing of students without much concern for quality of work. Issues of gender, race, and ethnicity heighten the strains with university life, and make such strains permanent features. Instead of liberalization, the university becomes a fulcrum for radicalization—again deepening the differences between administration, teaching, and learning functions.

The First New Nation (Lipset). A major interest and concern of Lipset has always been to explain why the United States is different from Europe in political outcome—in spite of having similar capitalist economic bases. In short, what is it about the political process in North America that has prevented the politics of the street from replacing the politics of legislative process? He located this in a nation that began with a political testament (the Bill of Rights and the Constitution) and developed its economy to conform to a politics of compassion and constraint. He also held that the American experience emphasized religious pluralism, broad public education (and through this upward mobility), and trade unionism rooted in economic issues rather than general strikes. As a result, *The First New Nation* describes a new civilization in the making, a conscious invention rather than an accidental or mystical fusion of linked inheritances.

Ideology and Utopia in the United States (Horowitz). The very choice of the Mannheim phrase indicates a view of the United States not quite as sharply demarcated from the European experience as Lipset holds. To start with, the larger issues of political power, economic system, and military might provide linkages to the European experience. Beyond that, the solidification of the United States did take place. It did so, however, not as a result of the founding fathers, but more so of the Civil War. The solidification of America was brought about not so much by Washington and his decision against a third term as president (or dictator) but by Lincoln and the decision to hold the nation together against states' rights and the slavery system of the South. In this view, what distinguishes the United States are the low level of ideological commitments and the high level of utopian expectations.

Consensus and Conflict in Political Sociology (Lipset). Political life is defined by value preferences and prejudices. These are played out in the advanced cultures on a party canvas. Political ideologies of left, center, and right are defined by these valuational grounds. In democratic systems, class values are absorbed in larger patterns of national considerations. In dictatorships, such class values become predominant. The evolution of political culture is generally toward increasing political autonomy from economic activities. Western systems tend toward centrist politics as a function of social consensus. The party system in America tends to underscore such functions. The legal order enshrines that consensus as a mechanism of legitimation and rationalization of society as a whole.

Foundations of Political Sociology (Horowitz). Political life is defined largely by interests—national, racial, religious, and ethnic. These are played out in advanced cultures as a clash of nations and regions. The key to politics is not the electoral process, but in examining how societies respond to the needs of law and order. Democracy and dictatorship alike establish military outposts and diplomatic initiatives. They are essentially the defining polarities of modern politics. As a result, a conflict model, rather than one of consensus, comes to define modern politics. Systems are changed more in war than in ballots. The legal order enshrines an ideology of the dominant authorities, and these serve as universal guideposts within the system—but not beyond that system. The political leadership establishes a mechanism of rationalism and legitimization that may vary from pure dictatorial rule, to a variety of subterfuges, that at the other end may yield democratic rule and electoral political and mass participation.

American Pluralism and the Jewish Community (Lipset). Lipset held to a lifelong interest in Jewish organizational life. For the most part, his work in this area centered on the Jewish experience in America, the ability of the Jewish people to become part of the political process and not simply an economic factor as in the European experience. Indeed, Lipset saw the American Jewish experience as the model of upward mobility for all Americans in the area of education and scientific advancement. Another element in Lipset's work was the role of the Jewish cadres in radical movements and groups, not the least how they migrated to left-wing causes. He held that Jewish universalism spared them the conventional parochialism of voting their interests, while instead voting their values. This dovetailed neatly with his overall belief in the role of values in shaping the political culture along Weberian lines.

Israeli Ecstasies and Jewish Agonies (Horowitz). My own emphasis was more on the Jewish experience in the Holocaust and in postwar European Jewish reclamation through national identification in Israel. There were important points of contact, such as the fact that the inability of European Jewry to play a role in the bureaucratic administrative apparatus served to make them vulnerable to attack, isolation, and ultimately annihilation. The emphasis on the Jewish factor was less national than global, that is, the diaspora of Jews to places like Argentina, France, and England, and the overall shift from religious to cultural and organizational identification with Jewish causes. The center of gravity in my work shifted from contemporary Israeli life to the Jewish American experience to the Holocaust as a defining hallmark of Jewry through the post-World War

Two epoch. If Lipset, following Sombart, was interested in the place of Jews in the development of capitalism and democracy, my own work centered on the place of Jews in the dreadful history of communism and fascism under dictatorship. That at any rate is the path my work took in *Taking Lives.*

Finally, an area of direct overlap is what Lipset, in an essay for a volume I edited on *Sociological Self Images*, described as his own odyssey from socialism to sociology as a defining set of beliefs and values. He felt keenly that the early training of communists, in particular the Stalinists, led them into economic pursuits and political reductionism, whereas the early identification with anti-authoritarian modes of socialism and social democracy, including the Trotskyists, led people such as himself into sociology. While Lipset has often been termed conservative, I find such a label hard to stick on him. Quite the contrary, his commitment to social democracy seems largely intact and certainly an extension of a general social welfare orientation to issues of minority rights and civil liberties. Lipset grew up in a CCNY in which political and ideological identification was important. His was the last prewar generation, and the most committed of all. But if colleagues of his such as Irving Kristol, Philip Selznick, Nathan Glazer, and Irving Howe tended to drift away from the sociological into the cultural, they all retained a lively sense of the politics of socialism. They also carried with them scars of conflicts that helped to define ideological battle lines for generations to come. But the spirit of liberalism rather than fanatic radicalism at one end or an avuncular conservatism at the other clearly fueled Lipset's driving belief system.

My own generation, following a decade later, is the first postwar generation, and the returning soldiers had their belly full of ideologies and abstractions. The strong impulse to social reform gave way to an equally strong impulse for technical training and personal advancement. Nevertheless, as the so-called Davis-Knickerbocker affair (involving demands for the resignation of two professors accused of racism and anti-Semitism respectively) demonstrated, it was not that the postwar generation of students at CCNY was disinterested in public affairs. However, their animosity toward racism and anti-Semitism was precisely that—an animus for specific inequality, not a search for utopian communist solutions. In such an environment, my own role was essentially non-political on campus. Communist and socialist student clubs were cut down to size by the Cold

War in the late 1940s. The big factor was seeing how the social sciences were to be integrated in some sort of unified positivist standpoint. Wittgenstein's *Tractatus* rather than Marx's *Das Kapital* was the guiding text. The very idea of the honors program in social science (embracing all the major disciplines plus philosophy), and the degree itself (i.e., the Bachelor of Science in social science) was the defining ideology. It was one that put far behind itself the notion of socialism as the fulfillment of the sociological dream. We were further caught in the swirl of Karl Popper's work on *The Open Society and its Enemies* rather than the materialist messianism of an earlier generation. Hence the turn away from communism and socialism was much less of rupture for my generation than for the one Marty lived through and conquered with great aplomb. For the post-World War Two world, social science was an instrument to advance policy, a remedial rather than revolutionary device. What it resisted from the earlier, or last generation before World War Two, was an emphasis on seeing social science as a general ideology, a substitute for the religion of an earlier generation.

Throughout, Marty and I worked in each other's ballpark. I contributed to his *Elites in Latin America*, and later gave the first Elsie Lipset Memorial address at Stanford on the subject of philo-Semitism. At the same time, Marty was always a steady contributor—indeed an early investor—to Transaction Publishers and in *Society* magazine. We can boast that no fewer than eight of his book titles were either initially released or reprinted by our publishing enterprise. Also, as I earlier noted, Marty contributed a major statement of an autobiographical sort on his move from socialism to sociology for *Sociological Self Images*, a volume I edited on behalf of Sage Publishers.

Beyond the sense of collegiality, however, there was something deeper than a respect for one another. It resides in a common respect, indeed love, for the history of the social sciences—for that which came before us that permits intelligent dialogue and differences to make sense, not only in the larger world, but also in the inner world of a profession. In a series of introductions written over a diverse time period, Marty showed this reverence for people ranging from Roberto Michels, Harriet Martineau, Moises Ostrogorski, as well as his beloved Max Weber. I probably paid more attention to the history of ideas in a broader philosophical canvas, but that is because Marty in turn paid closer attention to empirical issues in sociology ranging from industrial unionism to workplace democracy. At the end of the day, I have grown to a greater appreciation of values and elections. I would like to believe that he in turn has achieved a greater appreciation of interests and movements.

All of this is to indicate that while our differences were real, and some remain as intense as when first expressed, the sense of cordiality, civility, and fidelity to a common sociological culture was a constant denominator. Throughout the long night of difference there is a sense of mutual and sincere respect. We appreciated that the dialogue as such enriched us both, sharpened us both, and made the professional audience to whom we appealed for succor and support aware that options exist—even if differences sometimes obscured them. I realize that we have both been tarred and scarred with labels. But neither of us seems to have really suffered in any consequential way from the labeling process. We have struggled with each other, argued with each other, but above all, learned from each other. And at this level, as Michael Oakeshott might say, we have come to appreciate, influence, and ultimately enrich each other. May it always be thus between us.

Works by Seymour Martin Lipset

American Pluralism and the Jewish Community
The First New Nation
Political Man
Rebellion in the University
Revolution and Counterrevolution

32

Robert S. Lynd and Helen Merrell Lynd: The Sociological Couple Par Excellence

Robert Staughton Lynd might be described as the Sinclair Lewis of sociology. His books *Middletown* (Lynd & Lynd 1929) and *Middletown in Transition* (Lynd & Lynd 1937) provide the sociological flesh that makes Lewis' satiric classics, *Babbitt* and *Main Street*, comprehensible as studies in the culture and mores of mid-western America.

Lynd was born in New Albany, Indiana on September 26, 1892. His major research works, undertaken and coauthored with his wife Helen Merrell, were actually performed in Muncie, Indiana, not far from his birthplace. His background was modest, but he graduated from Princeton University in 1914, and from there went on to earn a Bachelor of Divinity degree at Union Theological Seminary in 1923. A doctorate from Columbia University was granted in 1931, after the publication and in recognition of the first Middletown study. Until his retirement in 1965, he was associated with Columbia. He died on November 1, 1970.

Lynd's first major job was as managing editor of *Publisher's Weekly,* the trade magazine of the publishing industry. His next position was director of the small city project of the Institute of Social and Religious Research, which directly, albeit modestly, underwrote the Muncie research. *Middletown* may be the first sociological work to be distributed and promoted to the general public as a trade book. According to Helen Lynd, the book was displayed in bookstore windows alongside the leading novels of the time. The relationship between his sociology and the quality of writing was at least partially due to his vocational background in publishing, then a rare training ground for a sociologist. Recalling him at the time of his death in 1970, Seymour Martin Lipset noted that Lynd not only "devoted an enormous amount of time to his students," but that he was always available to help them rewrite, edit, and even restructure their papers. His publishing experience clearly remained with Lynd as pedagogue and as researcher.

Today, Lynd would probably be described as an anthropologist of complex organizations. Certainly his work defies easy labeling. Not since Alexis de Tocqueville's *Democracy in America* (1835) have we had such a careful analysis of the daily life of America; middle America in this case. The book subjects one Indiana community to the same kind of intense scrutiny that de Tocqueville gave the entire United States. *Middletown* illumined, for a generation of social science, the essence of the American way of life. Probably no other single work published between World War I and World War II so precisely and devastatingly delineated what the nation had become. *Middletown* was described by H. L. Mencken as "one of the richest and most valuable documents ever concocted by an American sociologist"; and by Stuart Chase as "an unparalleled work: nothing like it has ever been attempted; no such knowledge of how the average American community works and plays has ever been packed within the covers of one book."

Middletown makes little conscious effort to posit the centrality of one variable or factor over another. It is divided into six large sections. The first, on the economy, documents "Getting a Living." The second and third sections are concerned with family life, linking problems of housing, child rearing, food, clothing, and schooling. The fourth, and probably the most innovative section, is on leisure. This material includes early mass communication research. It analyzes the leisure activities of Middle Americans in pictures and periodicals, selecting and viewing, precisely in terms of mass communication. The fifth section concerns religious observance and practices, analyzing varieties of Protestant worship, but also, showing how organizations such as the YMCA (Young Men's Christian Association) link religion to community. The notion of community organizes the final section, showing how community is related to the machinery of government. The very fragmentation of community points out the insignificance of bureaucracy in the social life of Middletown. These last sections clearly owe much to Lynd's activities in the mid-1920s as a missionary preacher in the oil fields of Montana.

The book took several years to produce. Robert Lynd lived in Middletown with his wife Helen for one-and-a-half years; their assistants lived there for an additional half-year. Tables imaginatively illustrate the book; and while some of the data provide only a careful reworking of state and national data, other tables concern sources of disagreement between children and their parents, and books borrowed in the adult department of the public library. These show an imaginative concern with intimate detail rare in the annals of sociology up to that time.

What gives added character to *Middletown* is its historical specificity. The Lynds provide a documentary accounting of the life of a town at two selected periods: 1890 and 1924, rather than attempting to do a detailed study of the history of the intervening years. Such cross-sectional analysis provides a sensitive appreciation of the cultural tension between past and present generations. Middletown is in retrospect best seen as an analysis of the secularization process in American society: a veritable model of why modernization occurs and how social change takes place in an advanced industrial society.

Middletown in Transition is another pathbreaking effort in a tradition of reevaluating and reanalyzing data. It examines what happened in the decade between 1924 and 1935. The Lynds took seriously critiques of their earlier work. Their follow-up study, while lacking some of the historical possibilities of the earlier effort, builds upon that earlier work and attempts to apply techniques that had evolved in social science in the intervening decade in sociological history. As John Madge sagaciously noted: "If Middletown had changed it is also necessary to substantiate the claim...that there had been a profound development in the thinking of the Lynds."

Not only did the Lynds return to study the same town; doing so they clearly changed their own estimates of what was important. The machinery of government, for example, was no longer subsumed under community activities, nor was religion given a whole section. It was reduced to a chapter. This reflected changing mores of American society, namely, progress in the secularization process that the Lynds discussed at the end of *Middletown*, and also a sense of new problems emerging in the depression of the 1930s. The world of Sinclair Lewis' early novels had broken down. Class bias gave way to class antagonisms, stating the facts yielded to making clear the sources of power. While Middletown's citizenry continued to retain the values by which it lived, the impact of economic chaos at home, and fascism and socialism abroad, compelled Middletown to face both ways. Trade unionism became acceptable; reluctant adaptation to the new world became inevitable. If the follow-up study ends on a note of uncertainty, taken together the *Middletown* studies remain a most significant record of this period in American social life. The Lynds's ability to weave ethnography, stratification, and quantitative data into a meaningful whole has rarely been equaled in sociological literature. One might wonder if their open-ended choice of methodologies makes such broad-ranging work currently suspect. There is strong evidence that Lynd himself had serious questions about how generalizable such field researches actually are.

In *Knowledge for What?* (1939), a book subtitled *The Place of Social Science in American Culture*, Lynd attempted to come to terms, indirectly at least, with a new methodological emphasis in American sociology. He argued that scholars have become technicians who would lecture on navigation while the ship goes down. This book has a bitter tone; it reveals pessimism that even if the new methodological sociologists should take the wheel, they would not really know how to steer a meaningful course. It is not that Lynd thought social scientists should go in for "pretentious soothsaying," still, he recognized that a sense of the fragility of the future should not result in the sorts of inhibitions that make broad-ranging social science research unpalatable.

Lynd clearly was a sociological pragmatist, urging a careful middle course between what C. Wright Mills was later to call "abstract empiricism" and "grand theory." This approach was underwritten by a strong Columbia tendency to emphasize culture over society—a tendency that Lynd very much shared. From John Dewey in philosophy to Franz Boas and Ruth Benedict in anthropology, the emphasis was on a cultural framework, subsumed under society, economy, and the polity. In a special way, Lynd was like a swan in a department where he seemed to be increasingly perceived, by some at least, as an ugly duckling. It was his philosophical anthropology, rather than a lack of statistical methodology, that ultimately frustrated Lynd and led him to shift his priorities from intellectual pursuits to departmental matters.

Lynd was involved in bringing the best scholars to the sociology department of Columbia, even when he doubted the efficacy of the methods used. The methodological wing represented by Paul F. Lazarsfeld and the Bureau of Applied Social Research had Lynd's unwavering support. Although they were intellectually on different lengths, Lazarsfeld and Lynd remained close personal friends. Lazarsfeld never forgot the role of Lynd in securing him a position at Columbia in 1940, nor the place of the *Middletown* study in his own community research efforts of the 1930s (Jahoda, Lazarsfeld, & Zeisel 1933). Lynd, for his part, made frequent reference to Lazarsfeld's study of the Austrian village of Marienthal in *Middletown in Transition* (Lynd & Lynd 1937, pp. 146, 179, 201, 254-255, 385). Lynd also shared with Robert K. Merton a concern for the middle range of social research. He was probably intellectually closer to Merton than to anyone else among the senior staff in the department of Columbia, and they worked closely on decision-making levels in the department. Lynd was also largely instrumental in bringing Mills to Columbia from the University of Maryland. He was central in a postwar crop of social scientists, headed by Lipset, who in many ways continued the dialogue about culture and democracy in new forms and in a postwar crisis period. Lynd, however, broke his silence between 1939 and 1956 long enough to write an extremely provocative, even crucial, critique (1956) of Mills's *Power Elite* (1956).

When one takes into account the paucity of Lynd's writings between *Knowledge for What?* in 1939 and his review essay on Mills in *The Nation* in 1956, the importance of the critique becomes self-evident. Lynd had been preoccupied with the development of a theory of power and democracy ever since *Middletown*. For Lynd, power as a social resource was absolutely necessary for the operation of society. Like physical energy, power could be harnessed for human welfare or corrupted by misuse. The development of democratic goals and the enhancement of a pluralistic national culture are, therefore, a responsibility of any sociological critique of power. Jeffersonian emphasis on democratic life is precisely the most outrageous hypothesis contained in *Knowledge for What?* Lynd shared with Mills a concern for the proper use and applications of power that he too had found much abused by elite groups. Yet he chides Mills for failing to undertake an analysis of power that extends its meaning for democracy. According to Lynd, the chief task for the observer of power is developing a theory of power for a given society. But according to Lynd, this was not what Mills aimed at. He was sorely out of sympathy with Mills's lack of commitment to a liberal democratic ethos and consequently finds that his ambiguous "expose" lacks concreteness with relation to America as well as any sense of meaningful alternatives. Lynd also found elite analysis in social science limited, if not distasteful, because it obscured or ignored the basic characteristics of a given social system. It bred a superficial analysis that amounted to a way out of dealing with capitalism, socialism, and class structure. In this sense, Lipset picked up on this sense of Lynd's frustration, and his *The First New Nation* (1963) in some sense proceeded along the lines indicated by Lynd in his critique of Mills.

It would be unfair to think of Lynd's contribution as residing solely in the work of his students. Lynd was close to present-day Marxist analysis of American society; certainly his claims that Mills over-looked important evidence linking present-day American capitalism and the capitalism of the nineteenth century struck that note. Lynd indicates that Mills did not systematically analyze the American economy, and that by focusing on great changes, Mills failed to ac-count for property as a power base linking the centuries. For Lynd, social science needed to understand the chief characteristics of the American system and not a given institution within the social order. Finally, Lynd breaks with Mills by assuming that the capitalist char-acter of the United States defines the quality of society in the United States from the outset.

By all reports, Lynd was fair and tough, deeply committed to the idea of graduate education and to sociology itself as a cultural trans-mission belt. He also had a lifelong commitment to the Columbia style of education as a civilizing process, civilization itself being measured by its advanced educational institutions. He was a plebe-ian comfortable in a world of patricians. To his lasting credit, the values he espoused and lived by remained consistent and conso-nant. He linked the sociological tradition and the problems of social science with the democratic culture and the larger problems of soci-ety.

Helen Merrell Lynd, two years his junior and his co-worker, carved out a career in many disciplines. She was born on St. Patrick's Day in 1894. Her parents were devoutly religious, with that element of social justice characteristic of many Midwestern Congregationalists. She graduated from Wellesley College in 1917, where the strongest single influence was Mary S. Case who introduced her to philoso-phy, particularly Hegel, and according to her colleague at Sarah Lawrence, Bert J. Loewenberg "gave her an abiding zest for both." She married Lynd in 1921, taught for many years at Sarah Lawrence College, and has remained in the New York City area since her re-tirement in 1965. If the word *polymath*, someone learned in many fields, has any meaning, it certainly applies to her. Not only is she coauthor of the famed *Middletown* series, which alone would make her a figure to contend with in sociology, but she can also claim a place in the disciplines of history, psychology, and philosophy. She was entirely at home with the poetry of Shelley, the plays of Shaw, and the novels of Dostoevsky. She was versed in the technical literature of an amazing variety of fields—from the philosophy of science to experimental psychology. Perhaps this breadth was essential to a work like *Middletown*, which in its very nature transcended many disciplines and imageries.

After the completion of *Middletown in Transition*, Helen Lynd carved a path of her own, starting with her remarkable book *England in the Eighteen-eighties* (1945), a work in social history done initially as a doctoral thesis under the supervision of the dean of history at Columbia, Carleton J. H. Hayes. The impact of *Middletown* showed in the organization of *England in the Eighteen-eighties*. It is divided into "Material Environment," "Environment of Ideas," "Political Parties," "Organized Labor," "Religious Education," and "Organization for Change." There is the same dialectical tension between the old and the new; the discrepancy between material abundance and satisfaction of human wants on the one hand, and the continued poverty of the masses on the other. Helen Lynd understood England in the 1880s as being involved with problems of social organization compatible with democratic individualism, a problem in England then and in the United States fifty years later.

Helen Lynd's style is wide-ranging, with a transparent clarity that disguises the seriousness of her efforts. She worked out the essential tension between freedom and authority in a series of discussions of party life: namely, the tension between conservatives and liberals, between organized labor and what might be described as agitators and reformers, and between the High Church and Methodist Quakers and other nonconformists, between the crude barbarism of the private schools and the tragedy of lower-class education, what were called the ragged schools for the ragged classes. The work is informed by a strong sense of the social contradictions in British society; a series of unresolved conflicts looked at from a decade involving the principal political actors, writers, and playwrights of the time, who illuminated the central themes of freedom and authority.

While this work seems remote from her classic volume a decade later, *On Shame and the Search for Identity* (1958), in a way it reveals the same sense of dialectical tension in concrete settings. Even in discussing such psychological categories as shame and guilt, the nature of language, and clues to identity, she retained a lively sense of the concrete, constantly illustrating her theme with wide-ranging references to the scientific and literary leaders of the time. It remained characteristic of Helen Lynd that she referred to work as wide-ranging as that of C. P. Snow, Norbert Wiener, and Alfred Korzybski, all with a gracious weaving of information and ideas that in lesser hands could easily have fallen apart. This book shares with her earlier work a strong democratic impulse. The authority of the earlier work became a search and realization of identity. Helen Lynd distinguishes between guilt, which is a response to standards that have been internalized, and shame, which is a response to criticism or ridicule by others. Guilt, she argues, is centrally a result of a transgression, a crime, a violation of a specific taboo or legal code by a definite voluntary act, whereas shame is linked to uncovering, to exposure, to wounding, to experiences of exposé, and to peculiarly sensitive and vulnerable aspects of the self.

This work is far more than a purely psychological account of pleasure and pain, and reward and punishment. It involves a general theory of personality development, linked to the evolution of historical thought. The work of Georg Simmel and Dorothy Lee plays a large part. Helen Lynd appreciated the extent to which concepts of psychological analysis are linked to mechanisms of social control intended to minimize conflict. But whether such reduction of conflict is good is warranted not by personality adjustment but by historical tendencies. This made Lynd's work quite different from conventional neo-Freudian writings of the 1950s. Her approach to questions of: "Who am I?; Where do I belong?" was strongly linked to sociology and history. Showing how such questions are formulated in ancient, medieval, and modern times, she observed that notions such as pride or shame are linked to general theories of religion, theology, and ideology. For Lynd, it is not the sin of pride but the capacity of pride to transcend shame, and therefore, to reach a new level of identity or even lucidity, that becomes central in raising consciousness. Unfortunately, she provided few clues as to how the guilt axis and the shame axis can be resolved by creating a pride-humility axis. Still, because at the time the social sciences emphasized intense social control and negative reaction to deviance, *On Shame and the Search for Identity* is more than a product of a generation in itself. It is also part of Helen Lynd's long-standing commitment to the idea that individual freedom is integrally linked to social democracy.

Critical acclaim for *On Shame and the Search for Identity* was widespread. Psychiatrists felt her work to be of seminal importance. Franz Alexander noted that "Mrs. Lynd's study goes further in depth and in comprehensiveness than any other contemporary writing on the subject. It is a sensitive, highly suggestive discourse on that most human of all faculties—reflection of the self on the self." And Theodor Reik added that "her perceptiveness and sensitiveness, especially felt in her differentiation of guilt and shame, as well as her intellectual sincerity and the originality of her observation, made her book a remarkable work." He might have added doubly so, since Helen Lynd was trained in history, did a pioneering work in sociology, and taught in philosophy. Helen Lynd, like Robert Lynd, revealed that powerful element of freethinking autodidacticism that was a family trademark.

A number of her important occasional writings were collected in *Toward Discovery* (1965). In his introductory essay, Bert J. Loewenberg properly notes that "Helen Lynd is concerned with the context of discovery; the environment of ideas; education in contemporary society; and the nature of historical objectivities." He also understands that ultimately, for Lynd, discovery was really a way of growth as well as a technique of inquiry, and that to discover in a true sense also involves a diversity of methods. In this collection of papers all of these themes are amply illustrated.

In the 1950s, Helen Merrell Lynd achieved political notoriety by becoming courageously involved in the response to McCarthyism within university life. Her essay "Truth at the University of Washington" (1949) took to task university administration and faculty supporters. Various tenured professors were found to be competent scholars, objective teachers without academic fault, but members of the Communist party and hence incapable of objectivity. Such issues deeply divided the academic community. Helen Lynd was always on the side of the victims of McCarthyism; even her occasional papers showed the same tension between freedom and authority, identity and guilt. Her writings went far beyond placid formalism. During a period when nearly any defense of Communist party members was tantamount to inviting disaster, she was able to write:

Freedom and truth must be sought in the world we live in, not in a vacuum. With the worst that anyone can say about the Communist Party, I cannot discover any reading of this evidence about what has happened at the University of Washington that supports the belief that there can be more dictatorial power over teachers in the United States by the Communist Party than by Boards of Regents; or that the search for truth is more threatened by Communists than by arbitrary action of Boards of Regents and Canwell Committees. I cannot discover any readings of this evidence which supports the belief that purging Communists is in the interests of independent teaching, or of democracy. (1949)

If Robert Lynd had a clear impact on his intellectual progeny, Helen Lynd had an equally powerful impact on familial progeny. They had two children, Andrea and Staughton. The latter in particular, as evidenced through his own writings in history and social science, and his involvement in everything from the anti-Vietnam War movement to legal advocacy of organized labor in the mid-West, exhibits a fusion of radical ideas and social action. Helen Lynd's final statement to the graduating class at Sarah Lawrence in 1964 stands a fit epithet to her careers and writing and those of her husband: "So we cross the bridge into a new country. We go alone. But we take with us some knowledge of what it means to probe deeply into new worlds of learning and to glimpse all that lies beyond and is yet unexplored. And we take with us the gaiety, the delight, the sustenance of having known each other here—a knowing that will continue with us. We go in expectation of what may lie ahead."

Work by Robert S. Lynd

Knowledge for What? The Place of Social Science in American Culture

Work by Helen Merrell Lynd

England in the Eighteen-eighties: Toward a Social Basis for Freedom

Work by Robert S. Lynd and Helen Merrell Lynd

Middletown in Transition: A Study in Cultural Conflicts

33

Joseph B. Maier:
Tradition, Modernity and the Last Hurrah
of the "Frankfurt School"

Joseph Maier was a scholar who died just shy of his 92nd birthday. One might take the easy path, the emotional way out, and salute a life well loved and long lived. But I am suspicious of fatuous commentaries that ease our consciences as we send the old to their final resting places. Whether one lives through the ninetieth year or dies at thirty, the problem of analysis remains the same: how to summarize the *lebenswerke* of a colleague—and to do so with tact, grace, and above all, accuracy. Joe lived a long life, but he carried within himself the contradictions of classical liberalism that defined his career from start to finish. He knew as much. But I would suggest that it was history, not society, which carried the grains of resolution for Maier. I suspect that this is what led Enrique Krauze to call his interview with Joe that appeared in the festschrift "The Fury of Historical Redemptionism"—an awkward but accurate critique of the fanatic style in much that passed for social theory.

To start with, Joseph Maier was a colleague of mine at the Rutgers graduate program in sociology for many years. It pains me to note that few members of that department have paused for a moment of silence in his memory, much less offered even a word in tribute, at least none whom I have encountered. He deserves more than silence from a department and a university he served with honor and distinction over the years. It must be said in candor that Joe's alienation from Rutgers, sadly enough, was mutual. In a festschrift honoring Joe issued five years ago, entitled *Surviving the Twentieth Century*, the sub-title is telling: *Social Philosophy from the Frankfurt School to the Columbia Faculty Seminars*. I gave the book its main title. But the subtitle was very much what Joe insisted upon. And to be sure, it well defined the intellectual bookends of his long and distinguished career.

213

Joe invested tremendous energy in the Columbia Seminars. There seemed to be at least three parts to his deep involvement: First, they were tribute to his own mentor, Frank Tannenbaum—a person he greatly cared for and respected. They also represented a need to remain intellectually active after his retirement from Rutgers in 1980. And finally, they exemplified Joe's belief that these seminars—targeted as they were on specific subject areas domestic and foreign, theoretical and applied—carried the full weight of the sociological tradition. For him that tradition included Mannheim, Toennies, Lukacs, Cahnman, and the invincible Weber. It must be said that Joe had respect for the Marxian socialist tradition. It would have been virtually impossible in a world of the late 1920s and early 1930s dominated by the likes of Max Horkheimer and Theodor Adorno not to be so influenced. But he remained skeptical and increasingly critical of totalitarian tendencies in Soviet life, and in the proclivities of socialist doctrine to veer to an eschatological ideology, a pseudo-religion that paralleled rather than overcame fascist doctrine. In the world of Columbia, he saw "emancipation" from the Frankfurt School, as Judith Marcus rightly notes, not in personal but in political terms. His break was intellectual, not idiosyncratic—itself the mark of the man. Joe freely admitted his indebtedness to the pragmatic philosophic tradition extending from John Dewey, John Herman Randall and Horace Friess, and Ernest Nagel. I came at the tail end of that grand collection of philosophers. This helped us span our substantial generation differences.

The impact of Frank Tannenbaum started with various University seminars at Columbia and extended to a lifelong interest in Latin America. While Joe's final efforts were concentrated on European social theory, his work at the Columbia Faculty Seminars was centered on problems of development, and especially those that are linked to Latin America social mobility and educational systems. His work was especially located on the emergence of an independent labor movement—one that had characteristics of the European world, such as the general strike and mass mobilizations for political ends. But these movements also grafted on the North American notion of labor—the bread and butter pragmatic issues characteristic of the AFL and CIO. How differential forms of secular organizations met in global contexts, especially the more advanced nations of South America, was a lifelong concern for Joe. In this area, aided and abetted as he was by a huge capacity for languages and literature, he performed yeoman service. Indeed, he is one of the very few—perhaps the only—"member" of the Frankfurt School of social research to exhibit an early and wide interest in and knowledge of emerging areas called the Third World.

Joe was not simply of the Frankfurt School or of Columbia University. He was very much a Jewish survivor with a powerful appreciation of the American democratic credo. His skepticism about political placebos was thus well grounded. The tendencies of Hitler and Stalin bode ill for the Jewish people. But Joe was different in this regard as well. He eschewed the sort of blasé "enlightened" Jewish anti-Semitism of the Horkheimer Circle, bought whole hog from Marx's early diatribes on "The Jewish Question." In this he may not have been fashionable, but he was consistent with core values of democracy. His military experiences in postwar German reconstruction stimulated his passionate commitment to the restoration of Jewish burial sites, synagogues, and institutional places of congregation that gave Jewish life its meaning before the Nazi effort to destroy Judaism as History. The search for physical restoration, for representation in artifacts as well as ideas, gave special meaning to Joe's post-academic career in America. It permitted him to see history as memory, the unique instrument for resolving the contradictions of tradition and modernity. In this he understood Vico well. It is a tribute to Joe that a brief piece on Vico, with its sly, but unmistakable critique of the Frankfurt School, represented his own contribution to the Festschrift edited by Judith Marcus.

It would be inappropriate to skip over Joe's special relationship to Transaction during the final years of his life. Indeed, my continuing presence at Rutgers provided some sort of institutional thread that may have played a role in his interest in seeing his efforts lodged with our Press. To pay tribute to Joe's rich life of service is also to honor his own sense of who mattered as well as what mattered. Indeed, the five works to which Joe was connected that were published by Transaction each reflected his deep interest in the best of the European sociological tradition, and how it reflected the Jewish cultural formations that underwrote so many of these efforts at *Aufklarung*. Joe did not escape the tensions and strains of this marriage of tradition and modernity, lay and clerical traditions, but he recognized contradictions as the stuff of living cultures. His work gave expression to them. And through the amazing fortitude of Judith Marcus and Zoltan Tarr, it saw the light of print.

The most relaxed atmosphere in which I saw Joe was actually in his years of partial exile as a "snowbird" in Florida. Because of my own connections with the University of Miami, we always managed at least one meal during my own sojourns to its Cuban and Cuban-American Studies program. Despite serious medical problems, he and his wife maintained a youthful, outgoing posture. Their pleasure in each other's presence was clear and transparent. An outsider could only imagine that the death of his wife was very painful to him. It took away not just the other half, but arguably a good deal of the reason for his own sense of living. Toward the end, he was inspired by efforts to make things right, to come to terms with himself in a world from which he was indeed *Entfremdung*. Joe Maier helped give meaning to twentieth century social research. He was a child of its evolution from near start to finish. Its greatness in science, technology, and democratic credos were embedded in his mind. Its horror, militarism, totalitarianism, Holocausts, seared his soul. No one who knew Joe could fail to detect the self-contradictory series of strains tearing at him. They were neither his issues alone, nor his sufferings alone. They were and remain the liberal consensus of the past century in the Western tradition. In thinking about Joe Maier, it is perhaps wise to acknowledge the durability of human imperfection, even error, in our lives. But far more important, it is to at least seek the higher truths of human creation. In this way, Joe becomes part of the eternal return that history promises but happily never quite fulfills.

Works by Joseph B. Maier

Ethnicity, Identity, and History (with Judith Marcus and Chaim I. Waxman)
German Jewry: Its History and Sociology (with Judith Marcus and Chaim I. Waxman)
Sociology: The Science of Society (with Jay Rumney)
Weber and Toennies (with Judith Marcus and Chaim I. Waxman)

34

John D. Martz:
North American Latin Americanist

Let me start with an admission—the likes of which I have a hard time interpreting. When I first learned that I would be appearing at this memorial service for John, I stopped all else, indeed it was difficult to think of academic business as usual, until I prepared a brief comment for this occasion. Before being able to print out the diskette on which the work was saved, the program temporarily crashed, and along with it everything I had written for the occasion was lost. And despite the best efforts of computer mavens, the material could not be resurrected. I suppose they remain hidden somewhere—may the words rest in hard drive privacy, if not in eternal peace.

But if the truth were said, I was less than satisfied with what I had first written. It was reasonable enough in tone and sufficiently accurate in content, but it lacked contact with the living mind of John. It was just too formalistic. In short, it lacked heart. So I take the computer crash as God's will that I try again, work harder, be less glib, and come closer to the sources of a friendship that extended for well over a quarter-century. This interaction included writing published reports and reviews (and unpublished evaluations) for John while he was editor of the *Latin American Research Review*, and in reverse, his writing three books for Transaction on Colombia, Venezuela, and Ecuador. This in turn mushroomed into his extraordinary, near decade long stewardship of *Studies in Comparative International Development*. Since I founded that journal, while he was the catalyst that propelled it into first place in the area of research and theory covered, we were and remain locked in a professional relationship for all time.

There is something prima facie absurd in attempting to summarize the rich life of a special person in a few moments. It is more an act of desperation revealing the impatience of our age with speechifying among other things, and shortcuts to knowledge, the dark side of making the act of learning a pleasure that knows no pain. But

217

there is also a value in such an exercise, since in such memorial services held in university chapels we free ourselves of personal anguish and moral sensibilities. Our forefathers had far less trouble with such defining events since they were far more religious in their understanding of life, death, and the conduct of activities in between the two great poles that guide our collective stars. So now that I have this second chance, let me make the most of it by speaking from the heart as well as the head about what John Martz meant to me personally.

John's most apparent and perhaps most enduring characteristic was his fair-mindedness. He was an innate Aristotelian, a scholar for whom the golden mean was just that, golden. I have reviewed more than one hundred and fifty letters he wrote to me, and in every one of them this sense of being fair—to the thought of those with whom he disagreed, to the needs of the public he was serving as writer or editor, and to his own vision of the way the world functioned—uniformly prevailed. To be a good scholar and great editor requires just that innate or acquired concept of fair-mindedness. For lacking that characteristic, scholarship becomes ideology, truth is subverted by opinion, and universality is displaced by idiosyncrasy. We live in an imperfect world, and doubtlessly, one can fault this or that decision of John to publish or not publish a particular article. But I do not know how one can fault his unfailing striving to be equitable. This is not in John's case a matter of vacuous liberalism, or a search to simply avoid combat or controversy. Quite the reverse, it was a principle—to look at options, not just polarities, however many there are, before leaping to conclusions. John came to strong conclusions about all-important and even less-important matters. In Jamesian terms, he may have been tenderhearted but he was no less tough-minded.

John had a powerful sense of tradition—as is characteristic of our tribe, more of the academic than the religious. His loyalty to his North Carolina cohort during the "golden era" was ferocious and abiding. Indeed, to read his moving, impassioned obituary on behalf of his colleague from the University of Miami, Enrique [Kike] Baloyra, who preceded him in death by a year, is to gain an appreciation of what the culture of university life has meant in the formation of the Western tradition from Desiderius Erasmus of Rotterdam to Ortega y Gasset of Madrid. But for John this sense of tradition was far more than an abstract humanism or a metaphysic of reason:

it was at rock bottom a sense of common pursuits for its own end. North Carolina, under the stewardship of Federico G. Gil, was one of the very few places in which the study of Latin America was not undertaken as a function of missionary work as it was for most of the nineteenth century, or of foreign policy as it became for most of the twentieth century. It was a pure act of appreciation for that broad linkage of language, culture, geography, and people, that however diverse, seemed to add up to a frame of analysis that was also a window on the world that deserved study in its own terms. I suspect that his frustrated efforts to build a similar cohort and framework at Penn State were a deep source of his uncharacteristic anger. Not personal ambitions, but institutional goals were at the core of his strong ties to Latin American studies as a culture of its own.

John retained a life-long dedication to ethnography, to working in the field. It is hardly a secret that for many lesser academics, going overseas is a necessary chore undertaken to write a dissertation. Rarely was it internalized as an opportunity to return to the scene of the intellectual crimes committed in youth. But for John, to study the northern tier of South America meant to retain physical contact with its peoples and its powers. At one level, that he died in Venezuela was an accident, but at a deeper level, it was a function of his constant commitment to empirical work as ethnographic work.

All types of people uniquely respected him. He established levels of confidentiality as to the meaning of events, derived in substantial measure from knowing that the field is the larger turf on which we write our tableaus, and not the narrow range of academic politics that are better left to smalltime power brokers. Mark Twain in *How to Tell a Story* (1897) reminds us of the naturalistic fallacy. "History has shown that when he [the observer] is abroad observing unfamiliar peoples the chances are heavily against him. He is then a naturalist observing a bug." That is why John tried mightily and so successfully to change the odds by making the field a home and not a painful and temporary tour of graduate student duty. That was the North Carolina way of doing Latin American studies, and that was John's way.

John forcefully expressed this sentiment not only in Twain's way, but also in his own way. In a 1989 essay on "The Conduct of Social Research," he wrote that "the opportunity to carry out intellectual inquiry abroad is a special, even unique circumstance which does not fall to all social scientists. Its professional and personal rewards are great, if primarily in non-material ways. To maximize the experience, and to make possible further efforts by other researchers, the scholar must exercise constant self-examination and the best of rational judgment. If even this has its occasional problems, it is the most that can be demanded of the human condition and its enduring capacity for fallibility."

It would be incorrect to think of John as observer and ethnographer pure and simple. Indeed, the purpose of all his painful amassing of data and detail was to come up with some general theory—not just of the area, but of political life as such. John was, after all, a social scientist, a political scientist, and not merely a journalist. I hasten to add that the word "merely" is not used in a pejorative sense, for John held such steady and serious overseas-based reporters in the highest regard. Alas, John did not live long enough to fully articulate his theoretical framework. But he left enough materials in published form to add up to a powerful theory—what I would like to think of as an institutional political science equivalent in meaning to the institutional economics of an earlier period in American academic life. Indeed, his ability to write brilliantly on Taiwan and parts of the world removed from his usual haunts derives from this search for general theory. That it may also be a response to a beautiful marriage to his Philippine wife, Cora, only served to further articulate a need for theory, not as a summing up, but as an operational foothold in the real world of rough and tumble politics.

What then is the theoretical legacy of John Martz? I dare to submit that it ultimately rests upon a theory of democracy as a delicate set of institutional arrangements built up over time by decent and unheralded public servants. Too often democracy is spoken about as some sort of dialogue between people and a process of accommodation to live and let live. But John well knew from his Latin American experiences that if this were the case, the area would be subject to far less turmoil and tribulations. Democracy is more than that—it is a system as well as a process, a set of institutional structures built up over time that become the measure and the touchstone for accommodation. It was the failure in so many parts of Latin America to translate constitutional documents into everyday practices that prevented or stunted democratic growth in the region. It is also the lack of such institutionalization that made the area easy prey for English lords, Spanish conquistadors, and yes, American imperialists.

Dictatorships easily accommodate to the needs of foreign bandits, especially when doing so permits them to retain local, regional, or national controls. Caudillos and caciques are inherently anti-democratic because they make the growth of democratic institutions virtually impossible. Unlike the Weberian formula for successful transition from the charismatic to the rationalistic, such personalized leadership removed from the needs of ordinary people leads to cycles of irrationalism, of rule by edict, by bribery, and by force. The political institutions of democratic rule are hard to establish, and take years to nourish. But John lived through a process of just this evolution in many sectors of the Third World. He was not foolish enough to think that Venezuela, Ecuador, and Colombia are exemplars of democratic order, but he was smart enough to appreciate that changes in Argentina, Chile, Brazil, and even Mexico, were pointing the way to the linkup of democratic institutions with liberal values. As John himself wrote prior to his death: "Underlying all the preceding is a passionate belief in the profound significance of Democracy, as defined in broad terms and deserving of a capital D. In the long and inexorable unfolding of history, the democratic ethos must ultimately prevail."

This brings me to a final word about John himself: his own sense of liberality—not some cheap sloganeering "ism," but a personal decency that he emitted. This he did in the simplest of ways: by the ability to listen, to avoid contradiction as a humiliation ritual. It is not that he suffered fools easily; rather it is that he appreciated how few humans can claim infallibility and wisdom as an everyday companion. That he sometimes made mistakes in intellectual as well as personal judgments is a foregone conclusion. To spend part of a lifetime editing the work of others is a sure guarantee of such a mixed bag of results. But he was such a rare treasure of a man, so easy to be around, because he was genuinely interested in the work of others, and how that could be incorporated into his own sense of the world. Personal pursuits and public performance was so easily meshed in John that it sometimes became all too easy to ignore his magisterial contributions to our own growth. John Martz was my friend, my colleague, and my leader. That he performed each of these three roles with unfailing modesty and moral probity makes his loss all the more difficult to accept. It also makes his goals difficult to achieve. But the living has few options but to keep trying. John could never imagine the tangled tasks of life to be otherwise.

What John, in a moment of revealing his passionate core, said of his colleague Enrique A. Baloyra can stand as the final word about John as well. "He was a preeminent political scientist and Latin Americanist. His publications were numerous and consistently outstanding in quality. He also provided counsel and advice to a host of other entities.... He remained the scholar and academic, teaching and guiding students while performing administrative and curricular tasks.... Most of all, those who knew and loved him, will always remember 'Kike' as the complete human being, one whose intellectual accomplishments were paralleled by the example of his values, principles, and ideals. With the passing of a true brother, words are inadequate. *Combatiente*, we will always remember you." The same must now be said of our fallen colleague: John D. Martz.

Works by John D. Martz

The Dynamics of Change in Latin American Politics
Politics and Petroleum in Ecuador
The Politics of Clientelism
United States Policy in Latin America
Venezuela

35

Robert K. Merton:
Passionate Professional

The death of Robert K. Merton in early 2003 was for me, and I suspect for countless others for whom social research matters, a dreaded event. The field of sociology lost perhaps the most civilized gentleman in the profession. But it also lost its most persuasive figure, one who kept up a lifelong struggle for sociology as a profession. The devastating balkanization of the field, papered over by celebration of cacophony in the guise of democracy, has sapped the field of its centripetal forces and figures. In its stead has emerged a series of vaguely affiliated interest groups united by factionalism, fanaticism, and common hatreds. Shadow boxing with political leaders and cultural icons replaced the emotional force behind the field.

In the early 1990s, when sociology was increasingly torn asunder by its departure from the norms that earlier had given the discipline its strength, few people in the field were prepared to make a public statement of support for my book, *The Decomposition of Sociology*. Even good friends told me that the situation was not as bad as I made it out to be, and anyhow, the exaggerations of the time would pass into oblivion. Those less friendly generally viewed my work as a type of treason to the field—as some Latin Americanists had earlier responded to my 1964 article on the "Stalinization of Cuba." In that difficult professional climate, Merton stated for the record and in public that my volume was "absolutely in the tradition so luminously described by Max Weber in his two great addresses on *Politics as a Vocation* and *Science as a Vocation*."

All who knew Merton also know that he chose his words—certainly his words for public release—with great care. He understood all too well that the burden of my concerns was the reconstitution of the field, not a celebration of its dilemmas. In correspondence, he wrote of the need to recall what Max Weber was arguing for and the forces of evil he was struggling against. He also invoked the Great Instauration of Francis Bacon—viewing it as the task of the modern

223

world to free itself from medieval theological straightjackets. I have not a shred of doubt that Merton saw contemporary political ideologies as the same sort of straightjackets that stand in the way of reasoned thought embodied in the social science enterprise. He was a man for whom history is measured less in terms of issues of war and peace and more in terms of irrational strictures imposed by the method of authority. In contrast, he was enough of a Deweyian to believe that rational discourse was best made possible by the method of science.

Merton spent a lifetime trying to understand the role of science in the evolution of capitalism and democracy in the West. He saw social research as not simply an adventure in the history of ideas, but as a new stage in the evolution of consciousness. It was a framework for establishing science as a basis for human action. His enormous regard for his many students, such as James Coleman and Seymour Martin Lipset, derived not only from their research contributions, but even more from their ability to make the grand mission from Bacon to Weber a living entity. I emphasize this element in Merton's work in part to avoid the trap of reciting his work in everything from mass persuasion to social problems as detachment from quotidian life. It was no such thing. Rather, the research agenda that every serious scholar engages is measured by this sense of the public good, which in turn is derived from the ethical bases of scientific production as such. The Bureau of Applied Social Research embodied the Mertonian credo. And if others like Paul Lazarsfeld were crucial to the research designs of many projects, Merton was no less central to the social mission of such projects.

As I indicated in my book *An American Utopian*, the work of C. Wright Mills, along with that of the late Talcott Parsons, and of course, the effort of Robert Merton in social theory and research, formed a core triptych that defined, if not exhausted, the legacy bequeathed by Max Weber. Protean figures like Weber allowed for different emphases. For Mills, it was stratification in society; for Parsons it was the systemic and institutional fabric of whole societies; while for Merton it was the search for an explanation of how the parts of society, when faced with innovation and invention adjust to new circumstances. "Middle range" theory with which Merton was so closely identified is not some Aristotelian golden mean, a center between polarities. Rather it offers a way to understand how people can meet challenges of a sometimes cataclysmic and at other times revolutionary sort. Merton's lifelong interest in the scientific revolution is characteristic of his ability to address big themes and bring them down to a bite size level. His canvas is big—science, religion, economy—much like Weber himself. The explanations are on a human scale—improving profits, making beauty, modernizing liturgy—again like Weber himself.

The naturalistic, pragmatic tradition was especially strong at a Columbia University that boasted John Dewey, Frederick Woodbridge, Ernest Nagel, and John Herman Randall in philosophy, Richard Hofstadter, Jacques Barzun, and Allan Nevins in history, Wesley Mitchell, John Maurice Clark, and Eli Ginzberg in economics. They, along with many others, gave a sharp edge to Merton's thinking, compelling him to look with care on the experiential and experimental side of things, and to do so with the spirit of liberal reform. This perspective sat well with Merton, since he saw democracy as a likely consequence of scientific research. This sense that science produces social betterment, without the need for preaching about what constitutes such betterment, was part of the long march of Enlightenment, of the making of the modern mind. Not even the scourge of Nazism could disabuse Merton from the scientific way of doing sociology. If a certain optimism is characteristic of Merton's work on science and society, he can be forgiven. Indeed, it underscored his naturalistic faith. He was after all a child of the Enlightenment. For him it was the French tradition ranging from Voltaire to Diderot that served as the critical American bridge to Europe, rather than the more austere and totalistic tradition of nineteenth-century German philosophy of Hegel and Fichte. I suspect that this was a deep difference in orientation between Parsons and Merton—despite a common identification with the functional structural view of the world.

This broad mosaic of practical assumptions—naturalism in philosophy, welfare reform in economics, the democratic credo in politics, and the place of human agencies in fashioning history—made Merton the quintessential *American* sociologist. While Parsons was admired for carrying on the Germanic tradition and Mills perhaps less admired but nonetheless widely appreciated for his radical critique of his own society, it was Merton who struck the notes that made sociological music the world over. His choice of themes started with commitment to the inductive study of actual conditions. His work increasingly centered on aspects of American life that attracted worldwide attention. His work covered public opinion, mass persuasion, serendipitous relations, scientific bases of economic change, the notions of self-fulfilling prophecy, opportunity structures, functional-structural systems, and a host of other terms and concepts. He pioneered areas that became part of the folklore of sociology no less than the common currency of people who knew little and cared less for the field. Because of his pellucid style, it was easy to feel at home with Merton's work. Moreover it was difficult to ignore the accuracy of his observations and conclusions.

This is neither the time nor place to review old battles, though honesty requires admission that there were strong differences between us. Then again, this is probably the case for a great many people in sociology who recognize that moving forward requires going through the writings of a giant. Perhaps my strongest critique of Merton came in *The Journal of Politics*, in a 1963 article on "Functionalist Sociology and Political Ideologies." I challenged the idea that functionalism was value neutral, an often-made claim in his *Social Theory and Social Structure*. I argued then, and would still argue now, that although functionalism retains biological neutrality of sorts, that on a conservative-liberal axis, it carries a political baggage that remains entirely unresolved. The appeal to instrumental or pragmatic criteria of workability entails a series of value perspectives that simply conflates de facto worldly success with values worth struggling for.

Merton himself well appreciated his epistemological cul-de-sac. He often decried the "motley company" in which his commitment to functionalism placed him. A type of functionalism that gave succor to rabid biological reductionism that fascists and racialists employed disquieted Merton. Indeed, over time, Bob moved away from the language of functionalism and toward broadly empirical guidelines for research. One can only look fondly upon a functional theory that took seriously the fact that the social world is a stubborn place presenting severe limits on the wildest flights of fancy of ideologists disguised as sociologists. Reviewing those discussions of forty years ago—in light of the rise of a rancid subjectivism coated over as postmodernity, and a rhetoric of "the social construction of…" in which nothing is any longer real out there and everything is the invention of clever wags—is a bracing experience. Merton not only understood the risks and threats to such a social science by moving far beyond the strictures of science, he tolerated with uncommon decency critics who singled him out for advocating a sociology of science that presumably failed to take account of ideological values. At the risk of engaging in hyperbole, there is strong evidence that anti-Americanism in European intellectual circles not infrequently took the form of anti-Mertonian assaults.

This is not to say that Merton lacked supporters. Few American social scientists can boast more translations into foreign languages, including several *festschriften* emanating from European lands. Indeed, one of my early tasks in Buenos Aires in 1958 was to supervise translations into Spanish of *Social Theory and Social Structure*. It was well understood that overcoming a decade of Peronist dictatorship meant retracing some intellectual steps—and paramount of these were the writings of Merton in sociology. Indeed, when I once asked a class of young post-Peronist Argentine students what they thought of in relation to the United States, they uniformly mentioned the early titles of The Free Press rather than the Statue of Liberty! Merton's writings were synonymous with a philosophy of science no less than sociology of science. He knew and appreciated that, and I believe that it steeled him in the face of those seeking to take the discipline of sociology to the dark places of subjectivism from which it had emerged. It was his quiet achievement to move the discipline to a higher sense of the place of science and technology in the study of advanced societies. It was also to his credit that he struggled against the lower depths of anti-science and clever Ludditism. His naturalistic framework was the epistemological background that gave meaning to his sociological theory and method.

There were several other occasions when I found myself responding directly to Merton's themes. The first was in several articles in the 1960s that tried to synthesize the idea of sociology as a profession on one hand and the Everett Hughes position of sociology as an occupation on the other, e.g., *Philosophy of Science* (1964). There can be no question that Merton's impact on sociology derived in no small part from his efforts to codify professional life. From defining the field and criteria of membership to delineating the ethical bases on which the field must proceed, Merton simply extended to sociology the values to which he had been committed to in a wide variety of fields, from nursing to communication. For he well understood that the power of a field to define the world, not to mention determine the reward system for the field, depends on professionalization. This was a bitterly contested subject, especially within the Chicago

School for whom such codes of conduct and styles of research spelled the death knell of participation, observation, and research into dangerous places and areas.

With the establishment of *The American Sociological Review*, one can readily see that such a difference in opinion had wide ramifications. It was a sort of Columbia answer to *The American Journal of Sociology*. And to this day, some seventy years later, the character of sociology has been shaped by a bifurcated vision. On one hand there was the view of the field as an occupational activity with freewheeling participation and observation, in contrast to a professional style of work with rigorous adherence to well-established methods of research and theories based on the conversion of big chunks of social matter into variables. These bitter fault lines passed into other publications. The professional crowd populated sociology at older publishing firms in the East. The occupationalists found solace in newer firms, like The Free Press of Glencoe, Illinois and Aldine-Atherton of Chicago.

One should not make too much of a geographical distribution of ideological tendencies within the field. Yet, it is the case that special polarities appeared in sociology that were unique to the field, and that reflected its special history, and it must be said, its unique personalities. None loomed larger than Robert Merton, and perhaps none suffered the consequences more widely than did he. For with professionalism an accomplished fact, it became easier for the sociological associations to be taken over by forces unsympathetic to the commitments of Merton and other early professionals. The latter type was more eager to see the codifying of the field as a mechanism for curbing rather than encouraging new forms of research. New orthodoxies replaced old ones, and with them the worst fears of those urging an occupational model based on work performed instead of authority presumed. It is not that the disastrous evolution of the profession can be laid on Merton's doorstep. It most emphatically cannot be. The drive toward a credentialized model was simply too powerful for any force to oppose, or for any individual to claim as his own. That said, the struggle for an honest sociology became more intense and more extreme in Merton's final years. He saw the erosion of the consensus that he was central to creating. But he also lived to see the emergence of a professional life in think tanks, research institutes, foundations, and in entirely new areas that carries forth his legacy.

My other disagreement with Merton concerned my effort to move beyond the consensus position, on which functional doctrine rested, and toward a conflictual position, on which just about every shade of dialectical doctrine rested. My own view was that cooperation was a better and truer guide in understanding social cohesion than either conflict or consensus. But again in retrospect, I seriously doubt that Merton was especially wedded to consensus as a theory. More to the point, he saw consensus as a basis for human association. It was the outcome of rather than the input to scientific discourse. It was also the ground upon which academic life could move ahead in something resembling an orderly democratic fashion. In this, Merton was a better and truer guide than the Franco-Italian School from Michels to Mosca. For it was the consensual position that carried prospects for both democratic improvement and democratic survival. It provides the legal framework for social order. In this, Merton's work with Robert Nisbet in the social problems area—a part of his work too readily forgotten and ignored—played a large part in showing how Durkheim's work influenced Merton no less than Weber. Without order, the cement to managing change dissolves. And what is imperiled is the idea of civility at the personal level and civilization at the macroscopic level. Here my evidence is more from correspondence between us rather than published writings, in which Bob was careful not to exceed the evidence.

These were hard issues for Bob to confront at the end. Our correspondence touched on such themes gingerly. It is not that we disagreed—that was a rare occurrence in the last thirty years of our relationship. Rather, we shared dismay at the disintegration of a field so carefully crafted to play an imperial role in the construction of a new America. I may be reading into Merton certain sentiments that he either did not possess or felt only marginally. He certainly lived through the worst of times as well as defined the best of times with the same assured equanimity. He has been the subject of many books and articles and reviews. Indeed, if one takes a citation index view of sociology, he probably ranks at the very top or certainly near the top. But it is also clear that even against his preferred judgment, his work has become the touchstone of what sociology should be, not simply what a life in sociology has been. And in that effort, it is no longer within his domain to define the character of the struggle or its limits. That remains a task for the living. For me, and I believe for many others, his was a voice for scientific clarity, sociological modesty, and democratic participation. The struggle for reason in science and sanctity in society had no more forceful advocate and no finer soul.

Works by Robert K. Merton

On Social Structure and Science
On the Shoulders of Giants
Science, Technology and Society in 17th-Century England
Social Research and the Practicing Professions
Social Theory and Social Structure

36

C. Wright Mills: Sociologist of American Stratification

C[harles] Wright Mills (August 28, 1916 – March 20, 1962) was born in Waco, Texas. His boyhood was spent in Sherman, Fort Worth, and Dallas, where he attended Catholic parochial schools and public high schools. His father, Charles Grover Mills, was an insurance agent and his mother, Frances Ursula Wright, a housekeeper. The upbringing was distinctly urban. Mills was married four times: twice to Dorothy Helen ("Freya") Smith, from 1937 to 1940 and then from 1941 to 1947; to Ruth Harper, from 1947 to 1959; and to Gloria ("Yaroslava") Surmach, from 1959 until his death. He had a daughter by each of his first two wives and a son by the third.

After an unproductive year as an engineering student at Texas A&M, Wright enrolled at the University of Texas, where he received a B.A. in 1938, and M.A. in philosophy and sociology in 1939. From Texas he went to the University of Wisconsin, where, working under Howard Becker and Hans Gerth, he received the Ph.D. for a study of pragmatism and the rise of professionalism in America in 1942. He taught sociology at the University of Maryland from 1942 to 1946, and also conducted research for a variety of government agencies such as the Small Administration. He went to Columbia University in New York where he taught sociology for the remainder of his life. Much of his time was spent at the Bureau of Applied Social Research, where he worked closely with Paul Lazarsfeld, its director. During his years at Columbia he had a variety of visiting professorships, including stints at the London School of Economics, the national University of Mexico, Brandeis University, among others. Mills was highly regarded as a teacher—especially at the undergraduate level. A number of his pupils selected themes for essays that later became books and journal articles.

Mills' work can best be seen in tripartite terms, roughly corresponding with three periods of his life. His earlier work at the Universities of Texas and Wisconsin was dominated by a concern with themes in the sociology of knowledge such as his essays on philosophical sociology, ranging from Chinese thought to German *Wissensoziologie* (these are readily available in two collections of Mills' essays edited by Irving Louis Horowitz, titled *Power Politics and People* [1962] and *On Social Men and Political Movements* [1965]). It was also during this period that *Sociology and Pragmatism* (written in 1939-41 but only published in 1964) appeared. In this period he displayed a deep regard for the relationship of power to culture on a vertical axis, and professionalism to advanced industrial society on a horizontal axis. Mills put to good use his interdisciplinary training. Some scholars in the history of sociology feel his contribution was a unique effort to bring the abstractions of the European tradition in the sociology of knowledge into a concrete American setting of broad social meaning.

The years Mills spent at Columbia and the Bureau constitute the second period of Mills' life. Between 1948 and 1956 he produced the three books on social and political stratification on which much of his posthumous reputation rests. The first was *The New Men of Power* (1948), a study of labor leaders and their political attitudes. It stayed closely in touch with the currents of the 1940s in terms of integrating narrative and data characteristic of the work of people like Samuel Stouffer, Robert K. Merton, Robert S. Lynd, as well as Paul Lazarsfeld. *White Collar: The American Middle Classes* (1951), his classic study of varieties of professional labor, continued his concern with work and society, but introduced a concern with alienation, culture, and anxiety, that derived in part from his work with Hans Gerth on *Character and Social Structure: The Psychology of Social Institutions* (1953) and his growing interest in problems of contemporary American capitalism. Mills caught the concerns of a postwar generation caught up in the business of service rather than production. His third contribution to stratification added a political dimension derived from the European tradition of Pareto, Mosca, and Michels, in which the theme of power displaced the earlier interest in the Weberian view of authority displayed in *From Max Weber* (1946). In this work, *The Power Elite* (1956), Mills also exhibited a tendency toward didacticism and tendentiousness, which characterized his final period. It had an enormous impact on the social and political theorizing of the Eisenhower years, emphasizing as it did the relationship of military, industrial, and executive power. Even the president took note of this when, in his farewell address, he expressed concern about the "military-industrial complex" emerging in the 1950s.

The last period of Mills' brief life is identified with his increasing concerns with the threat of nuclear warfare, best observed in *The Causes of World War Three* (1958). This was followed by a polemic tract in support of the Castro Revolution in Cuba, which was published as *Listen Yankee! The Revolution in Cuba* (1960). This work had a galvanizing impact on Mills's reputation—it was widely read and it caused strong critical responses from colleagues. Mills became a pariah to the point of being viewed as not a bona fide sociologist at all. His final work was a collection, *The Marxists* (1962), which appeared within days of his untimely death. In it, Mills sought to link the Marxist tradition with the open society—offering hope for the socialist critics of Stalinism, and showing the thread of pragmatic concerns that characterized Marxist leaders such as Marshall Tito of Yugoslavia. This work also closed out a period of intense political concerns first put forth in *The Sociological Imagination* (1959) in which he sought to mix history and biography in order to create a sociology more global in perspective and more personally important than the established orthodoxies of the time.

Mills left a variety of unfinished tasks and incomplete manuscripts, including *Contacting the Enemy*, which was to be a study of the Soviet Power Elite similar in tone and substance to his analysis of the American power elite. He had also begun to think about problems of underdeveloped regions, and he contemplated a multi-volume work on international social stratification. He had also contracted to do volumes complementing *The Marxists* on the anarchists and the Trotskyists, and other "deviant" socialist and libertarian types. He was diagnosed as having heart problems in 1942, but apparently did little about it. His fourth and fatal heart attack came at his home in West Nyack, a suburb of New York City.

* * *

American sociology has lost an enormous talent with the death of C. Wright Mills on March 21, 1962, at the age of forty-six. But American society lost even more—an authentic voice of an authentic liberalism. Mills' sociological imagination stood for a style of intellectual work inherited from the French Enlightenment. Like Diderot, Voltaire, Helvetius, and the men of the *Encyclopédie*, Mills saw the essential task of sociology (and intellect generally) as the confrontation of the action situation with critical intelligence. Theory was not a sop to action but, in its critical function, was itself a species of action—and a dangerous species at that.

This strong Enlightenment belief in the autonomy and utility of critical intelligence had a practical side. Just as the *Encyclopédie* was intended to cut through the morass of inherited oracular academicism, so Mills envisioned his mission as necessarily being limited only by the number of people who could be reached intellectually and touched emotionally. It is for this reason that Mills felt a keen need to relate sociological imagination to what heretofore has been a "bad word": journalism. It is no accident that in Mills' collection of writings of political sociology and social stratification, the lead article is by Walter Lippmann. For here was the embodiment of how the journalist can function when he reaches the highest point of his profession: a scholar. Mills clearly sought to get to the same point in reverse direction—to get from sociology to his beloved "public" through the employment of journalism of Lippmann's type. Sociology was good if it helped the student better understand what was going on in the world—and that world is revealed most directly and organically in the daily press.

Mills was prepared to accept the fact that almost all sociological inquiry is comparative and relative in nature. What he insisted upon was not an absolute measuring rod of a predeterminist historical variety but simply that the comparative method is itself necessarily historical in character. "To compare" means to do so in time no less than in space. His objection to "narrow empiricism" was that it compared spatially as if time had no reality or bearing on the human subject. He also remained untouched by Hegelianism—as it emerges, in sociology as "grand theory"—wherein time is substituted for space, rather than the two being fused.

The uses of historical sociology (for Mills *all* sociology is historical) guarantee sociology a place in the scientific sun because it need no longer be assumed that there is an "essential human nature" or a "mysterious core" to men in their social interaction. "Abstractions" of this kind, or any other kind for that matter, disturbed Mills. He was empiricist enough to understand that what sociologists observe are men struggling, men battling, men killing, men making revolutions. The sociologist does not observe inevitabilities, equilibrium systems, or any parceling of men into neat sub-specializations of sociology. This accounts in good measure for the practical need of

Mills to write on revolution, on thermonuclear war, on minority migrations, on middle-class life in America, and on the growth of an elite in the American labor movement.

Sociology helps men "know where they stand, where they may be going, and what—if anything—they can do about the present as history and the future as responsibility." Mills boldly employed the "neo-Machiavellians"—the great sociologists of the Franco-Italian tradition as no other American sociologist before him. The work of Mosca, Pareto, Michels, and Sorel deeply influenced his thinking on questions, not because they demonstrated that men were often irrational in their behavioral patterns. This he knew without them. What they did was offer sociology what Freud and his circle offered psychology: a *rational explanation* for irrational behavior. What made these men important was their development of a scale of measuring irrational behavior which to his mind was unsurpassed, and was basically left unaccounted for in the calculations of the "biographers" who wrote the *Chroniques scandaleuses*, and the "historians" who wrote of ideology and *Wissenssoziologie*. That the "manipulation" of men was possible Mills did not doubt. But that the message of the great sociologists of the past not only dealt with the *mechanisms of persuasion*, but also in this very process provided a *system of clarification*, proved for Mills that sociology could *cure* social ills as well as account for them. And any science of human beings had to have this prescriptive value—just as does medicine and psychology.

I have saved for last an accounting of Mills' relation to Weber and Marx. Of the former, little can be added to Mills' already masterful introduction to *From Max Weber*. The use of multivariate analysis in political sociology, the irreducibility of class, status, and power as sociological variables, the role of charisma and rational authority in the organization of social life, the place of bureaucracy in the modern corporate State—all of these are embodied in Mills' writings—not as formal elaborations, or as "systems of sociology," but as working tools in the analysis of observable facts of human intercourse. With Marx, the situation is different. Mills came to a serious accounting of Marx very late in his career. Only in his last work does he offer an analysis of Marx on his own terms and not simply as part of the "classic tradition." And like latecomers, he tended to allow his enthusiasm to interfere with his judgment so that every nondescript piece of romantic, pre-revolutionary fancy tended to capture his fancy. For Mills, the writings of the Marxists—Luxemburg, Kautsky, Bebel, etc.—were like an uncovering of the Dead Sea Scrolls.

The impact of these writings on Mills' general vision of sociology can be grasped only in light of his conviction concerning the bankruptcy of the liberal tradition with which he was in such sympathy. The blasphemy of liberalism as a credo was that it succeeded, and in its success occurred the natural history of a dominant force—a conservative bias in all critical spheres of life. To find meaning in liberalism, to redefine it in terms of modern needs, meant to turn to the Marxians.

For Mills, the Marxians were *every* shading of radical opinion claiming to represent the truth of Marx and the truth of socialism. Marx was the only legitimate Marxist. The others—from Joseph Stalin and Leon Trotsky, to Ernesto Guevara and Mao Tse-tung—were "revisionists." And revision is a good thing to Mills. It prevents a doctrine from stagnating, it keeps alive the critical spirit. It makes for a lively dialogue. Thus, in his last period Mills became convinced that the real options for a social science still concerned with the realities of history and power were *within* Marxism, rather than between Marxism and liberalism, or Marxism and conservatism. Liberalism, in the sense of differences of opinion, concern for problems of real men, interest in problems of democracy, authority, and power, was thus embodied within the varieties of Marxism. In this sense, Mills was in his last days to become a Marxian. But this entailed no party affiliations, no ritualistic attachment to dogma, and no pieties for any one figure over another. To the end, Mills harbored deep antagonisms for Marxians of the Communist variety. In Cuba, he accused them of jingoism and cowardice for failure to go to the Sierra Maestra with his beloved "Fidel" on the limp excuse that such would be romanticism. In Russia, he accused Khrushchev and his fellow leaders of cowardice in the face of Stalinism, and calumny afterward. In fact, Mills' personal feelings ran high for the "romantic reformers" in Yugoslavia, Cuba, and Poland. In this he saw the continuation of the liberal dialogue at another level, suitable for another stage of historical development.

At the time of his death, Mills had several manuscripts in preparation. He was most anxious to follow his volume on *The Marxians* with one to be called *The Anarchists* and another on *The Trotskyists*. And how he adored these people, Bakunin, Sorel, Kropotkin, Thoreau, De Leon, and Emma Goldman, who made up in political posture what they lacked in sociological sophistication. Another work in preparation—tentatively entitled *Tovarisch: Letters to Ivan*—was going to fuse all of this sociological understanding and anarchist philosophy into a critical statement of the Russian polity, from the viewpoint of an American radical, a free spirit, and a dedicated social scientist.

What is indisputably clear, however, is that Mills never ceased being a sociologist. True enough, he eschewed graduate teaching for undergraduate teaching (he once explained this by saying: "why should I teach three casehardened and crystallized people when I can teach three hundred young and open minds with the same expenditure of energy?"). It is also true that he paid little heed to the politics of the American Sociological Association. But these hardly form a basis for dismissing him (symbolically, to be sure) from the sociological community. Mills offered a provocative frame of reference that demanded (and did not always receive) straight answers. He pushed his conclusions beyond the evidence because only in this way could the dialogue ("thinking in opposites") that nourishes the sociological imagination be extended. It is casuistry to say that Mills divided sociologists into camps. What he did was help make possible a sociological dialogue.

In outlining the essential content of intellectual craftsmanship, Mills reveals the motivating force behind his own work, thus providing perhaps the most fitting and the final epitaph to it:

> Know that you inherit and are carrying on the tradition of classic social analysis; so try to understand man not as an isolated fragment, not as an intelligible field or system in and of itself. Try to understand men and women as historical and social actors, and the ways in which the variety of men and women are intricately selected and intricately formed by the variety of human societies. Before you are through with any piece of work, no matter how indirectly on occasion, orient it to the central and continuing task of understanding the structure and the drift, the shaping and the meanings, of your own period, the terrible and magnificent world of human society in the second half of the twentieth century (*The Sociological Imagination*, p. 225).

Works by C. Wright Mills

Character and Social Structure (with Hans Gerth)
New Men of Power
The Power Elite
The Sociological Imagination
White Collar

37

Daniel Patrick Moynihan:
The Last Hurrah of Liberal Sociology

Unlike the overwhelming majority of social scientists, Daniel Patrick Moynihan lived in the public arena no less than the professional world. Indeed, the ways in which he managed this duality of roles is itself an object of interest. He is a man about whom much has been written, and who himself has hardly been shy about his extraordinary life. This makes it possible to speak of microscopic details instead of macroscopic generalities with relative ease. What is especially noteworthy is not so much a background in international relations and social policy, but how, once Moynihan entered the quotidian existence of a political man, he remained true to the calling and constraints of social science. He brought honor to the field precisely because he avoided or at least managed to disregard the trimming, hemming, and hawing that characterizes so many officials in public life. The moral foundations of social science were not imported into the political process like some excess baggage. It was in fact endemic to the tasks of social research and public policy.

The death of Patrick Daniel Moynihan is so stunning because he represented in his person many of the hopes and dreams of sociology in its heyday in the middle of the century. Moynihan's sociology was to be scientifically grounded based on fact, and policy oriented based on human need. This dual perspective permitted Pat Moynihan to have a successful career as a Harvard professor and also a Washington politician without skipping a beat. In his person, he was almost a prototype of Edwin O'Connor's Boston politician even though, in his later years, he represented New York in the Senate. But curiously, in his sociology he was more the pugnacious New Yorker than the Cambridge don. Multiple roles served Pat well, and he in turn used his multiple roles to bring unique distinction to policy work.

His love of America was evident in his deep feeling for the immigrants who forged a new nation out of an old culture. An intellectual environment in which Oscar Handlin and Nathan Glazer looked about them and saw a world of Irish, Jewish, and Italian immigrants—all of them finding a way to carve out a space in the New World—stimulated Pat's work on ethnicity. Along with Seymour Martin Lipset, who called this "The First New Nation," Moynihan celebrated the fact that everything was made possible by the giant shift from inherited status to stratification based on education. America rewards what people know, not what they inherited. It was a good thing too, because inheritance is not what potato farmers from Ireland, peasant from Sicily, or shtetl Jews from Poland and Russia brought with them to the New World. Moynihan's work in this area, in collaboration with his colleague at Harvard, Nathan Glazer, was neither celebratory nor stereotypical. He saw in the immigration experience the essential model for everyone else. They democratized America, while the native English and Dutch speaking stock provided the institutional framework that allowed the country to burst the boundaries of the Old World in everything from economy to ideology.

The hardest theoretical challenge Moynihan faced was trying to figure out why the "experience" of European immigrants did not work at all times for all peoples. Because it did not, policymaking became difficult, if not impossible. Pat's interest in the Negro family was a source of inspiration as well as a challenge to all he dearly believed to be true. He was too sophisticated to explain black American differences exclusively on the break-up of the family under the terms of slavery. If this were the case, he reasoned, why was it that a black bourgeoisie managed to emerge in the first half of the twentieth century? What permitted rising class and ethnic differentiation within black life to flourish? At the same time, even acknowledging institutional racism as a reality of the 1960s, discrimination did not prevent, but only impeded, upward mobility for America's ethnic and religious minorities. The ever-pressing "Negro Question" served as the springboard for Moynihan to move from being a smart sociologist to a dedicated public servant. That he was criticized and at times even vilified by ideologists and extremists for his intellectual work did not deter him from his mission. Indeed, he lived long enough to convert many of his harshest critics into supporters. The plurality of votes that Pat received in New York's black communities increased each time he ran for the Senate—to the dismay of many rivals.

The family as a metaphor for moral virtue arguably caused him troubles long after the *Report on Black Families* was issued. In a memo to President Nixon, in whose administration he served as ambassador to India, he prepared a memo urging a cooling-off period in the rhetorical and street battles between black and white America. It was in that context that Pat used the phrase, "benign neglect," that was to cause him so much trouble. Such words make sense in the context of a family dispute in which husbands and wives, parents and children resolve problems not by enunciating new policies, but by keeping quiet, or simply cooling off. Pat's intentions notwithstanding, the phrase caused an immediate uproar. African American politicians saw the phrase as a fatuous effort to put the state of race relations on a back burner. It was no such thing. But it was at the heart of Moynihan's instinctive belief that beyond the melting pot may not be a bleaching of America into a singular personality type, but rather a harmonious balancing of different ethnicities with common values. I think it is fair to say that finding such shared goals proved far more elusive for Moynihan than identifying and mitigating the sources of different existences. Gunnar Myrdal's *American Dilemma* did not easily dissolve under the weight of new federal programs and policies.

Moynihan's report, *The Negro Family: The Case for National Action*, was completed in 1965, when he was assistant secretary of labor. It represented the culmination of his central role in shaping President Kennedy's New Frontier. But beyond the policy opportunity, the report was part of his continuing effort to explain the great difference between patterns of ethnicity and problems of race. He saw the roots of the problem in slavery, "the most awful the world has ever known." Reconstruction kept blacks in rural areas, thus denying them access to business and commerce. As a consequence, matriarchy, the reversal of roles of men and women was perpetuated. Urbanization brought about family pathologies, divorce, separation and desertion, children in broken homes, and illegitimacy rates far beyond the norm of the time. The wage system served black America badly, maintaining differentiation in roles and hence in family incomes. The result was rampant black-on-black crime, inadequate educational preparation as demonstrated by failure rates in the economy generally and in the armed forces in particular.

There were many criticisms of Moynihan's methodology and the databases he used, allegedly resulting in an exaggeration of both the weakness of the men and the strengths of the women in black families. Historians rushed to prove that family solidarity was somehow maintained throughout the slave epoch. But despite all of the criticisms, the result was a commonsense acceptance of the policy recommendations of Pat Moynihan. This deserves to be recalled as a measure of how far the American national effort came to be aligned with the goals of black America.

In a nutshell, Moynihan argued for a review of every federal program to determine whether it strengthened or weakened family life. He emphasized the need for special attention to employment for Negro men and adequate family housing—especially in the suburbs and beyond the ghetto walls. He argued for family planning services that could measure need and want, and programs that presaged affirmative action to address black under-representation, especially in university and military contexts. Pat was not alone in such recommendations. But he was unique in his ability to bring such new programs to reality, serving as assistant secretary of labor, and before that, as an assistant to Governor W. Averill Harriman in New York State—especially as head of the governor's task force while still completing his graduate studies at Syracuse University between 1959-1961.

I first met Moynihan at Hobart & William Smith—a stone's throw away from Syracuse at Geneva. We met through politics, not sociology. It was groundwork or trench time for Jack Kennedy's run at the White House and Moynihan was point man in the effort to mobilize younger academics in the New York area. It was a wonderful to be young enough to enjoy the experience and old enough to matter. As I recollect, the "chain of command," if it can be called that, was from Moynihan to Arthur Schlesinger, Jr. Arthur came and spoke several times. And I was delighted to do something, anything, to move the political process forward. I had a sense that the specter of McCarthyism, however well curbed by Eisenhower, could only be permanently lifted by a new turn in political party organization. Kennedy offered that hope through the magic of the New Frontier. I took this to mean a new generation of people in power, or at least close to power. Hobart at the time was an old-line denominational institution. It was probably best defined by its liberal Republicanism, but it was not exactly a hotbed of liberalism. The victory of John Fitzgerald Kennedy in November 1960 buoyed my spirits, and on campus at least, provided a new generation with an aura of political respectability. This was enhanced by the emergence of a sociology of relevance, as we liked to think of the Millsian pivot.

My most enduring personal recollection of Moynihan came eight years later, during the Bobby Kennedy presidential campaign in 1968. It was during the evening of the Oregon primary when a group of Kennedy supporters gathered to celebrate Bobby's anticipated victory. But to the great surprise of Moynihan, and the rest of us, the night belonged to Eugene McCarthy. It was only a week before the crucial California primary. Pat turned to me and said: "Irving, I have a room full of loyalists waiting to be addressed. How do I turn a defeat into a victory?" I replied by reminding him that the demographics of California, with its large African American and Mexican American populations, would move that state into Kennedy's column. "It would be tight, but our man should win," I said. Pat went downstairs to the ballroom and immediately thundered: "California is not Oregon. I have it on expert technical advice that the Hispanic and black voters will swing the state eight percentage points to our side. Now go out there, ring doorbells, and get out the vote. Next week is ours." And indeed it was. But who could possibly have known that it would be an evening that would turn from triumph to tragedy before the midnight hour. For me, my stay at Stanford and participation in the Kennedy campaign was the start and stop of politics. For Moynihan, the assassination only deepened his resolve to stay the course—which he did with the instinct and determination of one hundred years of the New York Irish Catholic tradition that he inherited.

Despite his increasing involvement and fame in the political arena, including serving three consecutive terms as a United States senator from New York, Pat remained very committed to academic and scholarly pursuits. In the middle of his first term as senator, I wrote an article critical of what I felt to be an exaggerated sense of the meliorative properties of policy. Pat both wrote and got on the telephone to tell me how disappointed he was with my position and assured me that his position did not rule out failure. Somehow, this call reassured me that I meant something more to Pat than the earlier and later encomiums. For Pat certainly read widely and wrote often! He was very helpful to Transaction in the mid-1960s when I arranged for a new series to be published by MIT Press, in conjunction with Transaction (which at the time did not yet have an independent book program). His fabled report was the basis of the first of several policy-oriented books to be issued.

Lee Rainwater and William Yancey, who at the time were my colleagues at Washington University in St. Louis, prepared a full-scale analysis and critique of policy toward black families that had at its core the actual *Report* itself. The second volume that appeared almost simultaneously was my own volume on *The Rise and Fall of Project Camelot*. Both of these emanated from articles in *Society* (then still known as *Transaction*). Pat was unstinting in his support of the series, and waived any royalties, which indeed went to Transaction directly. I am not certain that MIT would have taken on the series were it not for Pat's direct support. He was also a founding member of our editorial board and an early contributor on a variety of topics and themes. I realize of course that these were secondary activities for Pat, but they were of primary value in the launching and early years of Transaction. Moynihan was an important figure, but never a suffocatingly self-important figure.

In reflecting on his legacy, I am led to his faith in democratic government to do good things for ordinary people, but beyond that, a deep and abiding belief that ultimately these good things reside in bettering the person and the family. Pat did not so much celebrate the values of ethnicity as a residual aspect of Old World nationalism, but as evidence of New World possibilities. The government programs he sponsored nearly always depended upon providing a support system for the family. This is what he found to be the common core of Irish, Jewish, and Italian life. This is what he wanted to restore in African American life. Toward the close of his life, Moynihan came to understand the limits of policymaking, of social engineering if you will. Perhaps the stubborn persistence of unique qualities in black life which retained its own validity and its own sense of family values quite apart from the immigrant model of which he was so enamored caused him to appreciate that social science was apart from, indeed higher than, public policy. He painfully describes the dreams of mid-century social science to convert social welfare from a profession into a cause in his little (in size) work, *Maximum Feasible Misunderstanding*.

That said, the effort was noble, however imperfect the results. Pat was a unique voice of social science in the highest councils of public service. He provided a dimension of meaning to the word *evidence*—one that derives less from the deductive system of law and more from the reality of life. Pat did what most sociologists simply prayed would be done by others. He became a force in the world, while retaining an appreciation for truth in the science. As a result, he was a mighty force for change in the social world while remaining a servant for continuity in the cultural fabric of America.

Of the countless letters that I have received over the years, only three of them hang for public display in my office. Two of them are directly related to Pat. The first is a letter written by Robert Kennedy on the last day of his life, thanking me for my support of his efforts, and assuring me of his support of the social sciences. I have always suspected that Pat either inspired or, for all I know, actually wrote the letter. It somehow summarized my brief experience in a political campaign, and demonstrated lasting regard for public service as akin to social research. The second letter came from Pat directly and thanked me for my critical work on Cuba. In his heart, he was an anti-totalitarian. And while he reminded me that he was not much for small wars to rectify matters, he also took the occasion to note that he stood shoulder to shoulder with me in the struggle against tin-horn totalitarianism.

Pat could be trusted as a political man, and had to be respected as a social commentator. This cannot be said of very many people. Perhaps that is why he made colleagues in both of his chosen professions uncomfortable—and delighted the rest of us by his presence in our imperfect world.

Works by Daniel Patrick Moynihan

Beyond the Melting Pot: The Negroes, Puerto Ricans, Jews, Italians and Irish of New York City
Coping: Essays on the Practice of Government
Maximum Feasible Misunderstanding: Community Action in the War on Poverty
The Negro Family: The Case for National Action
Secrecy: The American Experience

38

Robert A. Nisbet:
The Radical Conservative

Robert A. Nisbet is often described in shorthand references as a "conservative." But if he was such—and I sincerely doubt the word has much meaning in relation to him (any more than "liberal" would have for either Strauss or Baltzell)—it was of a rarefied sort. His strong suit was community rather than individualism, and his sense of order was derived from the consent of the governed, not the insistence of the governors. Bob was essentially a social historian. Much of his earlier work was rooted in the study of eighteenth-century politics and ideology, above all, the French Revolution and its consequences.

It was a result of such analysis that he became a critic of theories of progress—not that he was opposed to progress, so much as appreciating that the moral curve does not move in a straight line from evil to good, simply because we have advanced mechanisms for controlling disease or mass production methods for making cars. He sensed that whether in the hands of a Robespierre or a Lenin, the demand for a more perfect human being, the ordering of perfection as it were, resulted in grotesque malformations of the free spirit. Social engineering, while superficially the offshoot of social science, was its reverse: the subversion of honest research in favor of securing an end result we now know is totalitarianism writ plain and simple.

In place of the idea of progress Nisbet offered something less grandiose, but for him far more serviceable: the idea of community. It was this element in his work that attracted wide attention in the decade of the 1960s—one in which a new left turned away from larger forms of historicism, or from what was defined as the old left, into more intimate ways of living a life without an apocalyptical scaffold. And whatever criticisms can be launched at that earlier epoch, its sense that some balance had to be struck between the needs of a group and the desires of the person remains a linchpin in current youthful realities.

Where Nisbet and his adolescent would-be followers parted company was the parallel notion that along with community the individual requires a sense of broad obligations to valued institutions, or more bluntly, to preserve the moral order. To be sure, Nisbet's moral order was rooted in the tradition of American Protestantism—in which the varieties of belief somehow coalesced to form a marketplace of ideas that ran on a parallel track to the political system, with its own variations and disputations. There was something of the Jamesian in Nisbet. The varieties of religious experience became transformed into varieties of moral experience. But however freewheeling one wanted to be with the word "varieties" its context was circumstanced by belief—not so much in a heavenly father as in an earthly president.

However uneasy was the relationship of community and order, the cement that held these two big concepts together was the democratic society as such. That is why he was an iconoclast in his choice of politicians and parties alike. He could be as severe on federally sponsored social science projects—such as Project Camelot—as any radical critic. He could denounce the corruption of government represented by Nixon and Watergate along with politicians far to the left of him. Having so little party loyalty meant he could hardly expect political appointment. Nor did he, unlike not a few others who made the final trek to Washington D.C., crave any such emolument. His final years at the American Enterprise Institute somehow heightened the sense of remoteness and distance from his more orthodox colleagues among those amazingly talented colleagues who comprised that think tank. Perhaps life was simpler for Nisbet than it was in hard reality, and hence choices between good and evil easier to discern. That as it may be, he offered a model of the scholar as a public servant throughout his life.

Nisbet saw the world in dialectical polarities: on one side were the values of community, moral authority, hierarchy, and the sacred. On the other side were individualism, equality, moral release from authority, and rationalist techniques of organization and power. While Nisbet left little doubt where he stood on these major concerns, he was astonishingly fair-minded in the presentation of those tendencies in modern society that he held up to ridicule. Perhaps this is because he viewed the sources of such polarities as themselves residing on the twin towers of the English industrial revolution and the French political revolution. The "particularities" of the old order dissolved with these twin developments. But left in their wake were the same moral choices to be made that plagued Western civilization since its founding in ancient Greece.

The place of sociology in the long tradition was the essence of the Nisbet contribution. Weber was the sociological equivalent of John Milton—still read and revered, not because he was correct in every judgment, but because every judgment was framed in terms of the polarities Nisbet identifies. The community and authority with which Nisbet wrote had their source in the writings of Emile Durkheim. And as with his master, so too with Nisbet: one is never quite sure whether the implications of the findings are reactionary or revolution. I suspect that again as with Durkheim, they were neither. Rather it was what Nisbet called the "passion for reality" that drove him. And such a passion goes far beyond methods and techniques into the structure of idea formations as such. His was a reality unmediated by layers of convention—but rather a direct look at the world as it is—straight, no chaser.

It might well be that Nisbet's idea of the sociological as some sort of extension into the post-industrial and post-revolutionary world of the late twentieth century is but a feeling more for the literary than the scientific. While this may well have been the case, until the hard scientific empiricism of the present, or its counterpart, the soft-subjectivist and individualist modes of post-modernism, can come up with figures who match Weber, Durkheim, Simmel, Mannheim, Tocqueville, Toennies, and yes, Marx, it will difficult to dismiss Nisbet's brand of the democratic culture. It is perhaps not entirely inconsequential that individuals who had in common personal beliefs, such as C. Wright Mills to the L0eft or Crane Brinton to the Right, came up with the same pantheon of greats from which to start a discourse on modern man.

It might well be that the contradictions in Nisbet loom larger than the reabsorptions. It might also be that cutting down large-scale theory into small bites make possible a sociology that has its own integrity. But if the larger implications of such newer work are not soon uncovered, the public will have a right to know if there is any larger meaning to such professional discourses. Nisbet sensed that this would be a fault line of the modern era, and so fought hard and long for some sort of linkages between historians and sociologists—between tradition and modernity—before the inevitable questions would arise as to the need for such work altogether.

Works by Robert A. Nisbet

Conservatism: Dream and Reality
The Degradation of the Academic Dogma
The History of the Idea of Progress
The Sociological Tradition
Tradition and Revolt

39

David Riesman:
Educating the Middle Class

One of the few blessings of passing away is that one does not have to suffer the indignity of reading obituaries written in haste and all too often with thoughtless praise of improper things. The instant obituaries of David Riesman in both the *New York Times* and the *Wall Street Journal* each appeared to be more book reviews than life summaries. One would think that Riesman just about closed shop with his first book, the much heralded work in social psychology, *The Lonely Crowd.* That work certainly captured the imagination of a post-World War Two generation trying to cope with American success while being sensitive to European tragedy. He did so with remarkable insight by dividing the world by how people respond to their own needs. That work, however, was not the end, but rather the beginning of a remarkable career.

For me, David Riesman, along with a handful of other figures— as diverse in background and careers as Arthur Schlesinger, Jr., Eli Ginzberg, and Max Lerner—gave definition, and not incidentally, decency, to the term liberalism. Greatly influenced by a background in law dating from Justices Louis Brandeis to Felix Frankfurter, David in particular understood well that it was law, not custom, that made possible a stable, civil, and worthwhile society. For the desire to do right and good does not define people so much as doing right and good within the framework of law—of what can be done without doing violence to who we are as a people. He avoided plunging into a revolutionary attempt to institutionalize for all people and all time what the right and the good represented. David Riesman's liberalism stemmed from a commitment to a faith in the law of the land being upheld. Like many of his intellectual predecessors, such as Morris Raphael Cohen, he believed that law had to do with guaranteeing the same starting point and the same opportunities for all people embraced by, and embracing, the American Constitution.

If Riesman seemed out of synch, even odd, by the close of his life, it was largely a function of changes in the American value system. He dismissed the idea that norms must trump law in order for the nation to keep pace with demands for a piece of the American pie. To do this, present-day liberalism has turned the classical model on its head: the task became not seeking a common starting point for all, but handicapping those advantaged so that, ideally speaking, everyone would finish at the same place. One of David's colleagues and co-workers on *The Lonely Crowd* who properly caught this special sense of liberal beliefs is Nathan Glazer. His comments in the June 3, 2002 issue of *The New Republic* were both persuasive and appreciative. Riesman, he wrote, "was a liberal with a difference. He was suspicious of the smugness of much liberalism and willing to go further than, or perhaps not as far as, the prevailing liberalism of the day." Glazer highlighted this special quality in Riesman's critique of higher education. "Riesman saw a degree of self-indulgence and sloppy thinking that he did not like, even thought he himself was a strong advocate of higher education reform, women's education, and civil rights."

He opposed those who advocated not winning and losing through talent and struggle, but finishing at the same place through the direct or indirect intervention of the state and its legislative, executive, and yes, judicial powers. Riesman's concerns about mandating equity are simply an extension of his fear of the totalitarian temptation at large. The experiences of the twentieth century, of Nazism and Communism, have made it patently evident that the usage of state power—however noble its stated aims—too often results in ignoble and even punishing outcomes. Riesman's steady devotion to classical notions of liberalism, derived from the utilitarian tradition of John Locke to John Stuart Mill, made him appear old fashioned and downright obsolete in the new world of race, gender, and class politics.

In some measure, his general outlook was underwritten by his life at Harvard University. He was not so much a figure in its sociology department as an icon that belonged to the university as a whole. Arthur Schlesinger, Jr., Bernard Bailyn, and Oscar Handlin in history, John Kenneth Galbraith in economics, Willard van Orman Quine in philosophy, Alan Dershowitz in law, and Harry Levin in comparative literature not so much defined schools of thought or departmental imperialism as provided Harvard with an unusual texture and blend of the life of the mind and commitment to public service.

Riesman shared many of the value preferences of the "greats" within sociology—including a general faith in pluralism with Talcott Parsons at one end and an appreciation of the person with George Homans at the other. But it was that special sense of the public good that existed beyond the professional world that set him apart from his departmental members. It also made him central to his beloved university. It is hard to know whether New England varieties of liberalism defined the Harvard style, or whether Harvard gave body to a New England vision of the world. But whatever the cause and effect in the interaction, the end result was the type of liberalism he thought to be superficial. It was the stuff of the second half of the twentieth century, at least that voted Democratic, took egalitarianism as an article of faith, and was skeptical of the free market, but was unusually indulgent in the so-called of planned economies. Within such broad parameters there was room for creativity and distinction. Beyond such parameters was presumably fanaticism. In such a closed universe, Riesman extended the boundaries of scholarship as policy in so far as possible without pushing them out of Cambridge Square.

Liberalism is far more than a set of principles, and certainly more than an institutional convention. It is just as much a series of contexts. That is why the American pragmatic tradition accommodated so neatly the classical liberal heritage of England. I became acutely aware of this contextual element while writing for Riesman's singular venture into editorial publishing. He started a rather informal publication in 1960; it might even be called crude by present-day standards. He called it *The Correspondent*. The choice of title stemmed from the Committees of Correspondence, that pre-Revolutionary group that alerted the colonists of British excesses and American rights. This may appear a rather odd choice for a title by one so dedicated to principles of classical liberalism. But of course, it is a title that those who took the British tradition in its exact meaning would have adopted. But David Riesman's publication was far less concerned about English problems with colonists of the eighteenth century than with American problems with Southeast Asia, especially Vietnam, in the mid-twentieth century.

The Correspondent keenly reflected Riesman's commitment to Enlightenment, as well as liberal, premises. The presumption in believing that a small publication, written and edited by intellectuals—mainly, but not exclusively, social scientists, could influence government decisions was breathtaking. *The Correspondent* debated the costs of involvement in a new war, attempting to extricate America from what was perceived as a dangerous trend within the executive branch of government, especially its Department of Defense, toward involvement in a Southeast Asian entanglement. The melange of individuals that Riesman brought together ranged from academics and pacifists, to Quakers, and the like. They managed to produce the first serious effort to deal with the premises, as well as practices, of the "war game" crowd—that group of so-called "whiz kids" that dominated defense policy with its theories of how to fight and win post-nuclear warfare. The publication made up for what it lacked in glitz with good reasoning. There was an element of Cambridge versus Washington, D.C. in the enterprise. David proved himself quite knowledgeable about how symbols can affect policy. For against all odds, *The Correspondent* did just that.

Its success depended in no small part on David's own sense of the context and content of liberalism. The publication was strongly opposed to United States military intervention in Southeast Asia, especially Vietnam. However, it drew a line between opposition to military adventurism and fawning support for the dictatorship of Ho Chi Minh that ruled North Vietnam or Pol Pot and the tyrants that were emerging in Cambodia. The same was the case with David's anti-nuclear stance, and later, his opposition to anti-nuclear missile shield forces. He was strongly opposed to militarization, but recognized full well that the Soviet Union was precisely a military-dominated dictatorship, lacking in the elements of democratic discourse. I suspect in retrospect that David was taken seriously in high quarters precisely because he never permitted opposition to United Stases foreign policy to degenerate into support for communist dictatorships—wherever they might be and whatever promises they held for a perfect proletarian future. In this, I would say that he was among that unique band of scholars—of whom Arthur Schlesinger, Jr. was the most prominent within the circles of power—for which liberalism was a way of life, not merely a set of slogans.

This same set of liberal guidelines characterized Riesman's more famous latter-day work on higher education. The liberalism was clearly evident in his strong support for black American rights to equal treatment, his close scrutiny of young women's participation in the educational process, and in general, his faith in education as a leveling device among social classes in all phases of learning and teaching. But when it came to affirmative action or infringement on the rights of the autonomy of universities, one saw a different Riesman. He became the anti-radical, the person for whom equity was sabotaged by notions of affirmative action, and university autonomy equally infringed upon by government mandates to admit women to all-male schools as in the Virginia Military Institute lawsuits. His suspicions about extremism on both sides of the ledger stemmed from an enormous regard for the legal tradition that dates to Oliver Wendell Holmes and later, his own mentor, Justice Felix Frankfurter. That his intellectual high wire act, based on Enlightenment values of faith in education, regard for the legal tradition, and advocacy of legislative relief for any and all inequities, angered some and infuriated others was of little consequence to Riesman. He was made of sturdy stuff, and perhaps a whiff of stuffiness as well, that simply would not countenance subverting principles to the whims of social pressure or political expediency.

Seen in context, *The Lonely Crowd was* part and parcel of this sense of principle. Riesman was not so much interested in making critical judgments as, say, Mills did in *White Collar*, as in examining the social psychology of postwar America as a whole. Just how difficult and complex an undertaking this was can best be appreciated by the fact that we have waited another half century for a similar effort, entitled *Bowling Alone*, by Robert Putnam, a political scientist also ensconced at the great Harvard University. Time will tell if the newer volume will have the staying power of its predecessor. But the same goal of capturing *Homo Americanus* whole is common to both efforts. Underneath the pursuit of happiness, each of these works sees the costs of that pursuit as estrangement from larger social moorings and alienation from private sentiments. Like Marx before him—the judgmental element aside—Riesman felt that social psychology may be a perfectly fine starting place, but it was not where a senior scholar necessarily wants to end up.

Given the strong proclivities of Americans to latch on to psychological explanations—to just about anything that can be converted into self-understanding, if not manifest self-help—Riesman's movement away from the subject of his mid-century classic may have made solid intellectual sense, but it also cost him the audience he so magically captured with his first book. For the themes of higher education, foreign policy, and race relations, which are enough for any ten scholars, much less a single individual, were simply not emotionally satisfying to the broad audience to whom David spoke. That said, his contributions to each of these big areas were immense. For he provided, with a small band of intellectual stalwarts, a continuing sense of liberalism as an evolving doctrine—one enriched rather than subverted by the social and behavioral sciences.

Riesman never made the fatal mistake of thinking that social science is simply political ideology writ in obscure language. Rather, he saw in its findings, in every sample of disparities arrived at in qualitative or quantitative terms, information that makes possible amelioration of ailments through policymaking based on those liberal premises. If the premises of the Enlightenment had run dry—or at least were subverted by the excesses taken, from Robespierre to Lenin, in bringing about a better day—it was not so much the fault of liberalism as ameliorative, but of the dictatorial impatience with democratic procedures. Indeed, the great divide of Riesman from the radicals was precisely with respect for procedures as such. For what is law if not a set of formally arrived at and agreed upon procedures? And it was this respect for the law, not just training in its canons, which separated Riesman from the political extremes that have engulfed sociology for so much of its tragic history. In this, Riesman fought for a social science free of posturing and exaggeration in much the same way as did Max Weber in his essays on science and politics as vocations. Indeed, they both shared a passion not so much for the law (which they had in common) as for justice as institutionalized fairness. The loss of David Riesman helps us realize in what terribly short supply a sense of the democratic imagination has become.

Works by David Riesman

Abundance for What
The Academic Revolution (with Christopher Jencks)
On Higher Education
The Lonely Crowd
Thorstein Veblen

40

Arnold M. Rose:
The Power Structure vs. the Power Elite

For more than twenty-five years Arnold Rose has fused the liberal ethos with the sociological imagination. An intellectual adventure that began in 1940 with his major role in *An American Dilemma* has now reached its intellectual culmination with *The Power Structure*. It might be added that, distinctly unlike most sociologists, Rose's knowledge of the civic culture and the political arena is authentic— an authenticity certified by his service as a representative in the Minnesota legislature and by his relentless defense of civil and academic freedoms in the courtroom no less than the classroom.

This aspect of Arnold Rose's career is not accidentally related to the book before you—since, like all good social scientists, Rose has transformed both personal profile and political commitment into scientific sociology. One may take issue with many of the hypotheses and conclusions he has drawn, but one may not easily contest either the sobriety of his intellectual viewpoint or the worth of the man behind it.

One genuine problem might well be that Professor Rose's involvement in politics at the local level tends to reinforce a populist image of government, which, while in fact present in American society, does not necessarily reflect the structural dilemmas of the society at the national, or even more noteworthy, at the international level. Thus, it may be that the degree of civilian control over the military appears greater from the shores of Lake Superior in Minnesota than from the Bay of Guanabara in Brazil. I doubt that the average American, infused as he is with populist values, and oblivious as he often is of overseas commitments, has the same perception of an American military or diplomatic presence as do those peoples who live in the midst of revolutions or counter-revolutions—successful or otherwise, depending on the attitudes of the United States military mission and the financial appraisals of United States trade groups, no less than on the civilian ambassadorial staff.

The attempt of Arnold Rose is clear enough: to effect a reconciliation of power theories by employing the political analyses of the pluralists, from Bentley to Key, and the sociological methods of the elitist school, particularly the contemporary work of Mills and Hunter. That neither of the contrasting schools of macro-political conflict theory will be much satisfied by Rose's analysis is a foregone conclusion, and clearly appreciated by the author himself. One must welcome Rose's calm and dispassionate examination of the available empirical information, and his willingness to speculate on the outcome of each theory in the light of the current discussion between pluralists and elitists. Without work such as his, the discussion could well become part of general ideology rather than part of systematic sociology.

In this connection, one of the most telling virtues of Rose's presentation is his appreciation of the generalized state of false consciousness in American society. There is an absence of a true appreciation of the nature of power, which is by no means confined to trade unionists or a proletarian class but extends throughout the business sectors, the political communities, and all of the intermediary classes that constantly examine their own power in evaluating their influence on social events.

I would not take issue with Arnold Rose on his shrewd observations concerning the generalized misconceptions about power, but rather I would emphasize more the actual disparity between the perception of power and the exercise of power. It might be true to say that the understanding of power on the part of big business is as fragile and limited as it is on the part of big unionism. However, from the point of view of social forces and not just social interactions, the actual dominion of power given over to business is considerably more than that given over to labor. This distinction between the perception and the execution of power is precisely what distinguishes pluralists from elitists, the latter being far more concerned with its exercise and the former far more concerned with its perception than is healthy for either. In this sense I view Professor Rose's book as an attempt to get each major theory of power to confront the other with its particular variety of false consciousness.

There is an ever-present confusion in political sociology between statements of fact (such as the existence of diverse and multi-channeled expressions of power in the United States) and judgments about the moral order (such as "the best way to study power in the United

States is by examining perceptions or life chances"). It is important to realize that power may be erroneously perceived not only in terms of underestimation but also in terms of exaggeration. Unionists may exaggerate their power. Militarists may overemphasize their warmaking potential. In these circumstances, perceptions may stimulate elitist sentiments rather than contribute to the pluralistic framework. Professor Rose's work does a great deal to clarify, or at least to catalogue, the present confusion between influence and power, between what is perceived and what is actual.

It might well be that there is a qualitative distinction to be made between voluntary community organizations and a bureaucratic national system. From a community point of view, voluntary organizations seem effective and powerful, but from the national perspective these same kinds of organizations often appear impotent. The nature of power, or at least the perception of power, shifts as the levels of analysis alter. Thus, the power structure in the United States may require one kind of examination when viewed in terms of voluntary community organization, while the United States as a power may bring out different features when considered internationally. Although even at the community level I venture to say that the degree of interlocking political-economic control is impressive.

One serendipitous finding made by Rose is the degree to which his empirical researches demonstrate a gap between civics and politics, between perceptions of influence and basic political issues within the nation. It is clear that the United States suffers not so much from power concentrations as from a breakdown in political dialogue resulting partly from a celebration of civic activities. The civic culture may not only vary from actual political behavior, but often represents an antithetical frame of reference. Civics often dulls the political sensibilities of the American public. This fact is clearly evident in Rose's work.

One of the most impressive facets of Professor Rose's book on the power structure is its revelation of his intimacy with the nature of power. The last sections, on Minnesota, Texas, the Kennedy presidential campaign, and the Medicare legislation, represent four case studies in political sociology. The case study method is often talked about but too rarely used. In Rose's hands political sociology is not reduced to cross-tabulating electoral results. He does not suffer from the fallacy of electoral determinism, of assuming that important political events are necessarily linked to electoral behavior. Quite the contrary. There is a strong undertone to Rose's remarks which clearly places him, no matter how dissatisfied he is with the results of Mills, on the side of the "classical" tradition, precisely because political sociology comes to represent the study of social interaction among political men, and not the study of electoral victories among nonpolitical men.

In this sense, the significance of *The Power Structure* is as much heuristic as theoretical. Chapter XIV may well be considered a guide for the perplexed liberal and for the confused sociologist. Written in the optative mood, it forms a basis for social and political action. Perhaps it is necessary to make constant references to democratic values in order to make good on the various propositions politicians proclaim to be existential fact. If the hopeful mood generated by Professor Rose's book produces a self-fulfilling prophesy based on liberal values, well and good. But if this same mood produces a smug acceptance of the American political system, both internally and in its effects on the rest of the world, then I would find this self-fulfilling prophesy more in the nature of a self-destructive fantasy.

Arnold Rose is a shrewd man. He appreciates and understands these various dilemmas. That is why his book manages to remain within the framework of a multi-influence approach without indulging in the kind of flatulent, self-congratulatory conclusions so often recorded in the work of those scholars adhering to pluralism.

This is a serious book deserving of attention and argument. If a political-economic elite theory of American society is to regain favor among students of the social sciences, the empirical and theoretical formulations of the multi-influence school as put forward so cogently by Professor Rose will have to be coped with squarely. Just as Rose engages in a symbolic dialogue with men like Mills and Hunter, so too will the future writers on political sociology have to come to terms in an equally serious dialogue with Arnold Rose's newest effort to construct a bridge between society and polity—or more to the point—between sociology and political analysis.

Works by Arnold M. Rose

Institutions of Advanced Societies
Mental Health and Mental Disorder
Organizing for Equality
Power Structure and Political Process in American Society
Race Prejudice and Discrimination

41

R.J. Rummel:
Death by Government

It has often and properly been bemoaned, by its champions and critics alike, that the social sciences, unlike the physical sciences, do not travel. By that I presume is meant that they lack an absence of universal properties that would permit an observer in one place to readily identify the parameters of research and findings in another place half way around the world. Indeed, if such parochialism is endemic to the nature of the social sciences then the very notion of science as social is itself in dispute.

However, there is one great and noble exception to this complaint (I should qualify this by saying that there may be others as well, for example the work done in experimental psychology) in the realm of large-scale analysis of whole societies: namely the study of life and death and the forms of inflicted nasty behaviors in-between. For in the measurement of life-taking propensities of states, societies, and communities, we come upon the universal property that links all humankind.

In this small world of specialized researchers on the arbitrary foreclosure and termination of human life, national boundaries and linguistic differences amongst the social scientists seem magically to melt. We have social historian, Alex P. Schmid in The Netherlands and his work on the politics of pain and punishment; famed psychologist Herbert C. Kelman from the United States and his studies of crimes of obedience and authority; Mika Haritos-Fatouros, also a psychologist, in Greece working on the psychology of torture; Israel W. Charny in Israel amassing worldwide studies of comparative genocides with a special emphases on holocausts directed at the Jewish and Armenian peoples. To be sure, this is a small universe of shared information about the terrible aspects of the large universe.

These names are more illustrative than exhaustive. One might just as well mention scholars of equal rank in Canada, Japan, England, France, and Germany also hard at work on similar and related subjects. The key is not disciplinary or national boundaries, but the human subject writ large—the taking of life, the maiming of life, the deformation of life—not as a morbid preoccupation, but as mechanism by which social science can join the pure and applied fields of science and medicine to heal and repair, and, ultimately, to just leave alone! For those who work in this area have as a common bond a recognition that issues of life and death are critical to social research, and that the prolongation of life and the postponement of death is a common meeting ground not just for people of good will but of researchers of good research habit.

In this specialized world at which the grim side of the twentieth century is explored in depth and with a special poignancy that often defies words—but does not escape numbers—none stand taller than R.J. Rummel, political scientist at the University of Hawaii. He has brought to the study of genocide the quantitative range of figures that is truly staggering by any measurement; and the qualitative meaning of all these numbers in the study of the comparative worth of civilizations.

What Rudy has done in this book above all others is provide a conceptual map to make future studies easier. He has made the sort of hard distinctions that are data driven between legal and outlaw states; between genocide and democide; between democratic and authoritarian systems—all anchored firmly in numbers. To be sure, numbers matter. All societies are in their nature imperfect artifacts. But those that hold as their highest value the sanctity of the person are different in their nature and essence from those who see their ultimate mission as obedience and punishment for the transgressors. This easy movement of different types of social scientists converging on the problem of life and death is fueled by the sort of data provided and distinctions made by Rudy Rummel. Indeed, we can no longer work in this area without reference to this massive, yet singular effort.

Just prior to the publication of *Death by Government* I wrote to Rudy to express my appreciation for his effort, mentioning that subsequent editions of my own work in the 1970s in this area summed up in *Taking Lives* were not needed—thanks largely to his own extraordinary efforts. I suspect that it is a rare and exhilarating feeling to be able to say with Weber: what I fail to make, others will, and then have this come true in one's own lifetime. To be sure, in my own most recent effort, an essay on "Counting Bodies," it was the spirit of Rudy's work that permitted me to better understand the wellsprings of Nazism, and no less, the source of Jewish survival.

Rudy's work needs no elaboration. But I would like to point to one crucial aspect that stands out above all others: the need to revise our sense of the depth of horrors inculcated by communist regimes on ordinary humanity. The numbers are so grotesque at this level, that we must actually revise our sense and sensibilities about the comparative study of totalitarianisms to appreciate that of the two supreme systemic horrors of the century, the communist regimes hold a measurable edge over the fascist regimes in their life-taking propensities. For buried in the datum on totalitarian death mills as a whole is the terrible sense that communism is not "Left" and fascism is not "Right"—both are horrors—and the former, by virtue of its capacities for destroying more of its own nationals, holds an unenviable "lead" over the latter in life taking.

One might argue that the fascists had a greater sense of technological modes of destruction, but the communists utilized the natural hardships of life, the better to destroy individual capacities for survival. Thus, those for whom the technology of death remains central may still prefer to think of the Nazis as worse offenders, whereas those for whom an elaborate prison system forever enshrined as the Gulag by Solzhenitsyn will see the communists as worse offenders. But it is the wisdom of Rummel to urge us beyond such dubious honors into an appreciation of the linkages of totalitarian systems in the murderous pursuit of worthless objectives.

Rudy rarely speaks about morality and virtue. His concerns are not fixated on "normative" concerns of equity and liberty, or the uneven rankings of people in societies. He is not describing the imperfections of democracies or the weakness of Western liberalism. Rather, he is by implication saying that societies in which debate and discussion do not lead to death and decimation will somehow find a means to care for themselves. In that sense, his trilogy on *Lethal Politics*, *Democide*, and *Death by Government* represent, by extension, a study of the forms of democracy—the ways in which systems operate to sustain themselves without destroying opposition. This was made perfectly plain in a specialized volume he wrote on *China's Bloody Century*.

It might be that the study of positive concepts like democracy and freedom will forever remain as spongy as they seem elusive. But it may also be that we will get a better "fix" on the positive aspects of social systems once we enlist the aid of data to help us arrive at a sense of which societies can truly be called decent. Not all issues are resolved: we are not told whether centralized or decentralized societies are better or worse, whether the impulses to one or another form of societies are driven by external modes of power or internal guides of authority, whether democracy operates best in small or large states, or whether legal or ethical varieties of rule are best. But all these, while important considerations, are secondary—at least in the sense that they presuppose an environment in which life taking is suspended and life giving becomes a large norm.

We all walk a little taller by climbing on the shoulders of Rummel's work. He has helped us to redeem the highest aspirations of the founders of social science, and yet remain perfectly true to the latest techniques of formal analysis. It is a pleasure to write these words as a fellow laborer in the vineyards of social research. It is no less a privilege to add that, as president of Transaction, it has been a privilege to serve as publisher of nearly all the major works of Professor Rummel. If we published nothing other than Rummel's works, the rationale for the existence of Transaction as a publisher of social science would be vouchsafed. I can think of no more fitting tribute to this singular scholar in search of collective life.

Works by R.J. Rummel

China's Bloody Century
Death by Government
Lethal Politics
Power Kills
Statistics of Democide

42

Peter Shaw:
The Political Vision of a Literary Scholar

Being the editor of several *festschriften*, contributor to at least a dozen others, publisher of yet eighteen more, and, lo, the recipient of one, I have developed a hard set of standards for participation in or publication of this odd literary duck, often found drifting among the academic swans. Let me outline my personal criteria quickly before addressing Peter Shaw, the real and worthy subject of this essay. The outline may be salutary in that Peter is a model for such an exercise, meeting all my criteria handily.

The recipient of a *festschrift* must have probed into new, uncharted realms, widening the frontiers of knowledge and assuming the consequent risks. And, it is not enough for him to have recited the opinions of others or to have floated above the fray as some remote paragon of virtue. Finally, the corpus of his work should demonstrate a coherence so that an homage not appear as a simple cluster of views unconnected to any larger driving force. These are my requisites. Others might describe them differently, but I suspect that the same elements appear, implicitly at least, on the list of attributes of any life fit to be celebrated.

As I have said, measured by my checklist above, the life and work of Peter Shaw merit celebration. And so, it falls to me here to highlight and underscore certain characteristics—there are four—that lent continuing importance and captivating force to his work. Detailing them, it is hoped, will provide insight on Peter's unique philosophy that might inform us as we seek better to perform our daily tasks.

First, Peter Shaw was essentially an essayist. It follows then, along the lines of Montaigne, that he was also a moralist, for, just as the short story has to have a "punch line," so too the critical essay requires a "moral lesson." Peter did not start out moralizing, as his dissertation on John Adams would indicate, but in the final decade his essays sought increasingly to distinguish between right and wrong.

Of course, the trick is to state such lessons with subtlety and in a nuanced way that does not bludgeon others into acquiescence but persuades by force of reason. The balanced relationship between the narrative and the normative is what Peter was all about.

Second, Peter Shaw loved American values and the tradition that nourished American culture. His work on John Adams is far more than a narrative of the thought and character of our second president; it is an appreciation of how the American Revolution became institutionalized, or, if you will, constitutionalized. Those early concerns remained with him even during the high polemicism of his last ten years. And, by promoting that about America which he cherished, Peter distinguished his views from the fashionable post-1960 *anti-politique*.

Third, his was an enduring love affair with the splendid English language and its distinctly American offshoot. To Peter, the structure of language was intimately related to the character of a people, so he delved into the historical foundations of our speech, going deeper than mere patriotic rhetoric to plumb the extents to which public discourse about politics, law, and government were invariably linked to the private language of the novel. In these scholarly endeavors, he was something of a Menckenite.

Fourth, Peter Shaw cared not a jot or a tittle for such bureaucratic managers of culture as the Modern Language Association, whose very name implies some claim to authority or influence over our native tongue. The culture wars were fought out on a larger canvas. As a result, boundaries between narrow disciplines counted for little to Peter, as the parochial fiefdoms they outlined were subsumed by the living force of popular persuasion. So, his assault on the extremists became a powerful critique of the entrenched effete intelligentsia.

If we turn to Peter's most purely literary work, where one might excuse departures from the strict application of the four above-listed building blocks, we see that they are nonetheless fully operative. Thus, *Recovering American Literature* exemplifies the essayist. Indeed, the work is essentially a compilation of papers written over time on *The Scarlet Letter* by Hawthorne; *Moby Dick*, *Billy Budd*, and *Typee* by Melville (clearly Peter's favorite writer); Mark Twain's *Huckleberry Finn*; and *The Bostonians* by Henry James. I will leave for my literary colleagues to gauge the quality of his analyses. But it is evident that these works, as a whole, summarized Peter's emphasis on literature as a basis for estimating value—in this case, of the contributions these figures made to American language, politics, and custom.

In his opening statement, Peter makes plain the grounds of his analysis:

> As things now stand, critical discussion has succeeded in putting America's literature on a plane with America's shortcomings. The critics have achieved a self-fulfilling denigration in which they impose on what they regard as a vulgarly acquisitive America a vulgarized literature. Yet whatever one may think of the nation's political record, its literature is not vulgar except in the uses to which contemporary critics put it.

He caps the point by concluding that

> recovering American literature does not mean neglecting these extraliterary impulses. But it does mean treating each of them in its literary as well as its political dimensions.

And in his wonderful conclusion to the essay on Melville's *Typee*, "at once less ideological and more subversive than his recent critics imagine," Peter returns to a central motivating thrust: the universal and durable core of American values. This he defends with a critique of those who "subordinate their critical understanding to their political conviction." The work ends with a stinging assault on a relativism that leaves America denuded of the values that made it a great civilization.

> So powerful have the imperatives of relativism grown, in fact, that not only can the norms of logic be suspended in its service, but also the cultivated sensibility that turns us away in disgust from cannibalism. For the critics of *Typee*, virtually any abandonment of values has been preferable to admitting an allegiance to civilization.

An intellectual career that started with his biography of John Adams as an affirmation of a distinctly American culture—a culture that both underlines and transcends personal motives with a sense of historical objectivity and public duty—concluded with a reaffirmation of just values in the guise of a critique of its opposite: extreme relativism and subjectivism that would deny either distinctive national traits or universal values. Even in his very last essay, Shaw struck this theme. "Downward Mobility and Praise Inflation" indicated that "as academic scholarship devolved into crude political proselytizing, hundreds of academic books were yearly declared to be paradigm-bursting major revelations of age-old historical and philosophical questions."

This theme of impoverished scholarship and inflated rhetoric, which became the leitmotif in so much of Peter's later work, was struck first and most forcibly in his 1979 essay for *Harper's* on the decline of criticism. It merits careful consideration, for it offers in broad outline the empirical grounds for his assault on presumptive radicalism.

> Certainty and piety of all kinds are systematically undermined in favor of a universal relativism of values and judgment. Just as the revisionists are led to reduce the act of criticism to a given critic's subjective preference, so do professors relegate judgment of all sorts to the students' subjective preferences.

Peter goes on to declare that

> college professors thus share a skepticism about art and knowledge, the intellect and culture, not only with revisionist critics but with anti-intellectuals outside academe as well. In the end, from this point of view nothing makes any sense; everything is relative, anyway; one person's opinion is as good as another's; moral distinctions are useless. They all reduce to power and desire—to my own opinion, the way I feel, what seems right to me. The diverse adherents of this philosophy, whether they be anti-intellectuals, revisionist critics, or professors at colleges and universities prestigious and obscure, come down to being part of the same descent into solipsism.

Shaw's politics, if it be so called, holds that the humanities have no intrinsic invulnerability against the twin evils of solipsism and extremism, which serve to vitiate literature and isolate it from the human mainstream—even if the substance of this mainstream is not always readily apparent. His concern with the "reconciliation" of culture and society led him into a broad naturalism in which social tradition alone imposed continuity on culture. The idea of "precedence" for Peter provided three great benefits: "The wish to preserve society, becoming skeptical of departures from its norms, and feeling more judged than judging of the past."

In this connection it is interesting to reflect on Peter's earlier, and to some degree curious, work on the symbolism of the American Revolution. In *American Patriots and the Rituals of Revolution*, he finds himself having to depart from the instinct to preserve society while observing its normative structure. In that work he reveals himself as supportive of America as a new civilization, but, at the same time, he appears less than content about forced departures from his reliance on precedence. In reviewing everything from the scapegoating of such commonly reviled political figures as Thomas Hutchinson, the governor of Massachusetts at the time of the American Revolution, to youth culture's turning into gangs of extortionists, Peter found himself reflecting a certain ambivalence about the American Revolution itself. He saw the symbolism as extending far beyond the cry for independence into a certain mob culture. In this, Peter was led to examine the consequences of the French Revolution of 1789, and why and how the American Revolution of 1776 did not end up eating its own in the same revolutionary quagmire.

What he arrived at was not the neat division between a French sense of passion and an American sense of compassion that often accompanies apologias for the American Revolution, but rather an impulse for liberty and freedom that exceeded its European boundaries and origins. Thus it was that the "ritual of revolution" rather than its substance became the subject of Peter's most troubled, and perhaps troubling, work. The insights of psychoanalysis, anthropology, and literary criticism softened the blow, as it were, of defining a revolution that was far from pretty, but that inescapable conclusion forced on Peter not only the reluctant commitment to an "eclectic approach," but also and more profoundly, it obliged him to respond ambiguously, straddling the fence in a position at once strange and uncomfortable. Extrapolating from what he wrote, one might say that Peter accepted the necessity of the American Revolution, but saw its success in limiting the influence of independent sovereigns while maintaining strong links to the source in a British "culture of liberty."

The seldom cited book *American Patriots and the Rituals of Revolution* reveals certain flaws in the conservative vision of America that Peter tended to shunt aside. It confronts poignant concerns that are not readily resolved. On one hand, he saw in the American Revolution a purity that set apart the American experience from all others. But the First New Nation emerged not with purity or innocence, but with a series of violent upheavals from the grim Stamp Act riots of 1765 to the mob assaults on legitimate government in Massachusetts in 1774 that saw the expulsion of Governor Hutchinson after the Boston Tea Party. Just how one can win freedom and do so within the framework of law was a problem for the founding fathers, and it was certainly a point of deep concern for Peter Shaw, the quintessential radical moralist and conservative jurist.

One can only speculate about Peter's internal resolution of the dilemma of a bloody revolution made for the purpose of establishing a just order. His answer would seem to posit the simultaneous workings of public and private rituals so that the American Revolution was "enacted both by crowds and in the minds and hearts of patriots." Making such a distinction—creating such a duality—is not to resolve the troubling theoretical technicalities, but it allowed Peter to let the dust of time settle on and obscure them while he turned his attention to the more pressing business of effecting a "passage from one state of being to another: from the reign of a king to that of the American people."

A writer often elects or is drawn to model his own behavior on that of his subject. Careful, rigorous deliberation on a life, an event, or a time, and the subsequent usage or treatment of those reflections in words, have a way of transfiguring the observer. To some extent, therefore, when Peter wrote of the second American president that "intensity of feelings remained with Adams to the end as surely as it marked his personality from the beginning," he was penning one epitaph that might be a particularly apt summation of his own life. But quite beyond sentiments are the similitudes of sense. Writing in 1815, John Adams said that, "I must think myself independent, as long as I live. The feeling is essential to my existence." I suspect that Peter Shaw would not object to being bracketed with John Adams on this final tough-minded sentiment.

Works by Peter Shaw

American Patriots and the Rituals of Revolution
The Character of John Adams
Recovering American Literature
The War Against the Intellect

43

Kalman H. Silvert:
Democracy as Human Rights

If Kalman Silvert's great and good friend, Leonard Reissman, were alive, it would be his role to speak here before you and tender this farewell to our beloved friend on behalf of the social science community. But his death late last year was also a tremendous loss, one that I know was deeply felt by Kalman in particular. They worked together for many years, dating back to the Tulane period, and I believe each gave to the other a broader sense of the social sciences—a sense of the redemptive power of addressing real issues and problems without being overly concerned by disciplinary boundaries or bureaucratic departmental notions.

I take it as fortunate that Kal had this special affection for social science as a whole and wayward sociologists in particular, for, were that not the case, I do not believe I could have possibly made it through those first years in South America, especially Buenos Aires. It was such a lonely period for me, not only because I was cut adrift from my own family, but, more profoundly, because I was so ignorant of all things foreign. In the late 1950s, it was Kalman Silvert who provided the proverbial helping hand. His family, especially his wife Frieda, and everyone else at home, made it possible for me to live out those early years abroad with a sense of tranquility. The most important thing at that time was the reminder that there really was such a place as home, even in a distant part of the world relatively unknown to me.

Kal was most at ease in metropolitan centers. What he loved about Buenos Aires, perhaps the same affection he had for New York City, was a feeling of not being estranged from his environment, of being in tune with the pulse and vibration of what is the center of civilization in our times: the big city. Kal also understood the nature of universities in large cities, the special character of students who drifted to the University of Buenos Aires or to New York University, as part of a large metropolitan center, rather than the center of a universe detached from the metropole. As a result, he had a special feeling for teaching urban students. He well understood the nature of formal learning and the limits to teaching, and vice versa.

Let me dwell for a moment on this aspect, since Kal Silvert provided a model for how one should live in a great city. He had a spectacular sense for living in, and not just observing, an urban setting, which many of us who go abroad, even repeatedly, oftentimes forget. We get caught up in the exotic and we lose the sense of ordinary beauty and intimate connections between living things, institutions, and peoples. Kalman's special gift was an ability to step off an airplane from New York to Buenos Aires the way most of us step off the platform of a subway or bus from Manhattan to Brooklyn. His sense of how those two cities in particular were connected by their ethnicity, by their secularization of learning, and even by the unsavory aspects of city life was profound. All of this wisdom he made part of my own life, and that of anyone else who listened and learned from him. Because of this understanding, it was possible for me to survive a very difficult period, and ultimately know what it is to love another environment.

The kindness that Kal and his family showed to me during this period is particularly touching in retrospect since the late 1950s and early 1960s were a period of deep desperation, even financial crisis, for the Silvert family. It was right after their son Henry (Hank) had sustained a frightful accident under circumstances that could easily have led a lesser man to abandon the idea of the family and go into a sense of cynicism, not just pessimism. Along with Frieda, the Silvert family never abandoned that hope. Kal had a kind of iron will and ferocious sense of the family that was very important to him: far more important than the casual humor about the foibles and fallacies of family life with which he could regale his friends and colleagues. For underneath that skeptical humor was a tremendous sense of the best, not just in the family tradition, but more exactly, in the Jewish family tradition. There was no effort spared—no money, no remedy, no love—to help his children survive. Though he loved all his children deeply, he had a special feeling for Hank. In that oldest, physically damaged child, the culmination and fruition of love and will came together.

Adversity brought forth the fire in the man. At that time it took someone with incredible love and will to have sustained such a passion for family life. Kal gave up everything: financial security, personal rewards, and attractive job opportunities, to do what had to be done. So he lived in a very special way as both a universal scholar and as a highly particularistic family man. Because he gave life where none could have been expected, he also provides a sense of the immortality of life and its triumph over death through that strange phrase: "next of kin."

Kalman was, as everyone who knew him recognized at first sight, a remarkable man. He had been a fine musician, highly literate in the world of letters, and a most unusual cartoonist. I recollect that whenever we sat next to each other at conferences (and this was nearly every time around) he had an extraordinary way of diagramming everyone's exaggerations. If anyone were making a particular fool of himself by using a word or a phrase repeatedly, that word or phrase would be captured perfectly in a quick sketch or cartoon. I remember one particular scholar using the word "indicator" five times in about one minute. Kal drew a series of indicators, from highway signs to weathervanes, that were so amusing I had to take leave of the room amid frowns of the other participants. These conferences we attended were often dominated by Kal, not because he spoke first, or last, or most, but because what he had to say was invariably a cut above the people he was addressing or for that matter listening to. Not only did he have an unusual bent of mind, but he spoke and behaved without pomposity and the customary conceit so typical of academic life in its higher reaches. Egotism was the enemy of intellect for him, and that made him a very special person: the target of wrath as well as of admiration.

As the years rolled by and both of us moved along, our paths crossed less frequently. However, our interests continued to run in a parallel course. Both of us became more involved with the structure of American society, and both of us began to view the hemisphere in more organic terms. We saw one another less frequently, but perhaps at far greater events than at an earlier period. We were both critical and highly immersed in the critique of Project Camelot, and all other efforts at harnessing the social sciences to national counterinsurgency efforts. Independently of each other, we wrote essays quite similar in sense and sentiment, if not in content. In the early 1970s problems shifted, and we both attended several conferences on the place and position of Jews in Latin America and the world over. Our positions tended to be far closer than in the past, despite the absence of much direct contact. Perhaps the last time we saw each other was at the preview performance of Costa Gavras' film *State of Siege*. Each time we met there was a feeling of continuity with the past. There was never a feeling of estrangement, not only because we followed each other's work, but because a solid sense of knowing one another pervaded our interaction. I never had the feeling that I had to get to know Kal over again. He was always there, and he was always providing help whenever needed.

It was strange to read the *New York Times* obituary on Kal, since I never thought of him as only, or even primarily, a Latin Americanist, even though I had gotten to know him in South America and we were both continuously involved in the world of overseas research and university life. In part, I presume that my surprise at his being defined as a Latin Americanist was for the aforementioned reason of his cosmopolitan persuasion. In part, too, it was because he had such a consuming interest in social science as a whole, unbridled by parochial "area specialist" connotations. He was an absolutely first-rate theorist who knew the literature of political science, sociology, and economics with equal fluency: precisely the kind of fluency often absent in area people.

There are so many aspects of Kal's life that bear repetition and recollection. I can only hint at one or two more. Above all is his sense of the public nature of the social science performance, the linkage of politics to journalism. He transformed those years of financial necessity, as part of the American Universities Field Staff, into some of the spriteliest, most cogent writing on Latin America that appeared in the postwar era. Many of these writings ultimately found their way into books and scholarly essays, others into the briefing sessions of the Ford Foundation. But their initial form gave a sense of vibrancy and life that is typical of the best of the journalistic as well as the social science tradition. Ordinary events took on powerful meaning because of Kalman's psychological insights into character formation. Kal never forgot that whatever else society was ultimately composed of—economics, classes, military factions, political interest groups—the people behind all of these were real unto themselves. They acquired characteristics built up by virtue of language, body movement, and behavioral forms. Kal was a master of Latin American culture in these intimate senses. It is no exaggeration to say that he was one of the few people I have known who knew as much about the societies he went to as that from which he emanated.

I have learned a great deal from Kalman. We did not agree on every issue. Clearly, this is more than one could expect between colleagues. But neither did he or I ever expect agreement on issues to affect in any way the nature or depth of our friendship. What I am left with, the residual element in his life that I hope at least in part I was able to incorporate in my own, is a deep sense of personal loyalty; an appreciation for the Jewish factor in public as well as private life; the cosmopolitan ability, exemplified by *porteños*, to connect up with all manner of people by virtue of being an outsider and a member of the marginal group; and that quintessential democratic sensibility that Kal manifested, what might be called street-corner democracy, a loose structure in which people figure out ways to violate rules some of the time simply to point up the irrational streak in those professing bureaucratic rationality. Further, it involves obeying orders only when they make sense and under no other circumstances. This democratic persuasion, coupled as it was with social science vision, was the very essence of the noble life and the intellectual life combined. It was a privilege and an honor to have known Kal Silvert, and I shall cherish his memory.

Works by Kalman H. Silvert

Churches and States: The Religious Institution and Modernization
Education, Values, and Possibilities for Social Change in Chile
Essays in Understanding Latin America
Man's Power: A Biased Guide to Political Thought and Action
The Reason for Democracy

44

John Stanley:
Historian of Political Ideas

Let me express my deep appreciation to the University of California at Riverside, its fine political science department, and above all, the driving force of this event, Charlotte Stanley, for having me deliver this inaugural address on behalf of our departed friend and colleague, John Stanley. Many of the people in the room this afternoon were acquainted with John in far more intimate ways than I—and in closer quarters. Thus, it would be a presumption for me to describe John in strictly intimate terms. Let me confine these remarks to the public side of John, his service to the community of scholarship, or that wonderful conspiracy of excellence that defined his mission and remains our quest.

John Stanley may have been based in a political science department but he was essentially cast in the mold of an historian of ideas. In this, he was much like his early mentor, Robert A. Nisbet. To put a fine point on it, John was an historian of political ideas, especially those that had a moral edge. He was a master of what the discipline somewhat euphemistically now refers to as normative theory—the belief that everything from natural rights to natural law is subject to norms. Whether such norms are derived from a transcendental, historical, or empirical realm is a touchy matter. It defines one as a Kantian, Hegelian, or Marxian in the Germanic tradition at least.

But John bypassed much of this definitional squabbling for position by largely deriving his tradition from French and British sources. For while he had early on acquired an extraordinary knowledge of the Germanic philosophical tradition, or at least the Marxian wing of that tradition, it was not until his final decade that he turned to issues generated by that tradition. John pursued a distinctive line of inquiry. The eighteenth-century French tradition, from Montesquieu in 1748 through Condorcet in 1798, represented fifty years of concern with human rights rather than state obligations. John was interested in the empirical coordinates of behavior rather than the rational implications of dynastic power, and hence a consideration of bottom-up politics of society rather than top-down politics of the state. He was after all a Sorelian: "Tory" in theory but "populist" in practice.

John was very much a post-Enlightenment analyst. He had to confront not only major figures like Rousseau, Diderot, and Voltaire, but also the revolutionary practice of their strictures in the guise of Robespierre, Danton, and Marat—that is, with the makers of a revolution that failed. He also had to confront a socialist tradition of the nineteenth century that either did not come to pass, or came into being as a distorted version of what was promised in Marxism. Like Berlioz's *Symphonie Fantastique*, the beautiful waltz of the first movement turned into the draconian death dance of the fifth movement. Those who wrote political theory as history in the second half of the twentieth century were compelled to face up to the moral failure of political nerve. That is precisely what made John Stanley's work of such durable value.

Seen in such lights, the choice of Georges Sorel as a central figure seems quite rational rather than eccentric. For Sorel is that autodidactic political theorist of prophecies that failed. The French Revolutions of 1789, 1830, 1848, and 1871 were all followed by conservative and restoration regimes in politics and a consolidation of bourgeois power in economics. After so much carnage it would have been difficult to imagine a world without Sorel. In some similar sense, the twentieth-century world wars of 1914-1918 and 1939-1945, the Korean War, which stalemated, and the Vietnam War, which was lost by the powerful United States, also created an aura of pessimism and optimism. Add to this to the utter bankruptcy of Stalinism and Soviet power, leading to the collapse of communism in Europe between 1989-1991, and the sense of revolutionary failure hung large over the twentieth century.

For John, however, the situation was one that required not simply an appreciation of failure, or even why failure seemed to haunt the democratic and socialist powers alike. Rather, the challenge—one he gladly accepted—was how does this condition permit a radical posture to be maintained? As his life moved along, John upset the traditional model of moving from the radical to the conservative, and preferred to see himself as perhaps more radicalized at the end than the start of his career. How was that possible? What were the elements that permitted a radical framework to explain a conservative epoch? Here again, Sorel—sometimes described as a "radical conservative," other times as a "conservative radical," came to the rescue. For he provided a moral, in contrast to a scientific, framework for discoursing on politics that preserved radical sentiments by seeing sharply their conservative morals.

His attraction to Sorel was different than mine. I sought to explain Sorel as a post-socialist figure, i.e., what happens when prophecy fails; in short, what happened to the socialist ideology and movement between the death of Marx and Engels and the successful Bolshevik Revolution of Lenin and Stalin. So my *Radicalism and the Revolt Against Reason* was an effort to situate Sorel in that netherworld of *fin-de-siècle* radicalism—radicalism turned subjective, irrational, and anti-historical. John's concerns started from my premises, took them as a given, and asked essentially what was the moral basis of socialism, once its empirical content had been emptied, or, as he preferred to say, "dirempted." In so doing, in emphasizing the ethical rather than political bases, John gave life and coherence to the work of Sorel never before recognized.

John was a special sort of figure—he approached Marx, Engels, and Sorel as one would Byron, Keats, and Shelley. He enjoyed reveling in their world, entering it as a friendly critic, and conducting a dialogue with the dead, but not with the deaf. I have met few others like him; perhaps Tom Bottomore was closest. John tested his mettle against the grain. He viewed himself much as he saw Harold Laski, an outsider, the man of principle, the political theorist who saw theory as such as a form of activism. I confess to be not quite so Olympian and detached in my views on the same subjects. Perhaps background variables play a role. My family was hounded by the Czarists, imprisoned by the Soviets, and murdered by the Nazis—so my sense of totalitarian doctrine or statism is doubtless colored by those realities.

But we are not here to discuss comparisons, although they play a role in friendship and yes, in the limitations of friendship. John was an outstanding human being: gracious in his estimate of others, generous in his praise of others, but with a firm set of convictions on the soft underbelly of democratic theory linked to capitalist practice. This has been a characteristic of conservatives as well as revolutionaries—a disdain for the commercial world and its vanities. In the end, John, like Sorel, was a radical conservative, or a conservative radical. Whatever spin we place on that dichotomy between main currents in political ideology, the world of learning was fortunate to have one so talented; it was also misfortunate enough to lose one of such talent far too soon.

John evolved slowly over time: from a commentator on the work of classical figures in political doctrine and social theory to an interpreter of such figures and work. There is a distinction to be made, since interpretation opens up the commentator to risk—of being wrong and of being disliked even if liked! So it was with John. As he moved from Sorel to Marx in the pantheon in the sky he shifted roles. This volume of his seven papers on Marx by no means represents what he might have done had he had a seventh decade in which to write and study, but it holds lessons nonetheless. The move to Marx was an effort to redefine the Croce line of thought, namely, to determine what is living and what is dead in the Marxian tradition.

The primary lesson is that John's work was predicated on and dedicated to exactitude and rectitude. He actually read all the works he was interpreting. This gave great strength to his convictions. The major two papers on the relationship of Marx and Engels debunks the myth that they were differing souls, at loggerheads even on fundamental questions of philosophy. It might have been pleasant had they in fact disagreed on basic issues, but they did not. The orthodox communists who linked Marx and Engels constantly turn out to be correct—unpalatable though that may be the revisionist history.

John was careful not to claim too much for what was living in the philosophical legacy of Marx and Engels. He was not in the business of political correctness. But he was anxious to keep the record straight, so that criticism, no less than support, is based on what the documents and writings of both founders of scientific socialism detail. It is a fact that the two rarely quarreled, but it is a fact that they pursued separate lines of work. Engels emphasized issues in ontology, military affairs, and technology. Marx for his part spent most of his time on economic and political issues. There is also no doubt who between the two was a genius and who was a talent. Engels himself never tired of placing Marx at the forefront. But this is a different sort of inquiry. It was hard for John to get a hearing on the philosophical similarities between the two founding fathers of modern socialism. The common interpretation from Sidney Hook to present political theory is clearly intent on separating the political economy of Marx from the metaphysical philosophy of Engels.

However palatable or unpalatable the consequences, he let the chips fall where they may regarding Marxism as well as Sorelian doctrine. This quality, done with a minimal amount of pugnacity, gave his writings on the history of socialism as theory a special dimension, a freshness derived from the care and feeding of primary sources. So what we learn from these last writings of John is not simply about the shifting objects of his attention and affection, but about the author himself. And in the long pull of time, the lessons of being open-hearted and yet precise well translated into the proper way to study the intellectual history of our times, and for that matter, past times.

Works by John Stanley

From Georges Sorel (2 volumes)
The Illusions of Progress (ed.)
Mainlining Marx
The Sociology of Virtue

45

Anselm Strauss:
Democratizing Social Psychology

The passing of Anselm Strauss deprives American social science of a unique stylist no less than a special sort of researcher. It is insufficient to speak of him as some sort of product of the Chicago School of doing sociology; more realistically, he a product of a literate approach to the American language. He framed issues an open ended way, to tease out the questions rather than demand answers. He wrote like he thought: listen first, talk last; hear now, interpret later. The modesty of the man translated into the analysis of the scholar.

Preparing this statement on Anselm Strauss actually proved to be a daunting task. Every time I thought that I had hit upon an insight into Anselm and his sociological work, it turned out that he had written on the subject with an acuity and precision that exposed my own commentary as tepid and vague! Indeed, his opening essay is such a brilliant synthesis of the Chicago Tradition (not simply style, but tradition), placing it within a firm philosophical context, that there is little left to add for the amateur historian of ideas.

Anselm was and remained a social psychologist of a special sort, someone who appreciated the degree to which what takes place in the privacy of our minds translates into the public consequences of the social fabric. His opening statement is followed in quick succession by intensely sociological essays on "closed awareness" (meaning in this instance knowledge about situations and events that is not equally shared), face-to-face interaction, and structured interactions. The subtext distinguishes sociological from psychiatric conventions, seeing everything from daydreams to visions in interactionist frames rather than as pathological states. The implications of such probes into the medical are stated gently, but carry deep ramifications. For the act of people treating each other compassionately, no less than professionally, is also an act of awareness. Treating the human person as a creature of dignity, when generalized, becomes the basis for imaging human society.

So much sociological theory rests on premises of superordinate and subordinate, on the unequal distribution of status, power, and wealth, that we tend to forget or ignore the extent to which all individuals bring to the collective experience potential for changing such established relations. At the center of Anselm's effort is the democratization of sociology—not in some sentimental, flabby way that does away with distinctions by clever manipulation or working the system, but by making sure that we all recognize, in true pragmatic fashion, the relativities of status, power, and wealth in the conduct of everyday life. For, if no power or status is absolute, all collective life becomes subject to negotiation, rearrangement, and reconstruction.

In this sense, Anselm's work elevated the "Chicago style" above its own norms. He understood that "interaction" is not a flat, mechanical relation between persons, but a constantly shifting set of struggles between people and institutions of uneven power at different points in time. In this, his work came close to the "Eastern School" of Peter Blau. In addition, Anselm treated institutions as a player in the lives of persons. And hence, his work on hospitals and medical practice raised the public awareness of how agencies shape our lives—and our deaths. By extension, this strain in modern life between people and between persons and institutions can be and should be examined in contexts of schools and teachers, court rooms and lawyers, laboratories and chemists. And legions of Anselm's students did just this.

Whether dealing with work, leisure, culture, illness, or any form of human activity, Anselm makes certain that we understand that the actual experienced arrangements between people, and for that matter, by extension, between nations, are subject to negotiation. The "web of negotiation" is the human field upon which organizational arrangements can be changed. Anselm avoids current fashions by going far beyond the cynical idea that negotiating orders is the same as doing away with social structures as such. Quite the contrary: it is the very reverse. Negotiation is for Strauss the opposite of pure self-interest doctrine. It is a way to ensure that structures can be made to work, and better, as a result of the interaction. In building upon the volitional or, as Anselm calls them, the anti-deterministic elements, he squarely places his position and his vision of the Chicago School at the service of a democratic culture.

I find Anselm's work tremendously refreshing and even exhilarating—a relief from the European traditions that too often slyly move from statements of domination and control to passive acquiescence in the inevitability of such a situation or, as in some tragic cases, to the active pursuit and advocacy of hard-and-fast distinctions between social roles and political statuses. In his remarkable ability to distinguish the negotiation process from a pure lapse into a denial of the reality of structure as such, Anselm is able to avoid the manifold subjectivist pitfalls to which certain tendencies in the away-from-Chicago-School have fallen prey.

The deep philosophical reasoning Anselm brings and are brought to the fore on every topic covered deserves to be appreciated and emulated—especially at a time when the crude specificities of the empiricist tradition are being countered by equally crude specificities of the integrationist inheritance. If I understand him rightly, the need of the moment is "to build a general theory about social worlds rather than merely to aim at substantive research on particular ones." And that is exactly what Anselm has done throughout much of his career. His emphasis on professions, on urbanization, immigration, ethnicity, and a variety of everyday concerns links up a perspective that too readily lapses into dilettantism and egotism, and shows how the common quotidian considerations are the cornea in the sociological eye.

In the long swing of the twentieth century, Chicago-style work—from Dewey and Mead, to Hughes, Thomas, Park, Blumer, and the more recent contributors to whom Anselm pays tribute—has rested not only on theories of society, but on policies for society. Indeed, as he properly notes, the linkage to Chicago is organic, and not accidental. Anselm's own fierce positions on medical service and health care delivery form an area in which the symbolic interaction tradition, which emphasizes the body and its frailties, also deals with the human soul and its inviolabilities. I realize that, in introducing such a notion as the soul, I can be accused of importing Horowitz into Strauss. But I suspect not. For "taking the role of the other" entails an entire set of moral premises about the worth of all people embodied in the theme of self and other. After all, just how far is this from Martin's Buber's "I and Thou" relationship? Not too far, I would suggest.

That Anselm retained a lifelong concern for problems of method, consultation, and teaching may appear anticlimactic to some. But I think otherwise. For if Anselm is offering a general viewpoint about sociological practice based on the pragmatic tradition, he is also providing a specific framework for implementing such practice in school and society. Further, that methods end with questions of pedagogy is very much part of the Deweyan tradition of inquiry with which Anselm began his long journey. The end is thus linked to the beginning in a general mode of analysis, passing along valid information in a meaningful way to a next generation. In this way, pedagogical practice becomes the mortar linking generations and creating cultures. The circle of life becomes a spiral of thought. This personal processing of social structures permits the promise of social science to be fulfilled. In this difficult, sometimes tortuous path, one can scarcely hope for a better guide than the *lebenswerke* of Anselm Strauss.

Anselm was an intense man—easily disguised beneath a calm demeanor. He felt keenly issues of medical care for the poor, and health services for all Americans. It is a reflection of the field of sociology that it has shriveled as a general theory and mushroomed as a set of applications. Anselm understood this well, and through the study of health and medical care sought to bridge this gap by offering his work as part and parcel of a democratic policy approach. That those who read his work may not always share in the policy must not blind them to the higher purpose of linking social science to social policy. In this, Strauss continued the tradition established by one wing of the Chicago School, that of Park and Burgess and Hughes, but perhaps also defined himself apart from the more anthropological wing of Goffman. Strauss struggled with the ambiguities of his legacy, and moved beyond them by the simple device of holding in suspension ultimate judgments and worrying more about immediate assistance.

As an analyst and methodologist of looking at societies, Strauss had few peers. As a human being with a larger dose of compassion than passion, he was able to offer a positive message to a field rendered feeble by exaggerated notions of struggles and subjectivities. In the jumbled world of medical claims, hospital service, insurance forms, and above all, patient complaints, Strauss found his voice. He was able to fuse the disparate elements of empirical precision with moral aims—a not inconsequential achievement.

Works by Anselm Strauss

Creating Sociological Awareness
Images of the American City
Professions, Work, and Careers
Psychiatric Ideologies and Institutions
Where Medicine Fails

46

Thomas Szasz:
The Politics of Psychiatry and
the Ethics of a Psychiatrist

There is a strange and wondrous story called "The System of Doctor Tarr and Professor Fether" written by Edgar Allan Poe in which the reader is never quite certain, at least until the close of the story, just who is the superintendent and who is the patient in a Maison de Sant outside of Paris in the first half of the nineteenth century. Indeed, there is sufficient role reversal taking place so that the reader is unrelieved of doubt on the doctor-patient role even after the story is concluded. In the short story, Poe mixes terror and kindness, sickness with health, and lucidity with imaginings of all sorts. Over all, we are left with grave doubt as to the relationships of people to each other—especially in confined settings, or what Erving Goffman preferred to call total institutions. The human condition is neither comedic nor tragic—but some ever changing admixture of the two.

It is not that categories of sanity and insanity are fictitious; it is rather that the human bearers of such categories are all too real. They operate from a bag of motives which themselves require explication. This story by Poe might well be the appropriate fictive tale to the quite real concerns of Thomas Szasz in our day and age. For his interests range far beyond commonplace slogans about mental illness, into the painful ambiguities of everyday life—and the need to make decisions about what constitutes creative as well as destructive behavior, no less than what we mean by health and ailment as such. His work crosses over from law, medicine, and the social sciences with a frightening ease—frightening because Szasz is so knowledgeable about each of these broad areas, and even more, because he probes the sources of our intellectual boundaries in a challenging way.

If there is another living psychiatrist who has suffered more professional obloquy while sustaining great public recognition, his person escapes my recognition. To be sure, one could say that the work of Thomas Szasz has far greater support in allied disciplines such as sociology and political science than in his own native grounds. This is a two way street of course. For if people like Erving Goffman drew support in his *Asylums* from the earlier efforts of Szasz, so too has Szasz sought relief and comfort in the likes of George Herbert Mead and his *Mind, Self and Society.* To say the least, the life and career of Szasz is a tribute to the incredible moral spine of this individual, but also to the tangled web of professional relationships that have evolved over the century in the social and behavioral sciences.

Calling attention to the contributions of the social sciences may be the greatest sin committed by Szasz in the eyes of his critics. For it is the medical model of psychiatric practice that comes under the sharpest sort of critique in his work. This is not because Tom is against medicine—indeed his training and points of reference have always been the medical profession—but against the smuggling of categories of crime and punishment, for example, into the definition of mental illness. In a recent essay, Szasz adroitly sums up the dual edge to his critique of contemporary psychiatry. "The focus of my conceptual critique is the distinction between the literal and metaphorical use of language; and the focus of my moral-political critique is the distinction between dealing with grown persons as adults, possessing free will and rights and responsibilities, as against dealing with them as if they were infants or idiots lacking free will and rights and responsibilities."

One might claim that even the conceptual critique is saturated with political judgment—since the literal, and metaphorical use of language has, over time, been well understood to have a high political content. For what else has given George Orwell his permanent niche in the world of letters if not this deep appreciation of language as a symbolic tool of manipulation, no less than a prosaic tool in communication. It is the language of medicine—the certitude with which the idea of mental patients having mental diseases and medical claimants having scientific rigor is a basic source of the politics of mental health—that presumes that a subset of professionals can impose its will and judgments over a large set of medical practitioners.

The stakes in this intellectual struggle are so high—ranging from fees to be collected to worldviews to be protected—that it is little wonder that Szasz has been pilloried in a manner and with a drum beat that surely would have sent a less determined individual to Coventry and back. Samples of invective abound. Hardly a book he writes or an article he produces fails to produce a legion of critics. The lines of criticism seem to divide between the political and the professional.

In the former category, we are told that Szasz does not represent a consensus of opinion and is therefore wrong, or he so distorts psychiatry that the normative foundations of society would be rendered inoperative by his judgments. On the professional level, the usual criticism is that he is mistaken on specific points of psychiatric practice, to the more recent and fashionable critique that psychopharmacology has given precisely the sort of chemical basis to neurosis and psychoses that Szasz's work largely if not categorically denies. Since Szasz himself has responded with considerable verve and at great length to these other charges, I shall eschew a defense of his work as such, and move on to the political and economic sources of those assaults. But before doing so, it might be worthwhile to explain what elements in his work have sufficiently enraged his professional colleagues. At least in this way, the ethical battleground of psychiatric practice can perhaps be sharply etched.

Ultimately, the achievement of Szasz is the unique ability to bring into a discipline that, ostensibly at least, has come to pride itself on its indifference to moral claims, precisely a sense of morality—an ethic of responsibility. In a universe in which everyone claims a victim status, a liberal virus threatens to undermine a liberal society. When everyone from the street pusher to the university president can claim a victim status, it is precisely this sense of ethical responsibility that vanishes behind a cloud of psychiatric smoke. It should be noted that such vague notions as ethics are given operation meaning by Szasz, to wit, sufficient education to make discerning distinctions as to what is right and wrong, good and evil, no less than true and false.

And while Szasz has been, improperly in my view, classified as anti-Freudian, he is perhaps the most Freudian of the present lot of analysts—for to rekindle the phrase of Philip Rieff, Szasz shares with Freud the "mind of the moralist" in defining the field and developing scenarios for the determination of neurosis and normalcy in the conduct of everyday affairs. For without a moral sensibility, prospects for the reconstruction of society become null and void. Egoism comes to replace civilization, and the discontents are only able to undermine rather than restore that sense of purpose that gives reason its place in the human mind.

This is not to deny that Szasz has been critical of many propositions within the Freudian corpus, from the oedipal complex and notions of philogenetic memory traces to Freud's judgments about the analytic setting of doctor-patient relations; but these are hardly unique to Szasz. Indeed, there are many practitioners of psychiatry who are far more severe in their judgments of Freud, who nonetheless earn Szasz's wrath. It is the singular merit of Szasz that his concerns extend far beyond the parochial boundaries of biography or, for that matter, the dangers of digressing from an established corpus of the master's writings. Rather, in a sense of the goals of medicine, the prolongation of life, and even the goals of analysis, the ability of the person to make free and rational choices, however such big words are defined, I find the two far closer in spirit than those who believe that in attacking Szasz they are somehow protecting Freud from a harasser and interloper.

For in reviewing the constancy over thirty-five years of his major themes, one senses the "ought" behind the "is"—the impulse to liberty as free choice even more than the lack of efficacy of psychiatric treatment and counseling. Indeed, in his most recent book, *Cruel Compassion*, which can be viewed as an underscoring of his lifelong themes, there is a sharper polarity: caring for others by means of coercion, or doing so with their consent. The libertarian motif becomes text rather than subtext. And to those who claim that a theory of consent is not feasible with those labeled as mentally ill, he reminds his critics that it is they who continually utilize and invoke the medical analogies. And if this analogy between the physical and the psychic is accurate, then too, must the right of the patient to solicit treatment be viewed as inviolable by extension.

It might be argued that certain levels of coercion are required. But Szasz's answer—not always fully worked out—are two in number: if this be the case, then the analog to medicine in general must be abandoned or seriously revised. But more important, to argue the case for coercive practice is to move dangerously close to the identification of the scientific community with the police force. And here Szasz, in his full passion, returns to the ethical basis of all issues connected with health. It is worth quoting since it is both an apt summary of his ethical position, and no less, a warning to those in possession of a monopoly of power—including the power to treat patients.

It is dishonest to pretend that caring coercively for the mentally ill invariably helps him, and that abstaining from such coercion is tantamount to "withholding treatment" from him. Every social policy entails benefits as well as harms. Although our ideas about benefits and harms vary from time to time, all history teaches us to beware of benefactors who deprive their beneficiaries of liberty.

Of course, it might be argued that this is a straw man, that many individuals do indeed seek the very sort of treatment Szasz finds reprehensible. But that is another matter—having to do with the empirical efficacy of specific techniques of treatment. One might say that there is an ethical break between psychiatric control of society's unwanted, and psychiatric treatment of society's elite. One might say that "the myth of mental illness" may be common to all segments of society, while the reality of psychiatry as a more of coercion is unique to only special segments of an advanced society. I am not sure that Szasz has worked out the parameters of this relationship of voluntary and involuntary patients, and libertarian and authoritarian psychiatrists. Perhaps this is a work yet to come.

My own view is that the gap between psychology and psychiatry in general, and to psychoanalysis in particular, will both widen and deepen. The uses of psychology—from testing and measuring individual performance to defining the structure of perception and conception—have expanded over time. And while this expansion may not always be uniform, or for that matter, even welcome, it is real enough. One might well argue that far too much reliance on psychologists has crept into everything from evaluating career capabilities to defining students as having learning disabilities. Nonetheless, this aspect of professional psychology has expanded enormously— the size and outreach of professions and journals attest to this.

At the level of psychoanalysis, the situation is far different. It is a sub-branch of psychiatry, and one that has great strength only in isolated pockets—usually suburban areas where time and wealth conspire to permit its practice. The need to compress years into days has had a variety of consequences: much higher use of drug therapies on one hand and a reinterpretation of behavior to widen the area of the permissible and reduce that which is considered bizarre. And here it is not the moral assault by libertarian critics like Szasz that has proven effective so much as the economic assault of the marketplace and the social assault of contemporary relativism.

So Szasz can be said to have scored some substantial victories in his crusade for a libertarian option, but also a few major setbacks.

He himself realizes as much, since the rise of Medicare and Medicaid programs, inclusive of psychiatry, has expanded the payment basis for mental illness of all sorts; and this is coupled with the license given to psychiatrists to define huge numbers of society's unwanted under a classification of mental illness rather than as physically dangerous. There are, in short, dynamics at work within the society that tend to subvert the very goals Szasz seeks. But there are also tendencies that reinforce his position. Just how these social considerations impact the theory and practice of psychiatry is beginning to occupy many talented people—very much, including Szasz himself—for whom the larger context of the field has transformed the world of professional analysis into one of public discourse.

But quite beyond minoritarian fashions such as libertarianism lurks the mind of the moralist. And it is this that provides the umbilical cord between Szasz and Freud—one that cannot be severed, no matter how severe Szasz's reservations might be about the therapeutic process itself, or the conduct of its practitioners. I am reminded of the fact that Philip Rieff, some thirty-five years ago, wrote a book on *Freud: The Mind of the Moralist*. It is in the dramaturgy of good and evil that Rieff saw the staying power of Freudianism as an ideology. While Szasz's savage critique of "the manufacture of madness" by psychiatrists and witch hunters prevents him from exercising the power of an "ism" (nor I hasten to add would he desire such an appellation), the burden of his work is precisely to reannounce the dramaturgical aspects of psychiatry: the confrontation of oppressor to oppressed, of good and evil, of science versus mystification.

I would argue that this aspect of Szasz's work—his morally centered critique of a branch of both medical science and social science—has led to certain shifts in his objects of wrath over time. But these have been minor in contrast to the shifts in those who support and oppose him. I know of few figures in modern intellectual history who can enlist the wrath and support of conventional "Left" and "Right." And thus it is that an Edgar Z. Friedenberg, a grand guru of the 1960s and the anti-American generation, can praise "the depth of Szasz's commitment to human freedom and the precision with which he perceives that psychiatry has created highly effective forms of human bondage," while an equally powerful voice in the conservative movement, Ernest van den Haag, can claim to have been "entranced by the originality of Szasz's ideas and the brilliance and cogency of the presentation."

But what links scholars like Friedenberg on the Left and van den Haag on the Right—if one can still use such tattered terms in a meaningful way—is their marginality. And that must be said of Szasz at the end of the day as well. For what we have with Szasz is an attack on the center of a profession, on its established habits of advancement and promotion no less than patterns of professionalization. While so much of this paper centers on some of the relatively well known aspects of his critiques of the latter, it is the implicit assault on the former—on ways in which a profession awards and rewards—that so excites the opponents of Szasz. This is not a pleasant academic discourse, but a bitter struggle on the fate of a science on one side and its economic foundations on the other.

For what we have with Szasz is a direct appeal to a larger, intelligent public—the sort of individuals who might well frequent the psychiatrist for better or for worse—to give reconsideration to their basic notions of superordination and subordination. And to do so is a direct querying of trust. To pay money to an analyst, to allow the analyst to sit in judgment, whether through expert testimony in legal matters or direct decisions about incarceration in medical matters, are weighty concerns. I suspect that Szasz at the outset of his career, when he first started raising fundamental questions about the scientific status of psychiatry, thought little, if at all, about the politics and economics of such considerations. But as his analytic skills sharpened, and the target of his criticisms became increasingly focused, so too did the resistance of the psychiatric mainstream. This in turn fueled Szasz's sense of the political. He became involved in what, for want of a better word, the politics of libertarianism. For his work moved from a critique of a profession to a defense of the person; or as Szasz liked to frame matters: "to a struggle for self-esteem." His approving citation of C. S. Lewis serves Szasz as a final judgment, not on the scientific pretenses of a profession, but on its moral claims. "Of all the tyrannies a tyranny sincerely exercised for the good of its victims may be the most oppressive. To be 'cured' against one's will and cured of states which we may not regard as disease is to be put on a level with those who never will; to be classed with infants, imbeciles, and domestic animals." But in claiming that "these words still apply to psychiatry today" he only increased the level of his marginality. He became vulnerable to assaults in ways he could hardly have imagined in the late 1950s, when *The Myth of Mental Illness* first appeared.

This is not aimed to provide a brief history of Szasz; not at all. It is rather to make clear the meaning of the title of my contribution: the politics of psychiatry and the ethics of a psychiatrist. What emerges is hardly a pretty picture of professional and academic life in historical context in America. The best that can be said is that such a life is never desultory or wanting in fireworks; the worst that can be said is that those in charge of the control machinery of a profession are not by any means best fit to be the guardians of scientific considerations. The long and short of it is that Szasz has garnered the public rewards of his marginality, while at the same time, paying a heavy price in terms of the professional emoluments.

Nonetheless, it might be said more in sorrow than criticism that the psychiatry and psychoanalysis of the mid-1990s is radically different from that of the 1950s. When Szasz started writing on fundamental themes, American culture, no less than medical practice, still accepted electro-shock therapy as a norm, and took for granted the blessings of incarceration—forced and otherwise—upon those labeled as mentally ill. While the humanization of treatment has not been entirely even or steady, it is sufficiently noteworthy to raise questions about the tactics of critical analysis. One would like to see Szasz take some credit for such new developments rather than flog a dead, or at least badly injured, pseudo-scientific horse.

Given this combination of intellectual circumstances, it is little wonder then that Szasz, at the end of the day, and in the twilight of his life, can boast few of the acolytes of far lesser figures. In part this is a consequence of the double cutting edge of Szasz's works: it devastates totalitarianism, in its fascist and communist varieties with equal force, and it cuts down ideological humbug however meliorative or humane its social intentions or scientific pretensions. Beyond the negative or critical elements is his devotion to a democratic psychiatry, or at least an appropriately humane psychiatry befitting a democracy. Thus it is that Szasz must deal with the loneliness, the isolation, that comes from moralism as a personal posture no less than as an element in his analysis of a discipline. The "struggle for self esteem" which Szasz offers is a lonely struggle—and again, one that has a curious analog in Freud's notions of self-liberation through rather than against the therapeutic process. Thus it is that Szasz cannot quite free himself from his adversaries within psychiatry—in part because of a magnificent obsession with the subject, but in great measure, because he shares with a century of psychiatry, despite its own ambiguities and doubts, the search for human liberation—however fumbling and stumbling that search may be at different times and different places.

In what might well be called the anomaly of success, Szasz now takes his place in the pantheon of the very psychiatric movement he has so chastised and called to task over the years. But that is because the secret is out—due in part to Szasz's own efforts: the function and structure of psychiatry, especially psychoanalyses, belongs more to the search for ethical and pedagogical moorings in a secular world, than strictly speaking, empirical science as such.

The sooner the practice of psychoanalysis comes to terms with the limits of its theories about itself, the earlier we can all get on with the shared task of fashioning a new, and more modest, science of human nature. Curiously, Szasz put this search in quite elegant perspective in the Preface to his first, and perhaps still most enduring book, *The Myth of Mental Illness*: "I believe that psychiatry could be a science. I also believe that psychotherapy is an effective method of helping people—not to recover from an 'illness,' it is true, but rather to learn about themselves, others, and life."

Works by Thomas Szasz

Cruel Compassion
A Lexicon of Lunacy
The Manufacture of Madness
The Myth of Mental Illness
Our Right to Drugs

47

Jacob L. Talmon:
The Social Vision of Intellectual History

I first met Jacob Talmon in the fall of 1961, when we were both serving brief terms as visiting professors at the London School of Economics (LSE). For Talmon, who had been awarded a Ph.D. at the London School during the height of World War II, this was a happy as well as familiar ground. England represented that happy blend of civility and common sense that Talmon displayed in his personality as well as political temperament.

That occasion was my first visit to England, much less to a leading international institution such as the London School. My only previous overseas experience had been several tours of duty as a visiting professor at the University of Buenos Aires in the late 1950s. Everything, from the tempo of the two cities to the professional interactions, was different. What the two places did share in common was a vigorous belief in the power of ideas, and perhaps an exaggerated faith in education as the source of emancipation.

Along with David Glass, my sponsor at the London School, and Leonard Schapiro, the great historian of Soviet communism, Jacob Talmon became my best friend. Indeed, for those who know the place, establishing friendships at the LSE in terms of months rather than years is itself a tribute to the elemental needs of people for human association. The British art of looking past rather than at you was never so well perfected as at the Commons (otherwise known as restaurant and reading room combined) of the LSE.

Professor Talmon and I actually first conversed with each other at the home of a mutual colleague, a permanent member of the LSE academic staff, and not at the Commons. Only after that initial encounter on neutral ground did we become actively involved in discussions and meetings. Then I learned with much pleasure and surprise of Talmon's appreciation of my work on Sorel's *Radicalism and the Revolt Against Reason*. And only then did I, in turn, dare speak of my admiration for his classic study of *The Origins of Totalitarian Democracy*.

Only much later, with the appearance of the third and final volume in his massive trilogy of political and intellectual history, *The Myth of the Nation and the Vision of Revolution*, did I realize how very close was our thinking on the broad subjects of Marxism, Violence, Fascism, and Communism—and Sorel's role in providing the ideological mortar of this pre-Hitlerite effort to early work on *The Origins of Totalitarian Democracy* permitted me to see clearly the dialectic of radical ideology: the insistence on the need for total social reformation, but within a context of total political domination.

Talmon is one of a special group of Central European Jewish intellectuals who have helped define the nature of twentieth-century social and political life, giving shape to destructive potentials of our age only dimly understood by those who worship at the altar of absolute progress. Central neither to class enthusiasms below nor national hubris above, these people, who were actually outsiders, possessed a keen insight into the driving forces of the times—notably the unitary character of the totalitarian threat, the tragic gap between promise and performance in the revolutionary process and the failure of internationalist rhetoric to resolve national realities.

These émigrés from Berlin, Vienna, Warsaw, Budapest, and their environs were, for the most part, not speaking and writing from a conservative bias or defending constitutional tradition; there was little to defend in the world of crumbling empires in Central Europe. They were not concerned with restitution or restoration of an old order, for they knew old orders to be a threat to their own survival as Jews, intellectuals, and cosmopolitans.

They often discussed socialism and left-wing democracy. They were motivated by a passion for economic justice and elementary forms of democratic rule. Their involvement with the Socialist dream, minus the maddening character of Socialist practice, gave these people a special rhetoric.

Among this group were such persons as Hannah Arendt, Hans J. Morgenthau, Hans Kohn, Franz Neumann, George Lichtheim, Walter Laqueur, Henry Pachter, and Jacob L. Talmon. Talmon (who died in the late fall of 1980) was the author of many works. *The Myth of the Nation and the Vision of Revolution* is a key one because it is the final volume of a trilogy on 200 years of modern political life, begun a quarter of a century ago with *The Origins of Totalitarian Democracy* and followed a decade later with *Political Messianism*. In my judgment, *The Myth of the Nation and the Vision of Revolution* is the best of the three volumes, certainly the most sweeping and ambitious. In fact, it is nothing less than a masterpiece.

In this work, Talmon brings us to the twentieth century and ideological polarization as its central feature. In its eclecticism, it seems less concerned with establishing a thesis than the earlier volumes, and less subject with establishing a tension based on dialectical opposites that are not quite as reified as Talmon imagined, such as democracy and totalitarianism, or empirical politics and messianic relations. The complex nature of the political fabric sometimes got lost in earlier volumes of the trilogy. In *The Myth of the Nation and the Vision of Revolution*, Talmon displays a much greater sensitivity to the wide disparities within the same thinkers, the same nations, and the same classes.

Talmon did not write history in any conventional sense; strictly speaking, he transcended dynastic history and social history. His was a special kind of intellectual history, written by political ideologists who were either politicians or close enough to the political marrow to inform practicing politicians. *The Origins of Totalitarian Democracy* was peopled with figures of the Enlightenment such as Rousseau, Helvetius, and Diderot, and with great political actors such as Robespierre, Danton, and Saint-Just. *Political Messianism* ranged from technocrats to theocrats, from Saint-Simon to Blanqui, who were in and of themselves both political actors and intellectual leaders. *The Myth of the Nation* continues in this tradition; major figures include Marx and Engels, Lenin and Trotsky, and, in Western Europe, Mussolini and Hitler and their intellectual progenitors. Talmon weaves a tight interchange among social, political, and intellectual events, breaking down conventional distinctions that usually impede rather than enhance a sense of history.

Few genuinely heroic figures appear in Talmon's work, and those who continually announce a utopian future are dealt with severely. That is true for Marx, Engels, and Lenin in the current volume no less than in the previous volumes for Saint-Simon, Babeuf, and Fourier. But there does emerge in *The Myth of the Nation and the Vision of Revolution* a sense of the political leader as intellectual but not as ideologist. This distinction lends insight into Talmon and his notion of who constitutes the political prophets of peace no less than war.

In the figure of Jean Jaures, the nineteenth-century French socialist, one can sense Talmon's archetype. He describes Jaures as having had a passion for fairness, an extraordinary poetic capacity for empathy, a marvelous quickness of sympathy and imaginative insight, combined with an unmatched gift for words. Talmon shared those qualities. Those who knew him realized that his concerns were those of Jaures: a life of intellect and politics tempered by a survivalist attitude toward society. Talmon also read into Jaures what was true of himself: that these very characteristics made him yield easily to inferior men with narrower horizons or limited understanding but greater self-assurance. Fanaticism and dogmatism and not just democratic dogma were the true enemies of both Jaures and Talmon.

The Myth of the Nation and the Vision of Revolution is divided into nine parts, which I shall summarize briefly in the following paragraphs. The work begins with the growing dichotomization of class or nation that took place after the revolutions of 1848. Talmon gives particular emphasis to the dilemmas involved in post-utopian Socialist thinking on the role of the nation in the development of a revolution strategy based on pure class assumptions.

The work then moves dramatically to the world of Germany under Wilhelm I in the late nineteenth century, a world in which the question of the emancipation of the proletariat is dwarfed by the issue of national destiny. Between 1848 and 1914, Europe was driven by national cohesion more than class emancipation. Whether in Germany or Russia, Talmon saw revolutionary internationalism as a tenuous thread in the face of an overpowering demand for national hegemony and survival.

The third section of the book, which discusses Austria, is another case study of the issue of class or nation. The Austrian experience, while limited in global terms, was in fact prototypical with respect to what took place in Europe in the rest of the twentieth century.

The fourth part comprises the special role of the Jewish dimension. Talmon tells us that, while the Jewish role in European history was hardly new, Jews did become dramatically significant during the early part of the twentieth century. And, he says, the encounter between the gentile with the Jew was first as a bourgeois adversary, and second as a communist enemy. The Jew appeared as the *extremis*, an unstable element in the nationalist equation. The inability of large portions of European society to handle situations in which the Jew became a spokesman for forces contesting each other led to a breakdown of Enlightenment and Romantic rhetoric.

As Jews became archetypes, animosities against them crystallized from both the left and the right. Consequently, they became the enemy for national and class ideologies and interests, a source of tension rather than resolution. And, as extremism became the order of the day, Jewish centrism, along with gentile liberalism, became identified as the main foes of the totalitarians.

The fifth and sixth parts analyze how the dilemma between class and national was finally resolved in pre- and post-revolutionary Russian practice. The seventh deals with how the general will of the proletariat was translated by Lenin and Stalin into a particular Russian national will.

The last two sections point to the alternative fascist-Nazi resolution of class and nation, which emphasized the national question beyond that of class. The Fascists spotted the weakness in classical Marxism, its denial and denigration of nationalism, and their ideologists proved pivotal in developing a theory of socialism based on ultranationalist considerations. Nationalism, according to Talmon, permitted and even encouraged alliances between communists and fascists. It was also the factor that made the clash within Europe inevitable.

Finally, Talmon takes up the hard questions of the nature of post-World War II problems; he does so in a spirit of tentativeness. The themes of Third World development and modernization are clearly beyond the ken of his worldview. He asks: What is the role of Western democratic forms with respect to Third World demands for political equality? What is the place of the Soviet Union as midwife to national liberation movements and new totalitarian systems? What military formations are taking place in the Third World? What are the inner tensions within energy-rich and food-poor developing areas? The strictly European context of his thought offered few clues, much less firm answers.

Talmon's last work projects a feeling that a new world is unfolding, a world unfamiliar to him and his European colleagues. In that sense, *The Myth of the Nation and the Vision of Revolution*, his final book, is a fitting conclusion not only to a personal career of outstanding brilliance but also to the end of a social epoch, one in which the European sensibility could still impose cultural order upon social chaos. Talmon understood that his epoch began with the demands of the French Revolution for both a revolutionary process and democratic goals implemented from above. In his world, Europe became a center of political, social, and economic experimentation. A rising tide of new social classes tested Europe's commitment to transnational economic involvements in contrast to strictly national political goals. Finally, in Talmon's own century, nations destroyed all visions of class solidarity, much less of human brotherhood, and, in so doing, deprived Europe of the opportunity to fulfill its highest and noblest dreams.

Talmon's work deserves careful scrutiny. Whatever one thinks about his treatment of particular themes, he provides remarkable insight into an era of European preeminence that no longer exists, and that can no longer determine the fate of worlds. Yet, though the old conflicts may not have much bite, there may still be lessons to be learned in the continuing emotional tug of pan-Europeanism in the latter portion of the twentieth century, about the value of pluralism and survival in the face of national struggles that, until very recently, seem insuperable and unending.

That the price of the pacification of Europe proved so terribly high, exacting a toll in so many millions of lives, can only be reflected upon with a deep sense of tragedy. Still, a sense of triumph emerges from under the rubble. Talmon's trilogy informs us of the high risks of all forms of fanaticism. Perhaps the non-European world will profit by these lessons, but the chances of this happening, as Talmon himself makes perfectly clear, seem slim given the imperviousness of new nations to the history of older nations.

It was Talmon's extraordinary achievement to demonstrate, to the squirming discomfort of many other historians of the modern world, that the familiar and easy contrasts of reaction and revolution made little sense. In point of fact, the totalitarian drive to destroy the old order whole, to replace tradition with modernity, was the work of a similar mind-set. The futurism of a Mussolini or the prolecultism of a Stalin has the same source: a belief in the need to start the world anew. And this impulse was itself anything but new. The French Revolution, with its Robespierrist insistence on a new art, a new politics, a new calendar, announced a modernity seriously impaired from the outset, severed from any historical moorings.

For Talmon, *The Origins of Totalitarian Democracy* arose from the wellsprings of an impatient reformist impulse, matched with a certitude that political leadership could feel the pulse of a people and regulate the springs of social change. The revolutionaries were the good doctors; the people were the patients in need of healing. Together they would move toward the utopian future in lockstep. This was a dream that turned into the nightmare of terror, or bad medicine if you will. But it was also a dream that persisted beyond the terror into the utopian thinkers of the early nineteenth century.

The second volume in the trilogy, *Political Messianism*, permits Talmon to carry the story through the early portion of the nineteenth century, a period that corresponded to romanticism in art and music, and hence that invited mannerism and exaggeration in politics, but always in the name of the good heart. The world of Fourier and St. Simon and utopian socialism is seen by Talmon as little more than a benign version of the revolutionaries who came to purify French life fifty years earlier. Utopianism provided a gloss that permitted the messianists to work in a far more tolerant period of the warm and generous heart; and hence less subject to the exaggerations of cruel terror and overt assassination in the name of the anti-Christ as typified the extreme elements in the French Revolution.

Even though *Political Messianism* was by far a more thoughtful and persuasive work than *The Origins of Totalitarian Democracy*, it was received without fanfare and without favor. In talking about this in later years, Talmon told me that he thought the negative reception was a consequence of the radical fervor of the Generation of 1968; although I suspect that this explanation credits the *Zeitgeist* with more than it is entitled. My own feeling is that the second volume was more severe in its implications, since it in effect says that the utopianism with a human face, no less than the earlier revolution of a heartless sort, ends up in the same quagmire of bad thinking and fanatic action.

Whether the final volume of the trilogy on *The Myth of the Nation and the Vision of Revolution* could resolve some of the problems bequeathed by the earlier volumes became the single-minded issue for Talmon. He realized the vast continuities between the French Revolution and the Russian Revolution; he understood well the identical theoretical wellsprings of a democratic theory that issued into undemocratic practices; and he saw well how national liberation efforts sweep away claims about international and transnational claims of universal brotherhood.

Therefore, the final volume sought not so much to provide a narrative of current events as to give synthetic character to an epoch begun in 1789 and closed two hundred years later in 1989. Talmon, alas, did not live to see this development, although he understood its inevitability better than nearly any other intellectual of our time. The final irony of the century was also the final answer to despotism: the revolt of the peoples of Europe and Asia to rid themselves of saviors turned despots.

The great schism within revolutionary movements was the struggle between communism and fascism, which then pitted the supposed internationalism of the former against the nationalism of the latter. Talmon shrewdly understood that there was something chimeric about the mutually exclusive claims of proletarian internationalism and National Socialism. What the communist and fascist movements shared in common was a "bastard synthesis" of nationalism and internationalism. Their struggles with each other concerned who was to lead in this claim of exclusivity.

The totalitarian ideologies shared a Manichean view of history, possessed an all-embracing sense of truth and healing, never admitted to a middle ground. Consequently, no form of collusion between the fascists and communists could be permanent. What they shared in common ideology made for a deadly rivalry in military terms. Jacob Talmon shared with Hannah Arendt this special appreciation of the unitary character of twentieth-century totalitarianisms, albeit arriving at this common wisdom from a study by Talmon of the French case and by Arendt of the German case. Both well understood that the ultimate struggle of the century remained the same as in past centuries: between totalitarianism writ large and the various forms of democracy, between the external powers of people and in the received wisdom of God, between the collective Will and the individual conscience.

The Myth of the Nation and the Vision of Revolution is a work of irony ending in paradox. For that reason it appears inconclusive; a work without a clear thesis, like those characteristic of Talmon's earlier two books. But this is not the case. Rather, Talmon came to understand that the "thesis" is itself the paradox: the mutually incompatible claims shoved down the throats of an unhappy and unwilling humanity. In this sense, the struggles of the century do not end with the completion of the century. Only the forms change. Hence, the final volume of the trilogy is marked by intensity rather than decisiveness. Like the century itself, the work ends neither on a note of triumph nor of despair, but a call for further vigil and better sense. Implicitly, Talmon calls for myths to be countered by facts, vision to be overcome by insight, and passion to be beaten back by compassion.

In the earlier volumes of his famed trilogy, the Jewish Question is strangely muted. I say strangely because in some of his briefer papers collected under the title *The Universal and the Particular*, not to mention his own lifelong commitment to Israel and the Hebrew University in Jerusalem, there was hardly a question of his concerns or commitments. But in *The Myth of the Nation and the Vision of Revolution*, the question of Jews and Holocaust takes front and center. With anti-Semitism the official policy of Stalin and the Gulag, and the Holocaust the final solution of Hitler and the concentration camps, Talmon raises the hard questions: Why were the Jewish communities so divided on the nature of their tormentors? Indeed, why were some quite willing to entertain their own spiritual extermination in favor of a set of higher ideological truths?

These considerations were especially difficult with respect to the role of Jews in the evolution of Soviet Bolshevism. How was it possible for such a universal people to align themselves in part with such a particularistic regime? And the answer, of course, resides in the overall theme of *The Myth of the Nation and the Vision of Revolution*, namely the global, internationalist pretensions that made the Jewish people align itself with a regime promising universal moral values coupled with legal assurance of the survival of the Jewish people as an abstract whole. Czarism was the soil of Jewish emancipation. Stalinism was the frustration of that emancipation.

In many ways, the subtext of the book is the Jewish Question. Talmon's own deep-seated revulsion for universal and national varieties of totalitarianism alike stem from a deep appreciation that the Jewish people, like the black people in America to whom he alludes, are both victims and agents of chiliastic appeals. If the emphasis on the Jewish Question is more on the Soviet variety than the Nazi variety, it is because the Soviet treatment, in its very ambiguity, illustrates the larger themes of the century: participants in self-destruction through political myth no less than victims of destruction through holistic visions.

Let it be noted that Talmon's last book is unique among those that attempt to survey the century in its frank analysis of the place of the Holocaust in twentieth-century history. Lucy S. Dawidowicz, in *Social Studies Review* (Spring 1990), in a survey of texts in history, asks: "How can students grasp the horror of the Holocaust if they are unfamiliar with the biblical revulsion against murder as the primordial crime? How can young people understand the evil that is the murder of the European Jews, if they are not taught that all cultures abhor premeditated murder as the most heinous of all crimes?"

Such concerns are precisely taken to be the provenance of Talmon's *lebenswerke*. As a scholar of our age, and revealing this age to its actors, he remains quite unsurpassed.

Works by Jacob L. Talmon

Israel Among the Nations
Myth of the Nation and Vision of the Revolution
The Origins of Totalitarian Democracy
Romanticism and Revolt

48

Thorstein Veblen: Elitist as Populist

It may strike the reader as presumptuous for an editor to entitle this volume *Veblen's Century*. Every field of the sciences, humanities, and literature has its own heroes and icons. I have no wish to enter an absurd contest as to who is "better" or "more important" in the pantheon of scholars. Rather, I have chosen this admittedly flamboyant title to illustrate the themes that played out over the course of time that are indelibly stamped with Thorstein Veblen's imprint, not who owned the twentieth century in intellectual terms.

In doing so, I make no judgment that Veblen was a sage or a prophet, or as right as rain on every issue. Indeed, my own remarks on Veblen's briefer essays, and many of the essays on Veblen contained in this special collection, call attention to the weakness of his formulations and even egregious mistakes in his predictions. That being the case, in what sense then can we define the twentieth century as Veblen's? Indeed, he is rarely placed on the same pedestal as, say, Albert Einstein, Sigmund Freud, or even his fellow economist, John Maynard Keynes. Thus, the task of introducing is also an obligation to justify.

I am nonetheless confident that those who persevere in reading this collection will find its title appropriate. The special place of honor reserved for truly important figures is deserved by Thorstein Veblen— iconoclastic economist, social critic, and moral judge of the American way of life. That Veblen has attracted such an unusually diverse and disparate group of commentators should in itself warrant close attention to him. People from every spectrum of political ideology and every branch of the social sciences have been drawn to his work— sometimes in praise, sometimes in criticism, but always with a sense of measuring what he said and how, or if, his position can be trumped.

Institutions of higher learning have drifted from a stodgy conservatism to a militant radicalism. The leisure class has turned out to be something other than the ruling class. People of means seem to prefer privacy to ostentation—and pay a great deal to achieve it. The power of wealth and assets is at least as apparent in our awareness as the conspicuous consumption that Veblen claimed guides us. One can continue in this vein in field after field: errors in the assessment of German intentions or capabilities, the role of corporate owner-ship vis-à-vis corporate management, and no less, a critique rather than celebration of American culture. Alienation from the mainstream has become more of a counter-culture than Veblen ever imagined possible. But to fasten on such predictive shortcomings, as indeed we must at the sheer level of assessing truth, is to miss Veblen's unique contributions in sensitizing American intellectuals to the master strategies and issues of our time—his time and now ours.

It is hard to believe that Veblen died in August 1929, or one month before my own birth. He obviously missed, if that is the right word, the Depression, World War Two, nuclear weapons, the Nazi system and the Holocaust, the Stalinist phase of Soviet communism, the emergence of a Third World, a communications revolutions far be-yond anything he could imagine, the emergence of a post-industrial capitalism, and the collapse of the communist system worldwide. In purely domestic terms, he barely comprehended the enormous shift in racial relations in the larger society and gender relations in more intimate aspects of social life. This is not a matter of right or wrong prognostications, but simple shattering events that redefined the American landscape and the world system.

So what then are Veblen's contributions that have persisted through time? Each of the essays offers its own answer to such a question. My own assessment, and one that others have also called attention to, is not too hard to identify. First and foremost, is Veblen's keen linkage of psychology and economy, of mind and money as it were. For it remains a fact, or at least I would aver such, that at the end of the century, these two disciplines have most sharply characterized American life. Ours is not a political culture. Not that we do not have politics. Rather, our politics are all bunched up precisely in some middle ground, one that seeks precisely a fusion of personal sentiments and economic goals.

Because of this, Veblen was ultimately a student—an anthropolo-gist if you will—of the American culture. We share his emphasis, if not his alienation, his sense of the stranger within peering on at the complex foundation of behavior—whether such behavior is defined in terms of attitudes toward work and leisure, wealth and poverty, and finally war and peace. For better or worse, twentieth-century America showed the face of the proximate future to the world. Veblen knew this well, better than any other serious commentator. With all the emphasis on Veblen as an outsider, and even a foreigner within our midst, he probably was that thinker who most closely touched the inner core of what makes the American a different sort of person from, say, the European or the Asian. We have to look back to an Alexis de Tocqueville to come up with another student of American life who has looked so deeply into the soft underbelly of a culture formed in equal measure by psychological need and economical greed.

A casual look at the contributors to the Veblen literature serves to illustrate this point. Whatever their disciplinary background, whether they be David Riesman, Douglas Dowd, Max Lerner, E. Digby Baltzell, C. Wright Mills, Daniel Bell, or the other outstanding contributors, all share with Veblen a linkage between economic system, psychological propensity, and cultural formation. And that gets us to the amorphous world of "post-modernism" that in truth began with Veblen even if it may have ended with Foucault, Derrida, and Lacan. He caught a sense of the malleability of culture that broke the back of the nineteenth-century stranglehold on social analysis. He did so by simply seeing systems as volitional rather than deterministic in character, formed by human beings rather than by actors playing out preordained scripts.

Veblen was as close as America came in the twentieth century to producing a freewheeling intellectual; he was neither defined nor contained by a single university. He was not a product of an artifact such as the Chicago School, or any other departmental generated collectivity. For all his faith in socialism as a system, it was individualism that clearly made him stand apart as a man. Veblen was aware enough of this contradiction. He worked alone because only in this way could he emerge as a commentator to the social schools sciences but also a writer within the cultural setting of his age. It is little wonder that he stood closer to Theodore Dreiser than to Andrew Carnegie. He studied industrialists as a specimen, a literary type that merits scrutiny more than obedience. It was not that Veblen sought marginality, rather it was the combustion of native sentiment and natural resource that made the experience with nationhood so distinctive.

In an age that had just started to value specialization in its intellectual class, Veblen represented the reverse, the generalist who held the specialist in a nonchalant contempt. Although trained in economics, Veblen's work is more likely to be found being taught in sociology and psychology classes. He was the father of the "soft" social sciences, the "marginal" social scientists. Veblen will forever remain their special saint. Concern for how personal behaviors and public morals shape our economic systems is hardly likely to send shivers down the spines of the "hard" social scientists—except of course when their prophecies go awry, and when crises take place that seem to defy easy categorization.

At times of crisis, Veblen will be drawn out of the closets. This will be so because he expresses the innermost suspicion of those who believe that all social science is "soft" because indeterminacy is a fact of all human life. At the end of the day, Veblen gave voice to a time in which culture and civilization have returned to dominate the discourse of the wise and the best among us. A hundred years from now, someone will again come along with the bright idea for a compendium (or an *e-book*) entitled once again *Veblen's Century*. Veblen endures.

Works by Thorstein Veblen

Essays in Our Changing Order
The Higher Learning in America
The Nature of Peace
The Place of Science in Modern Civilization
The Theory of the Leisure Class

49

Aaron Wildavsky:
Facts, Policies, Morals

I have been an admirer of Aaron Wildavsky for so long that when he died a full decade ago, I felt a personal injury—something akin to losing a limb. Just who would take up leadership of the intellectual defense of the common culture? I am surely not the only person to ask such an admittedly rhetorical question. He gave backbone to so many people in public life and in academic pursuits, that the problem of Aaron not being among us was less the quality of his legacy—already assured—but the character of the remaining living. It was somehow always easier to be courageous knowing Aaron was in your corner. How would we fare with him gone? If this appears a strange way to open the new edition of *The Revolt Against the Masses*, it will, nonetheless, have to suffice. I hope that by the close of my remarks, the source of my personal concerns will be evident.

As *The Revolt Against the Masses* makes plain, Aaron compelled us to think in multiple tracks. He always asked first, what are the facts in any given situation?—whether it is the nature of presidential leadership in foreign affairs or political determinants of economic decisions. Second, he asked, what are the policy implications of any serious analysis? Since, in every major empirical study, the author is driven and the reader is taken for a ride in the fact lane, what are we to do about the affairs described? Third, Aaron compels us in nearly every essay to answer the moral call: what are the human consequences of events and then of policies? Like Herbert Croly, who started the century before him, what haunted Aaron Wildavsky was the "unrealized promise of American life" at the close of the twentieth century. In that phrase lies the moral goodness of a people still in search of its ethical moorings.

If there is a "secret" in Aaron's style of work, and I suspect that he would be properly dismissive of any sort of mystical turn to that phrase, it is a methodology that eases into a morality mediated by a policy. In my capacity as editorial director at Transaction, I have supervised the publication or the republication of no fewer than twelve of Aaron's titles in just about every field in which he worked—from public budgeting to the nature of representational politics. With the guidance of a variety of his former students and colleagues, we have also turned out five posthumous volumes of Aaron's papers—and have done so at considerable personal cost to people who put aside their own labors to complete the task. Aaron is worth it. For those with little time to spare and who are new to the wonders of Aaron, I would suggest two books—published while he was very much alive and with us: *Speak Truth to Power*, and now, *The Revolt Against the Masses*. These texts, available in new editions from Transaction, will make one either a convert to, or a critic of, Aaron. He would not mind either outcome. He never lacked for good friends, but he never shrunk from a good fight. Opponents no less than allies define who are and where we stand. This Aaron well knew.

Aaron's play of words on José Ortega y Gasset's *The Revolt of the Masses* should not be taken as more than that. His concerns in *The Revolt Against the Masses* are not the emergence of mass repudiation of inherited elitist notions of domination and power, and certainly not with the dangers in the accession of the masses to social power. Rather, Aaron's intuition is to show how elites have struggled within themselves to maintain their domination and power. Far from being a source of humanistic tradition as Ortega held, the new elites are a source of anti-populist efforts to re-divide the wealth. In these ideas, Wildavsky is largely indebted to the Franco-Italian tradition in political sociology—especially Gaetano Mosca, Roberto Michels, and Vilfredo Pareto—rather than to the tradition of Spanish humanistic education. He makes the intent of this volume, its organizing principle, quite clear early on, in the essay that bears the title of the book.

"The revolutionaries of contemporary America do not seek to redistribute privilege from those who have it to those who do not. These radicals wish to arrange a transfer of power from those elites who now exercise it to another elite, namely themselves, who do not. This aspiring elite is of the same race (white), the same class (upper middle and upper), and the same educational background (the best colleges and universities) as those they wish to displace. The goal of this white, radical, privileged elite is clear: a society purged by them of the values, tastes, preferences and policies desired by the mass of Americans, The white elite is in revolt against the masses." The incendiary character of this opening gambit is not accidental, but part of a deeply held conviction by Wildavsky that the masses in America represent the source of the democratic tradition. At one fell swoop, Aaron undercuts the idea of a conservative or restorationist bias—and affirms a deep suspicion of radical ideologies as the answer to that which needs curing.

Wildavsky's deep fear, fueled in large part by the Vietnam War, was the raw capacity of elites to undercut the survival of national legitimacy as such. "Ways of life are in contention; that is why our image of America as a single nation, indivisible, is shaken." In truth, the thirty years that have passed since Aaron's writing of this essay indicate that he was correct about breaks in the national fabric—its sources in a war that was poorly defined—and in his belief that the masses were the source of whatever cohesion and integration that existed. Arguably, it was not until the terror bombings of the World Trade Center and the Pentagon in September 2001 that the sense of urgency in regaining an integrated approach was realized. When the nation was perceived to be in danger and at risk, this, rather than any great political awakening, accounted for a rallying to the idea of national survival and protection.

Concluding in a prophetic mode, one that foreshadows events that would occur long after Aaron passed away, he instructs his readers not to panic. "The greatest weapon the radical elite possesses is its ability to convince others that society is falling apart. Fire-bombings, window breaking, and shooting at police, however deadly or upsetting they may be, are mere pinpricks. They cannot, by themselves, move the levers of power. Only inappropriate responses by those in power can do that. Neither capitulation to violence nor indiscriminate repression will help. So long as most Americans do not abandon their posts, the radical elite can only kill or annoy; it cannot rule." While most commentators on Wildavsky have focused on his work on the budgetary process, federal policymaking, overseas development, and issues of risk and efficiency—all themes fully covered in *The Revolt Against the Masses*—few have celebrated, or for that matter even confronted, Aaron's larger moral vision. Perhaps this is one reason why this marvelous collection of essays has received far less attention than his middle-range writings. In an age given over to technical solutions to manageable problems, this may be understandable—if indeed regrettable.

With the exception—and it turned out to be a rather large one—of Aaron's concerns with developing a modern political science vision of *Tanahk: The Holy Scriptures*, the essays gathered in *The Revolt Against the Masses* cover the major areas of his lifelong interests through the 1970s. His essay on "The Two Presidencies" may be the most widely cited work in the political science literature. That it was first published in *Transaction/Society* is, to be sure, a matter of personal pride. In the section demarcated as "Political Analysis" we find Aaron's essential method: get to the heart of things and move beyond the conventional rhetoric of the day. In those halcyon days of the mid-1960s, the talk was about the "imperial presidency," which followed a period of much talk about "constitutional dictatorship." Whatever the merits of those earlier formulations, it was clear to Aaron that the historians in particular were often generalizing from one president, with little relevance to the nature of the presidency (or for that matter, the Congress) as such.

The essence of Aaron's masterful essay—visited in later stage, with some modification—is that the presidency is the office that is guardian of foreign policy concerns. Indeed, in an era of rapid communication, transportation and delivery of weapons of mass destruction, the lodging of foreign policy decision-making in the executive branch is an absolute necessity. At the same time, the domestic affairs of the nation—from the budgetary process to the administration of social welfare—is essentially an activity lodged in the congressional realm. If this division of labor was not exactly what each branch of government would like to be known for, it does accord with the image of the founding fathers. The constitution provides precisely for the sort of dual role of president as commander-in-chief that gives him a special role to play in military and defense affairs. Congress, for its part, ever sensitive to public opinion, is in a better position to make decisions that have intimate consequences for the home front. The budgetary process underscores this division. So in a sense, both those who argue for (or against) notions of an imperial presidency and a logrolling Congress are right—but only within the realms of foreign and domestic policies respectively. Aaron looked at behavior rather than formal structure as the grounds of political analysis.

The sharp critique of policy programs driven by accounting and budgeting—the rage of government in the late 1960s—well illustrates Aaron's special quality of looking at the political culture writ large and not simply specialized bits and pieces. Indeed, PPBS (Planning, Programming and Budgeting System), as it was known, derived from the Defense Department model evolved in response to military procurement and manpower needs during the Vietnam War epoch. The New Civilian Militarists, as I dubbed them in *The War Game*, were convinced of the advantages of managing policy from Washington rather than in the field—otherwise known as the United States. Aaron felt that the ill-defined Vietnam War led to an even less well-articulated method of governance.

Wildavsky's withering critique of top-down approach to policymaking was made at a variety of levels. He argued that conditions in the national society that could permit management and manipulation of resources, were absent; there was no body of knowledge waiting to be applied in areas like welfare and crime the way there is in military confrontations; and the personnel running agencies simply lacked a policy culture. But even within agencies with a policy tradition, like the Department of Defense, there are problems. Not least of these are decisions about avoiding or simulating nuclear war. Areas in which there was no body of data to draw upon require something more than programming or implementing new policies. Finally, given the difficulty of achieving consensus on goals, advocates of policy programming and budgeting were reduced to fixing their gaze on very limited operational goals that different leaders and agencies could agree upon. In short, public programs and policies need something other than "a fashionable pretense." The virtual collapse of such mechanical contrivances reduced policy to zero-based budgeting techniques. This failure was better understood by Wildavsky than by those enthralled with the conversion of policy and evaluation research into technique.

Not everything in *The Revolt Against The Masses* remains politically relevant. The essays on the actual presidential politics of the 1960s clearly are of more historical than analytical interest. But even here, in noting the growing impatience of Left and Right with democratic policies, and their turn to leadership models divorced from party systems and practices, one can detect how the ghost of Goldwater reappeared in the physical presence of the Clinton presidency. Wildavsky found the tendency to subjectivism and an uncompromising attitude to compromise itself to be disturbing. It still remains so. Ultimately, what he most feared was a frontal assault on the legitimacy of the system. In his view, "the greater the attack on the legitimacy of the system, the less the willingness to accept responsibility for it."

Even so strong a democrat as Wildavsky was desperately seeking leaders who could rise to the level of a Charles de Gaulle—who salvaged the system from its destroyers. In reviewing *The Revolt Against the Masses*, one is brought sharply to the realization of how fractured and fragmented America was during the Vietnam War period—a war that corresponded with domestic developments that seriously weakened any sense of national cohesion, much less a new consensus. The classes alienated from American society were not about to urge a course of action based on racial harmony or ethnic unity. And the classes who directed American society were themselves so wrapped up in turf struggles with each other that they likewise could not be counted upon to direct the nation into a new dawn. This essentially pessimistic reading of American society may not remain warranted, but this is not the issue. Even more open to doubt is what these essays suggest about how Aaron himself would react to current events. It is assuredly wiser to read his essays in a way that enables us to adopt his multi-tracked approach: first the facts, then the policies, and finally, the moral consequences. That in itself would represent a great leap forward in the conduct of political science, and who knows, perhaps of politics as such.

There was a private side to Aaron not easily observed by casual acquaintances. He could appear gruff, blunt to a fault, with a touch of sarcasm in his voice. That he did not suffer fools readily was apparent. But there was another aspect to his private self: a deep reverence for tradition and family. In his delightful autobiographical essay "A Boy from Poltava," he told the story of his love and reverence for his father. It was evidently deep and lifelong. In the larger sphere, his belief in the Jewish tradition and religion in which he was reared governed his moral sensibility and informed his political judgments. His two books on the subject were as radical in their own way as Freud's *Moses and Monotheism*. If there were conjectural elements in the transmigration from Old Testament readings of the Jewish rulers and prices of the ancient kingdoms to modern issues, there was no question of the authenticity of his reading. He saw a world of political leadership superimposed on the struggles between Moses and Joseph to define the Jewish Project, of David and Solomon to provide not such laws but legitimacy to this Project.

This Jewish element showed up in various guises in his other writings: Aaron's deep animus for "lawless behavior," his dismissal of the fundamentalist fears of a Catholic in the White House, his invoking of the Jewish experience to explain African-American oppression. "When people have been disadvantaged for a long time, they (like the ghettoized Jews who refined self-hatred into a high art) may become carriers of their own victimization." But the clearest indication of his deep respect for tradition emerged in Aaron's constant acknowledgment of help and support from everyone and every place in which he taught. All honors were bestowed to Brooklyn College, Yale University, Oberlin College, the University of California at Berkeley—wherever Aaron landed. He always pointed out the positive benefits of his experience, his encounters, with little known, but outstanding teachers, in his many acknowledgments.

He was able to integrate his political and theological interests only in later life. In two works produced during the 1980s, well after the papers in *The Revolt Against the Masses*, he wrote *Assimilation versus Separation: Joseph the Administrator and the Politics of Religion in Biblical Israel* and *The Nursing Father: Moses as a Political Leader*. In both of these works Aaron broke new ground simply by ignoring the vast exegetical literature, and returning to the biblical sources of Jewish history. It might well be that these volumes included an admixture of apocryphal and actual events, but the result is a heightened sense of the place of culture in the formation of a nation. For beyond the Weberian issues of charisma and bureaucracy, or even customs and laws, is the deeper issue of what it takes for a people to survive and a national entity to emerge triumphant. The full panoply of emotions, sentiments, and interests weigh as heavily in modern America as in ancient Israel. And while we may find it hard to understand, the relationship of the universal to the particular, the legal to the empirical, the good and the evil, was clearly apparent to the ancients. Forms change, technology expands, scientific knowledge multiplies—but the problem of human survival remains painfully impervious to all such blandishments of modernism and post-modernism alike.

Aaron also translated his own affections into an ability to work with other people, especially younger scholars. I know of few scholars of his singular grandeur who wrote as many essays as joint papers—with a plethora of colleagues and students—some relatively well known, others now in obscurity. From Mary Douglas to Naomi Caiden and Max Singer who were beyond the pale of political science to Jeffrey Pressman, Nelson Polsby, and Richard Ellis within the discipline, Aaron was generous in acknowledging the role of others in his own work. And indeed, he worked with others in collegial enterprise more easily and naturally than most people in social research. Aaron's agenda was clear enough. He wanted to develop a group of people who recognized the need for political science in which the two words were equally weighted. It is fair to say that in the decade since his death we have seen the evolution of just such an army of followers. These are not acolytes, but people for whom working with him on an essay or under him on a dissertation theme was and remains a singular badge of honor and respect. This was gained without intimation, without imposing a sense of his authority—simply by emphasizing on the work object what it meant and what larger purposes it thereby served. This all sounds simple in the telling, but as I reflect on how few academics there are for whom one can speak equal words, the singular achievement of Wildavaky as a teacher becomes clear.

Culture was not simply a term of endearment for Aaron, but a peculiar transmission belt in which an older generation bestows on a younger generation the wisdom of the past, without enveloping that wisdom in mysticism or dogmatism. I am not sure in a world gone instrumental and electronic that this same sense of intimacy, of a human past informing a human present, will survive intact—at least not in the same way as was experienced by Aaron. Ultimately, the wisdom of the people serves as carrier of the core culture. In this "The Revolt against the Masses" led by narrow elites parading forth as guardians of the people is defeated. There is a touch of wish fulfillment in this paradigm of commoners trumping elites, since it is not always the case that the masses behave in quite as principled a way in other nations and lands as they supposedly do in the United States and the United Kingdom.

It was this faith in the commoner, this retention in the personality of those with the common touch, that made Aaron special in the private as well as the professional realm. He came armed in every intellectual battle with a belief that ordinary people carry the high virtues and not just the common touch. He also believed that those in the academy, who disdain ordinary virtues while masquerading as champions of the people, would be exposed and defeated. This indeed is what happened to the narrow band of Rightists whose isolationism disguised disdain for the democratic cause against the Axis powers. This rupture within the narrow band of ultra-Leftists, whose internationalism disguised a no less vile acceptance of the Communist International, also made leadership of the masses impossible.

His hatred for all forms of totalitarianism, coupled with a faith in the prospects of a democratic political culture, revealed Aaron's commitments most fully. Many of the essays in this volume started with a review of empirical information showing that ordinary people were not uniformly well served by their political directorates. This moved him to a belief that it was possible to forge policies that would alleviate common suffering and improve the lot of the people. He believed this was feasible precisely because the mechanisms of democratic government were entirely intact in the United States—shaky commitments and adventures in foreign lands notwithstanding. Finally, Aaron internalized a moral conviction as to the decency of ordinary people—especially the American people. That is evident in the many essays in *The Revolt Against the Masses*. The flinty vision that infused Aaron is a key to the legacy of measured hope that he left us with. Political science may have been the discipline that guided his efforts, but like Adam Smith long before him, it was moral philosophy, and not ideology, that made that discipline acceptable and worthy of emulation.

At the end of the day, if there *is* an end of the day in matters of fundamental doctrine, I suspect that what irritated Aaron's opponents most was not anything he said or wrote, but rather what he did not say or write. He was appalled by the posturing among social scientists that led them to advocate one or another form of liberal or conservative doctrines. "Ism" words left Aaron just plain cold. He was one of the few people in the field who took the word "science," as in political science, to mean precisely that: the scientific study of political behavior and its institutions. He is also one of the even rarer group of people in the discipline who expressed his moral preferences and concerns in plain words. The entitlement for doing so was the wealth of scientific evidence and shared experience in any of the fields properly covered by the discipline.

Nowhere are these beliefs more clearly exemplified than in Wildavsky's other late life efforts: the understanding of the relationship of innovating to conserving. In a series of works ranging from *Risk and Culture* (with Mary Douglas) to *Searching for Safety*, he made it perfectly clear that decisions made are policies advocated. Much of this originated in his 1976 study of *Dixon-Yates: A Study in Power Politics*, where it became evident that the advancement of utilities involves environmental risks. In turn, risk must be evaluated against the benefits to the larger society being promulgated. There is no progress without risk. There is no harnessing or control of nature without admitting to prospects of risk—or more bluntly, failure. Hence, ideological argumentation is utterly worthless. Only actual empirical analysis of the dangers incurred, the results obtained, the policies implemented, tell us whether to pursue or cancel any particular policy or program. Again, for Aaron, these decisions help defines the common sense of the common culture. It also allows us to think of political science precisely as a science.

In Aaron's mind, the pursuit of political science is simple and uncluttered: the creation of adequate policy outcomes, predicated on a grounded culture rooted in Western values. As complex a person as he was, Aaron also was a simple teacher of political science. His enemy was not right nor left, neither conservative nor liberal. Rather, it was those who reversed this causal chain—the people who made of political analysis an esoteric, complex chore, far removed from ordinary minds. The anomaly of people writing about democracy without the least interest in observing its canons never ceased to amaze him. The themes in *The Revolt Against the Masses* illustrate both sides of the equation as he saw it: the need for political science and the faith in the common culture. I can hardly imagine a better way to begin the serious study of Aaron Wildavsky than with this fine collection of his politically rooted and morally aware essays.

Works by Aaron Wildavsky

Assimilation versus Separation
The Beleaguered Presidency
Budgeting and Governing
Culture and Social Theory
Speaking Truth to Power

50

Ludwig Wittgenstein and Karl Popper: Poker Players

One of the niftiest tricks in academic writing is to take a tiny event and illumine an entire universe. This is precisely what David Edmonds and John Eidinow—two journalists with the British Broadcasting Corporation—have attempted. Let me say at the outset that they have largely, but not entirely, succeeded. In so doing, they have enlarged the world of knowledge, or at least the sociology of knowledge. On October 25, 1946, in a lecture hall at Cambridge University, Ludwig Wittgenstein and Karl Popper came together for their first and only engagement. The event lasted ten minutes. It was punctuated by sharp commentary, Wittgenstein brandishing a poker and leaving in a huff. It was mediated by no less a luminary than Bertrand Russell. The event was to become the stuff of academic mythology.

Indeed, in retrospect, the event is best seen as a case study of the *Rashomon Effect*. What took place is more in the eye of the beholder than on the stage of the conference hall in King's College. Even if we take Popper's account at face value, it hardly ranks with the horrors and tragedies of the twentieth century. In his intellectual autobiography Popper writes that he put forth a series of genuine philosophical problems. In turn, Wittgenstein "summarily dismissed them all." Popper claims that his adversary "had been nervously playing with the poker" which he used "like a conductor's baton to emphasize his assertions." When a question came up about the status of ethics, Wittgenstein supposedly challenged Popper to give an example of a moral rule. Popper presumably replied by invoking the injunction: "Thou shall not threaten visiting lecturers with pokers." Whereupon Wittgenstein, "in a rage, threw the poker down and stormed out of the room, banging the door behind him."

The belated response from Wittgenstein years later came in a personal note to Professor Rush Rhees, a former student and close friend. He called the event with Popper "a lousy meeting…at which an ass, Dr. Popper, from London, talked more mushy nonsense rubbish than I've heard for a long time. I talked a lot as usual.…" At a later time, in the minutes of the Moral Science Club, it is recorded that the purpose of Popper's presentation was to correct some misunderstandings about philosophy as practiced by the Cambridge School (that is, Wittgenstein himself). The minutes repeat Wittgenstein's caustic assertion that for Popper "the general form of a philosophical question is, 'I am in a muddle; I don't know my way.'"

Whether these competing renditions of events are entirely factual or fictitious is somewhat beside the point. Indeed, what actually took place became the stuff of a nearly endless round of letters in *The Times Literary Supplement* more than a half century after the event. Even distinguished figures present at the event disagree vehemently on the actual handling of the poker by Wittgenstein, the self-discipline under fire by Popper, or that the exchange terminated abruptly after ten minutes. The authors of this volume use this passing event to discuss fin-de-siècle Vienna, Jewish assimilationist families, wealth and poverty, and finally, philosophical influence. I will leave the reader to determine the business of the place, the witnesses, and their recollections. Rather, it is worth probing the larger issues, since they bear so heavily and directly on the knowledge base of an age only now starting to recede from memory.

Vienna was the center of world culture at the turn of the twentieth century as assuredly as New York or London can make such a claim at the turn of the twenty-first century. In every area of culture, Arthur Schnitzler, Karl Kraus, Otto Weininger, Jacques Offenbach, Sigmund Freud, Heinrich Hertz, and countless others made Vienna central to discovery in physics, debate in philosophy, and creativity in the arts. But this creativity so heavily weighted with Jewish contributors became itself the sore edge and raw nerve of the city and the nation. The murder in 1936, just a few years before the *Anschluss*, of Moritz Schlick, one of the founders of the Vienna Circle, linked Judaism with Positivism—and both with "a new and sinister strain in philosophy." Wittgenstein escaped the assaults by attempting to escape from being Jewish as such. He became a willing participant as well as a victim of the anthropology of mixed racial strain "theory." He searched the records for grandparents who had converted or were themselves Catholic in background, and distanced himself from the Nazi war against the Jews—already in its initial stages. Popper's parents had converted to evangelical Protestantism. Popper himself admitted to being of Jewish origin, but also of Christian persuasion.

Even after the Holocaust had been fully exposed, Popper would insist of his remoteness from the Jewish condition, even to the point of presuming that Jews themselves, by their collective behavior, share the blame of anti-Semitism. Haunted though he may have been, as Edmonds and Eidinow assert, he shared with Wittgenstein a detached alienation from his religious background. Vienna was the stomping ground of Jews in search of Catholic or Protestant identity—but only as a feeble tactic to avoid persecution and extermination. It must be said in candor that the two giant figures shared in the myopia of pure secularism, and were perfectly prepared to think that the battleground was between philosophy as language construction versus philosophy as problem solving. As a result, neither figure can be said to be part of a culture in which religion, metaphysics, and belief systems beyond the purely naturalistic could be given any credence. The authors of *Wittgenstein's Poker* never quite face up to a possibility that both combatants had feet of intellectual clay.

Illustrative of the profound shortcomings of both of these figures, as the authors of *Wittgenstein's Poker* make quite clear, is that both of these major figures took refuge in Jew baiting as a mechanism of personal advancement. Neither Wittgenstein nor Popper were above taking refuge in family backgrounds involving conversion from Judaism to Christianity or seeking baptismal papers from a maternal grandparent as a mechanism to escape the punishment that the Nazis meted out to those less fortunate with "mixed religious" backgrounds. For Wittgenstein, this process was not undertaken in a shame-faced way, but with an admixture of self-hatred and anti-Semitism, in which being Jewish became a "limiting or distorting mechanism." While for Popper, the rationale was simply that being Jewish was essentially incompatible of being identified with German culture. The high irony is that it was far easier to assert the claims of positivist philosophy and/or scientific rigor in defining the universe in Great Britain than in Central Europe. Wittgenstein in particular was reticent to admit even this elementary truth. Popper for his part simply employed conventional British political rhetoric as a way to do away with the troublesome Jewish Question.

Perhaps the largest issue this volume raises is the nature of knowledge as such. There was a powerful streak of solipsism tinged by arrogance in Wittgenstein. His position was so narrowly defined that all those who claimed the existence of real problems, or for that matter, a real society, like Popper, were thrown into a constant defensive posture. Even Wittgenstein's mentors and fellow logical empiricists were assaulted for making claims about the objective status of knowledge. Allan Janik, in his recent book, *Wittgenstein's Vienna Revisited*, reports the following statement by Wittgenstein: "I am sitting with a philosopher in the garden; he says again and again 'I know that that's a tree.' Someone else arrives and hears this, and I tell him: 'This fellow isn't insane. We are only doing philosophy.'" But of course, the imputation of insanity (in this case to G. E. Moore and Bertrand Russell) is an implicit assertion that they are at best engaging in therapeutic relief and at worse quite mad.

It was against such thinking within a confined frame of epistemological relevance that Popper entered the debate with Wittgenstein on that fateful day at Cambridge in 1946. The very ability to generate an emotive response was in itself Popper's victory, whatever the post-mortem analyses by other parties concerned. For Popper, whether the issue was the patterns of discovery of scientific truth, or the theoretical foundations of totalitarian doctrine from Plato to Marx, the existential nature of doctrines of science at one end and ideology at the other are attested to by consequences. For Wittgenstein, ideas have no meaning beyond the observer and hence no consequences, whereas for Popper ideas have great meaning for collectivities beyond the observer and hence considerable consequences. Thus it is while Wittgenstein will remain fashionable as long as pure subjectivism becomes the norm, it is a Pyrrhic victory, since philosophic grounds for knowledge remains a goal that continues to be pursued. To claim that such pursuits are sociological or extra-philosophical may remove by one stage the search for warrants for truth, but it only ensures that serious people leave philosophy and take up social science. And the actual course of events since mid-century have demonstrated that philosophy has moved sharply away from a narrow positivism, if for no other reason than to retain a sense of relevance—the very goal at which Wittgenstein scoffed.

One element that I found curiously underplayed in *Wittgenstein's Poker* is the role of Cambridge University and a postwar environment in which the deep wounds of the war had barely healed. Wittgenstein was the consummate professional philosopher, the epitome of positivism, and a virtual demigod at the university. Popper was, in contrast, a popularizer, an advocate of modern philosophy as something beyond linguistic controversy, and a person whose private tendencies and brusque manners left him without friends. He assuredly was more at home at the anomic London School of Economics than at clubby Cambridge. It is small wonder that the author of *The Open Society and its Enemies* would find little favor in an environment in which the so-called Cambridge spy network for the Soviet Union took root and flourished. Indeed, the willingness of even the authors, Edmonds and Eidinow, to accuse Popper of lying when examining conflicting accounts of events long past attests to a strong belief that the positivist tradition prevails.

But does it? The authors are all too quick to consign Popper to the dustbin of history. After all, the totalitarian menace receded, the Berlin Wall was toppled, and then the Soviet empire itself collapsed. Presumably, so too did the concern with the sort of political philosophy with which Popper dealt, and that Wittgenstein, in his dismissive manner, called sociological matters. Perhaps this is so, but then so too has the luster of Wittgenstein worn thin—something not acknowledged by the authors. The idea that nothing beyond linguistic controversy is a fit subject matter for philosophical concern is more an embarrassment for positivists than an actively pursued proposition. Then too, Wittgenstein's proposition form of writing raises many problems, not the least being the vast contradictions between the ultra rationalism of the *Tractatus Logico-Philosophicus* and the metaphysical ramblings of his later work, *Philosophical Investigations*. There is also the considerable gap between Wittgenstein who took easily to English agnosticism and modest secularity and Popper, whose sense of being Jewish was far more developed (if not exactly convincing) and who had a strong and continuing European sense. Wittgenstein lived in a world of British culture, whilst Popper continued to reside in the world of European politics. I suspect that were these differences less manifest, the events of the ten-minute meeting would hardly be recollected. But one gets the distinct and uncomfortable feeling that the defense of Wittgenstein's utter rudeness, malevolence, and assault on Popper as a liar would have been far less shrill had Wittgenstein not become an accepted member of the British academic elite.

At any rate, it seems far too simplistic to see Popper as the transient figure and Wittgenstein as the durable one. The authors have simply bought into the culture of pure subjectivism and solipsism that still claims to be fashionable among stray sections of Anglo-American intelligentsia. The death of Marxism and Communism did indeed cut into the historical determinism and philosophic materialism that permeated an earlier epoch. But the search for objective meaning and truth did not pass away with one strain of nineteenth-century thought. The synthesis of Fueurbach's materialism and Hegel's dialectics was a clever moment in the history of philosophy. But it was only a moment. It did not serve to demonstrate the correctness of logical positivism, which itself was a hybrid formation of earlier doctrines of Berkeley, Hume, and Kant. We continue to search out new forms of knowledge seeking. As a result, crowning Wittgenstein or, for that matter, Popper, victor is irrelevant—or better said, too late in the day to even matter. That sense of a long haul has not yet developed.

Indeed, on the face of it, philosophy has moved much further away from the concerns of Wittgenstein than has politics, or, for that matter, the methods of scientific discourse have moved away from Popper. Our vanities about the end of theory notwithstanding, the history of philosophy is still being written. What has changed is that chapters on logical positivism and the Vienna Circle simply grow shorter as we learn so much more about a world of technology and science unimagined by our forebears.

Works by Ludwig Wittgenstein

Blue and Brown Books
Philosophical Investigations
Tractatus Logico Philosophicus

Works by Karl Popper

The Logic of Scientific Discovery
Open Society and Its Enemies
The Poverty of Historicism

Postscript

The Popper-Wittgenstein debate at Cambridge calls to mind the legendary encounter between Thomas Henry Huxley and Bishop Samuel Wilberforce at the 1860 meetings of the British Association for the Advancement of Science on Charles Darwin's *Origin of Species* that appeared one year earlier in 1859. That public argument too was billed as the greatest of all events, and it still remains shrouded in hyperbole and hagiography. Far from bringing to closure the debate on the relationship of science and religion, the clash of titans only exposed the hollowness of so much that passed for debate and dialectic in the nineteenth century. The same is true of the debate between Karl Popper and Ludwig Wittgenstein that mistakenly presumed an end to the discourse on the relationship of science and ethics in the mid-twentieth century.

It might well be argued that *Tributes* heaps praise on all sorts of people with distinctive and radically different viewpoints. Assuredly, those who thirst for intellectual equivalents to bloodletting will come away from these essays disappointed if not entirely dismayed. Whatever happened to the old lion? Why does he not roar with certitude? How are we to assess conflict between social science and other forms of cultural expression? It is too late in the day, at least far too deep into this volume, to offer direct responses to such mighty and futile queries. So let me once more take refuge in the words of that most eloquent voice of popular writing in science, Stephen Jay Gould. Summarizing the Huxley-Wilberforce discussions, Gould restates the grounds of free inquiry in an open society. I am honored to be able to close this effort with his words.

"The struggle of free inquiry against authority is so central, so pervasive that we need all the help we can get from every side. Inquiring scientists must join hands with questioning theologians if we wish to preserve that most fragile of all reeds, liberty itself. If scientists lose their natural allies by casting entire institutions as enemies, and not seeking bonds with soul mates on other paths, then we only make a difficult struggle that much harder." (*Bully for Brontosaurus: Reflections in Natural History*, p. 400.)

51

Kurt H. Wolff:
His Phenomenal World

I have a dual relationship to this work and to this man: Transaction is the publisher of *Survival and Sociology*. And as president of this firm, I am ultimately responsible for accepting this work for publication. I am honored to have done so. At the same time, my comments as an academic sociologist require a more critical, or at least, a different type of appraisal than one provided in a decision to issue a new title.

I found the book of value as a publisher, and even more so as a professor. Indeed, reading the work anew makes me realize just how condensed and packed with insight this volume is. For what the student is presented with is a special primer on the main issues confronting classical European sociology.

Kurt refused to call these seven segments "chapters." He insisted on calling them "entries." He was right to do so. For in point of fact, they represent opening salvos for our consideration as readers. The segments are cryptic, and invite our own sense of the themes and people covered. What we bring to the table in our knowledge of Weber, Simmel, Scheler, Schutz, Mannheim, and Durkheim is critical to whether we walk away with a sense of a full plate.

This is not to say that Kurt himself does not provide us with a sense of these people. His efforts are sometimes critical, sometimes praising, but always fair-minded. Of course, this is the spirit of Kurt. As a crucial link between Mannheim and our times, one expects and one receives the best of European critical theory in a democratic form. The unusual rhetorical devices notwithstanding, it is the liberal imagination, at times the radical imagination, that informs his writings, just as much as the sociological persuasion.

Indeed, if one takes seriously his notions of surrender-and-catch, they refer to rather eccentric, but intriguing uses. For surrender is in no way abject collapse in the face of authority, but rather surrender to the experience of new and innovative ideas. And the catch is really just that: what one captures in the net or web of reality. Such catches may be filled with surprises and they may prove dismaying of inherited truths, but they again open one to new experiences.

In this, Wolff is as much a child of Husserl as he is of Durkheim. This combination in the hands of a lesser person could easily disintegrate. In Wolff's hands, it provides the basis for a critique of crude empiricism and no less of vague abstraction that strays too far afield from problems of life and death—of events that range from Auschwitz to Hiroshima with respect to survival. In short, a key to *Survival and Sociology* is how close the field remains, or departs, with regard to fundamental issues of life and death.

One could dwell at great length and take issue with Kurt's criticisms of classical thinkers. But I do not see this as a fruitful, but only a pedantic way to deal with this amazing figure. In any event, whether in defense of Mannheim or in criticism of Scheler, I find myself nodding yes, rather than shaking no—and certainly never nodding out!

My concerns with Kurt's effort in *Survival and Sociology*—which to be sure should be read in conjunction with *Surrender and Catch* and some of his other writings on the subject of sociological and phenomenological theory—is what I consider a serious flaw in many of the phenomenological masters: the use of psychological categories to explain sociological events. What I have in mind is the conversion of complex events into a reductionistic framework, one in which phenomena like being a stranger or an outsider is seen in terms of personal alienation rather than, say, ethnicity, language, and their demands. Kurt avoids that trap nicely—in part because of his Mannheim-derived insistence upon a contextual set of reference points that extend beyond the individual.

For whatever else can be said of this approach, surrender-and-catch are personal, individual choices, and tasks. That such a prelude is the baseline requirement to raising sociology to a higher level is difficult to accept, since it presupposes that a state of mind rather than a state of society is the critical element. Thus the demand for sociologists to reemerge in the Schutzian world of everyday life is predicated on personality rather than methodology.

Such dilemmas create the basis for a hyperbolic reaction to world catastrophes. For example, it is true that "everybody now writes, or can write, poems—but only as if there had been no Auschwitz." But in fact Auschwitz continues to haunt German culture—all culture—

as Wolff recognizes. He quotes Rainer Maria Rilke's first "Sonnet to Orpheus," and such a line as "shriek, bellow and roar had shrunk in their hearts...." may be heard as if anticipating the echo of Auschwitz. Poetry no less than prose continues to be written, since the drama of good and evil may hit certain peaks and valleys, the drama continues as long as life does. And the poetic no less than the prose forms help us better understand as much. After all, one might call this slim volume a poetic exegesis.

Wolff is right to note that philosophy and sociology have intersected one another all along. But for that very reason, we are entitled to speculate on the survival capacity or lack thereof of sociology—no less than poetry. Indeed, one can say that poetry has a better survival shot at immortality than sociology—precisely because its concerns with problems of survival have been so long standing.

Kurt ends his work with a paradox of mystery and secularization. Sociology, a child of enlightenment, is given the burden of sustaining the cause of innovation, growth and survival itself. I submit that this is too heavy a burden for such a slim volume to carry, and that in point of fact, the field has not been able to turn its gaze onto those larger themes that preoccupy the attention of both.

If I had a final problem with Kurt's effort, it is how it can serve as a survival kit to vindicate the human subject. The work simply lacks a sense of early warning signals that would notify us that dangers lurk and problems of great moment are upon us. If sociology is to serve as an instrument of human liberation, I suggest that its capacity to make some kind of warning system a reality is needed. Even if predictions are poor and explanations weak in sociology surely it should be possible to detect what to be on the lookout for. This is implicit in Kurt's work, but hardly fleshed out in this brief volume.

Finally, one has to say what a wonderful primer this is in terms of familiarizing ourselves with the European background of so much that we take for granted as uniquely our own set of issues. Wolff on Mannheim is a joy of respect for a master and serious critique of some missing elements. His unvarnished response to Weber cuts through to the heart of some major problems in a rhetoric that failed to distinguish the legitimate search for ultimate ends from the politics of fanaticism.

This is a thoroughly worthwhile book—one that requires that we enter a dialogue rather than have a diatribe foisted on us. There is much wisdom in the modesty with which the book is prepared. Its brevity should not be mistaken for cursory levels of analysis. It has been a privilege to be connected with this literary as well as sociological effort, and with a scholar of infinite decency such as Kurt H. Wolff. I worry less for Kurt's mortal soul than I do for the mortality of a discipline that has confused the mundane for the moral.

Works by Kurt H. Wolff

Beyond the Sociology of Knowledge
O Loma: Constituting a Self
Surrender and Catch
Survival and Sociology: Vindicating the Human Subject
Trying Sociology

Bibliography: Original Sources

Arendt, Hannah
"Hannah Arendt: Juridical Critic of Totalitarianism." *Modern Age*, Vol. 39, No. 4 (Fall 1997), pp. 397-403.

Aron, Raymond
"Raymond Aron: Tribune of the Intelligentsia." Review of *History, Truth, Liberty: Selected Writings of Raymond Aron*, Franciszek Draus, ed., with a memoir by Edward Shils. Chicago and London: The University of Chicago Press, 1985.

Baltzell, Digby
"Digby's Paradoxes and Our Losses." Statement delivered at a memorial service held for E. Digby Baltzell, at St. Paul's Chapel, Columbia University in the City of New York, on September 17, 1996.

Becker, Ernest
"Ernest Becker: An Appreciation of a Life that Began on September 27, 1924 and Ended March 6, 1974." *The American Sociologist*, Vol. 10, No. 1 (February 1975), pp. 25-28.

Blumer, Herbert
"Herbert Blumer: The Pragmatic Imagination." Comments delivered at a memorial address on behalf of Herbert Blumer by the faculty of sociology, held at the University of California, Berkeley, on December 2, 1987.

Brown, Claude
"Claude Brown Has Gone to the Promised Land: 1937-2002." *The Chronicle of Higher Education [The Chronicle Review]*, Vol. XLVIII, No. 31, April 12, 2002, p. B5.

Cohen, Morris Raphael
"Morris Raphael Cohen and the End of the Classical Liberal Tradition." Foreword to *The Faith of a Liberal*, by Morris R. Cohen. New Brunswick, NJ and London: Transaction Publishers, 1993.

Coleman, James S.
"Chance, Choice, Civility and Coleman." *Society*, Vol. 28, No. 2, January-February 1991, pp. 80-84.

Du Bois, W.E.B.
"Revisiting the Legacy of W.E.B. DuBois." Statement delivered to a special convocation on "A Celebration of the Life of Sociology at Atlanta University," on Thursday, November 5, 1987, at Atlanta University in Atlanta, Georgia.

Elazar, Daniel J.
"Daniel J. Elazar and the Covenant Tradition in Politics." *Publius: The Journal of Federalism*, Vol. 31, No. 3 (Winter 2001), pp. 1-7.

Eysenck, Hans J.
"The Liberality of Hans J. Eysenck." Remarks delivered on the occasion of a memorial service for Hans J. Eysenck at the Maudsley Hospital, The University of London, November 21, 1997.

Feuer, Lewis S.
"Left-Wing Fascism and Right-Wing Communism: The Fission-Fusion Effect in American Extremist Ideologies," in *Philosophy, History, and Social Action: Essays in Honor of Lewis Feuer*, Sidney Hook, William L. O'Neill, and Roger O'Toole, eds. Boston and London: Kluwer Academic Publishers, 1988.

Fletcher, Ronald
"Ronald Fletcher: 11 August 1921-2 May 1992." *The Psychologist*, Vol. 6, No. 2, (February) 1993, pp. 82-83.

Germani, Gino
"Gino Germani: 1911-1979—Sociologist from the Other America." *The American Sociologist*, Vol. 31, No. 3 (Fall 2000), pp. 72-79.

Ginzberg, Eli
Introduction to *Eli Ginzberg: The Economist as a Public Intellectual*, Irving Louis Horowitz, ed. New Brunswick, NJ and London: Transaction Publishers, 2002, pp. vii-x.

Graña, César
Introduction to *Meaning and Authenticity: Further Essays on the Sociology of Art*, by César Graña. New Brunswick, NJ and London: Transaction Publishers, 1989, pp. xv-xxiii.

Greer, Scott
"Scott Greer: The Dialectic of the Unique and the Universal." Lecture delivered on panel for "Globalization, Cities and Human Habitat" of New York 2001 Conference on *World Forum on Human Habitat*. Sponsored by International Research Foundation for Development and Center for Urban Research and Policy, at Columbia University in the City of New York, Tuesday, June 5, 2001.

Gross, Mason W.
Preface to *Philosophy, Science and the Higher Learning: The Selected Speeches of Mason W. Gross*, by Mason W. Gross, Richard P. McCormick and Richard Schlatter, eds. New Brunswick, NJ and London: Transaction Publishers, 2002.

Homans, George Caspar
Remarks delivered at Harvard University on the occasion of the publication of *Behavioral Theory in Sociology: Essays in Honor of George C. Homans*, William James Hall, October 1976. Revised in 1989 for an address at Harvard's Social Relations Department, December 1989 in memory of Homans' death.

Humphreys, Laud
Irving Louis Horowitz with Glenn A. Goodwin and Peter M. Nardi. "Laud Humphreys: A Pioneer in the Practice of Social Science." *Sociological Inquiry*, Vol. 61, No. 2 (May 1991), pp. 139-147.

Kaplan, Jeremiah
"The Mission of Social Science." *Society*, Vol. 25, No. 3, March-April 1988. *A Memorial Tribute to Jeremiah Kaplan*. New York and Washington: Association of American Publishers. September 22, 1993, pp. 9-12.

Kirk, Russell
"Russell Kirk: Past as Prologue," in *The Unbought Grace of Life: Essays in Honor of Russell Kirk*. Detroit: Sherwood Sugden & Company, 1993.

Kirkpatrick, Jeane J.
"Legitimacy, Force and Jeane J. Kirkpatrick" Comments delivered at the luncheon held on January 21, 1988 at the American Enterprise Institute for Public Policy Research in honor of the publication by Transaction Publishers of the two-volume work by Jeane J. Kirkpatrick entitled *Legitimacy and Force*.

Konvitz, Milton
"Konvitz in Context." Remarks delivered on the occasion of the 93rd birthday celebration of the life and work of Milton Konvitz at the Cornell University Club of New York City, held on March 20, 2001.

Laqueur, Walter
"Giving Cosmopolitanism a Good Name." *Aufbau*, 11, May 24, 2001, pp. 11-13.

Lasky, Melvin J.
Preface to *Utopia and Revolution*, by Melvin J. Lasky. New Brunswick, NJ and London: Transaction Publishers, 2004.

Lasswell, Harold
Preface to *Essays on the Garrison State*, by Harold Lasswell. New Brunswick, NJ and London: Transaction Publishers, 1997.

Lengyel, Peter
Introduction to *International Social Science: The UNESCO Experience*, by Peter Lengyel. New Brunswick, NJ and London: Transaction Publishers, 2003.

Lerner, Max
"Memorial Address in Honor of Max Lerner." Remarks delivered on the occasion of the celebration of the life and work of Max Lerner at The School for Social Research, New York City, New York.

Levy, Marion J., Jr.
"Marion J. Levy, Jr. Memorial Address." Remarks delivered on the occasion of the celebration of the life and work of Marion J. Levy, Jr. at Princeton, New Jersey, held on September 21, 2002.

Lipset, Seymour Martin
"The Social Uses of Anomaly: In Dialogue with Seymour Martin Lipset." Remarks delivered at a special session sponsored by the Eastern Sociological Society on Saturday, March 9, 2002 in honor of the work of Seymour Martin Lipset.

Lynd, Robert S. and Helen Merrell Lynd
Article in *International Encyclopedia of the Social Sciences: Biographical Supplement*, Volume 18, David L. Sills, ed. New York: Free Press, 1979.

Maier, Joseph B.
"Joseph B. Maier: Tradition, Modernity and the Last Hurrah of the "Frankfurt School." Remarks delivered at Columbia University on Wednesday, February 5, 2003. A memorial service to the life and work of Joseph B. Maier.

Martz, John D.
"John D. Martz: Recollections: July 8, 1934-August 15, 1998." Remarks delivered in Eisenhower Chapel at Pennsylvania State University on Friday, September 18, 1998. A memorial service to the life and work of John D. Martz.

Merton, Robert K.
"Robert K. Merton: The Passion of a Professional." Statement delivered at a memorial service held for Robert K. Merton, at St. Paul's Chapel, Columbia University in New York City, on February 5, 2003.

Mills, C. Wright
"C. Wright Mills." *American National Biography.* New York, North Carolina and Oxford: Oxford University Press, 1993; and "The Sociological Imagination of C. Wright Mills: In Memoriam." *The American Journal of Sociology,* Vol. LXVIII, No. 1, July 1962.

Moynihan, Daniel Patrick
Extracted from "Daniel Patrick Moynihan: The Last Hurrah of Liberal Sociology." *Society,* Vol. 40, No. 5, 2003, pp. 47-52.

Nisbet, Robert A.
Extracted from "Losing Giants: Baltzell, Nisbet and Strauss." *Society,* Vol. 34, No. 3, 1997, pp. 47-52.

Riesman, David
"Reflections on Riesman." Remarks delivered on the occasion of the celebration of the life and work of David Riesman at Harvard University, Cambridge, Massachusetts, held on November 15, 2002.

Rose, Arnold M.
Preface to *Persuasions and Prejudices: An Informal Compendium of Modern Social Science, 1953-1988*, by Irving Louis Horowitz. New Brunswick, NJ and London: Transaction Publishers, 1989, pp. xv-xix.

Rummel, R.J.
Foreword to *Death by Government*, by R.J. Rummel. New Brunswick, NJ and London: Transaction Publishers, 1994.

Shaw, Peter
"Universal Values and National Interests: The Political Vision of a Literary Scholar." *Academic Questions*, Vol. 9, No. 5, 1997, pp. 42-46.

Silvert, Kalman H.
Remarks delivered at the memorial service for Kalman H. Silvert at La Maison Française, New York City, on Thursday, June 17, 1976, sponsored by New York University, the Ford Foundation, and the Institute for Study of Human Issues.

Stanley, John
"John Stanley: Historian of Political Ideas." Opening remarks delivered at the inaugural memorial address of the John L Stanley Lecture in Political Theory, held at the University of California, Riverside on Thursday, March 9, 2000.

Strauss, Anselm
Extracted from "Losing Giants: Baltzell, Nisbet and Strauss." *Society*, Vol. 34, No. 3, 1997, pp. 47-52.

Szasz, Thomas
"The Politics of Psychiatry and the Ethics of a Psychiatrist." *Existentialist Psychology and Psychiatry*, Vol. XXIII, Nos. 1-3 (Special Issue), 1998, pp. 107-115.

Talmon, Jacob L.
Introduction to the Transaction edition of *Myth of the Nation and Vision of the Revolution: Ideological Polarization in the Twentieth Century*, by Jacob L. Talmon. New Brunswick, NJ and London: Transaction Publishers, 1991.

Veblen, Thorstein
Introduction to *Veblen's Century: A Collective Portrait*, Irving Louis Horowitz, ed. New Brunswick, NJ and London: Transaction Publishers, 2002.

Wildavsky, Aaron
"Facts, Policies, Morals." Introduction to the Transaction edition of *The Revolt Against the Masses: And Other Essays on Politics and Public Policy*, by Aaron Wildavsky. New Brunswick, NJ and London: Transaction Publishers, 2002.

Wittgenstein, Ludwig and Karl Popper
Review of "Wittgenstein's Poker: The Story of a Ten-Minute Argument Between Two Great Philosophers." *Knowledge, Technology & Policy*, Vol. 14, No. 3 (Fall 2001), pp. 152-156.

Wolff, Kurt H.
"The Phenomenal World of Kurt H. Wolff." *Human Studies*, 16, 1993, pp. 325-328.

Name Index

For Product Safety Concerns and Information please contact our EU
representative GPSR@taylorandfrancis.com Taylor & Francis Verlag GmbH,
Kaufingerstraße 24, 80331 München, Germany

Batch number: 08158441

Printed by Printforce, the Netherlands